Growth, Stagnation or Decline?
Agricultural Productivity in British India

OXFORD IN INDIA READINGS

Themes in Indian History

GROWTH, STAGNATION OR DECLINE? AGRICULTURAL PRODUCTIVITY IN BRITISH INDIA

Edited by
SUMIT GUHA

DELHI
OXFORD UNIVERSITY PRESS
BOMBAY CALCUTTA MADRAS
1992

Oxford University Press, Walton Street, Oxford OX2 6DP
New York Toronto
Delhi Bombay Calcutta Madras Karachi
Kuala Lampur Singapore Hong Kong Tokyo
Nairobi Dar es Salaam
Melbourne Auckland
and associates in
Berlin Ibadan

SBN 0 19 563019 X

Typeset by Spantech Publishers Pvt Ltd, New Delhi 110008
Printed at Rekha Printers Pvt Ltd, New Delhi 110020
and published by S. K. Mookerjee, Oxford University Press
YMCA Library Building, Jai Singh Road, New Delhi 110001

Contents

General Editors' Preface

This series focuses on important themes in Indian history, on those which have long been the subject of interest and debate, or which have acquired importance more recently.

Each volume in the series consists of, first, a detailed Introduction; second, a careful choice of the essays and book-extracts vital to a proper understanding of the theme; and, finally, an Annotated Bibliography.

Using this consistent format, each volume seeks as a whole to critically assess the state of the art on its theme, chart the historiographical shifts that have occurred since the theme emerged, rethink old problems, open up questions which were considered closed, locate the theme within wider historiographical debates, and pose new issues of inquiry by which further work may be made possible.

The question of growth and stagnation in Indian agriculture over the colonial period, which is the subject of this volume, has been central to the debates on the impact of colonialism. The early estimates of George Blyn and Sivasubramonian offered a gloomy scenario of twentieth-century Indian agriculture, with yields failing to keep pace with population. This pessimistic picture was subsequently questioned in two ways. Disputing the reliability of agricultural statistics, historians suggested that no calculation of trends in yields was possible. Others recalculated the figures and doubted the basis of Blyn's pessimism. Alan Heston argued that the apparent downward trend in yields was the result of flawed estimation procedures, and needed to be revised. This 'revisionist' thesis was, in turn, subsequently challenged by other historians.

This volume presents the important contributions of the participants in this debate. In the introduction, Sumit Guha, critically assesses both the pessimistic and optimistic assessments, and concludes with an important section on productivity trends in the pre-Blyn period.

Acknowledgements

We are grateful to the following for permission to reproduce the essays included in this volume:

Popular Book Depot, for R. C. Desai, 'Crop Production' originally titled 'Crops', in *The Standard of Living in India and Pakistan* (1953). *The Indian Economic and Social History Review*, for: Alan W. Heston, 'Official Yields per Acre in India, 1886–1947: Some Questions of Interpretation' (1973) and 'A Further Critique of Historical Yields per Acre in India' (1978); Ashok V. Desai, 'Revenue Administration and Agricultural Statistics in Bombay Presidency' (1978); Carl E. Pray, 'Accuracy of Official Agricultural Statistics and the Sources of Growth in the Punjab, 1907–47' (1984). Manohar Publishers for M. Mufakharul Islam, 'Trends in Crop Production in the Undivided Punjab: A Reassessment', in Clive J. Dewey (ed.), *Arrested Development in India* (1988). *The Indian Journal of Agricultural Economics* for quotations from: C. H. Shah, 'Comparison of Yield Estimates prepared on the Basis of Traditional and Crop-Cutting Methods', vol. 17, no. 4 (1962); V. G. Panse, 'Why Crop-Cutting Methods?', vol. 18, no. 2 (1963) and C. H. Shah, 'Reply' in the name issue. The University of Pennsylvania Press for the two Appendix tables from George Blyn, *Agricultural Trends in India 1891–1947*. The essays by Ashwani Saith and P. P. Mohapatra are being published for the first time.

Introduction

Part A

The papers reprinted in this volume concentrate on seemingly recherche issues concerning the agricultural statistics of a period now long past: on the quirks and foibles, the judgements and guesses of defunct Directors of Agriculture and deceased *Patwaris*. Matters that now appear almost as remote as what song the Sirens sang, and what name Achilles assumed when he hid himself among women. . . . Yet, as the reader will find, the debate on agricultural productivity is far from dead, and still generates considerable heat among the protagonists. And this is because a number of wider theories turn upon conclusions emerging from the controversy regarding the levels and trends of agricultural production in British India.

The first, and most obvious issue is that of the impact of colonial rule on India. Nationalist critiques of its economic effects had begun to appear in the mid-nineteenth century, and a considerable body of official writing sought to rebut these attacks. Much of the debate related to national income and standards of living, and both of these, are, of course, intimately connected with output and productivity in agriculture. The issue is still alive, being connected with the wider polemic regarding economic imperialism and core–periphery relations in the world economy. Evidence from the official production series was recently used by N. K. Chandra to argue that there had been no improvement in mass consumption levels in India since the beginning of the present century.[1] And an economic historian could publish in 1984 a large volume devoted to refuting the work of R. C. Dutt (published 1904).[2]

Other equally important, if not equally contentious theories depend at least in part on the view we take of India's agricultural performance in the modern era. L. G. Reynolds for instance, classifies economic growth into extensive and intensive: the first being characterized by a constant per capita product, and the second by

[1] N. K. Chandra, *The Retarded Economies*, Bombay, 1988, ch. 5.

[2] M. B. McAlpin, *Subject to Famine: Food Crises and Economic Change in Western India, 1860–1920*, Princeton, 1983.

a rising per capita product. For India and Pakistan he sees the transition from one to the other as occurring only after Independence, which is also the time when, if the official series are to be trusted, agricultural output begins to increase after a quarter-century of virtual stagnation.[3]

Malthusian theory is also involved in the controversy. Malthus argued that a population unrestrained by prudential checks expands to the limits of food supply, when positive checks come into operation.[4] This part of his doctrine is, with modifications and emendations—notably the dropping of his untenable geometrical and arithmetical progressions—still maintained today. The Indian record seems strangely at variance with the theory. The positive checks (famines, epidemics) occur almost entirely before the First World War, when agriculture was apparently expanding, and cease after 1920 when population is growing with food supply constant. The bulk of the Indian population was believed to be at a bare subsistence level at the beginning of the century, and this phenomenon of population growth with declining food availability calls into question the whole notion of a subsistence level of consumption i.e. a level below which life and reproduction cannot be sustained for any prolonged period of time. The 1920–50 population growth becomes all the more puzzling because it cannot even be attributed to improvements in medical facilities or sanitary conditions—a proposition demonstrated in a recent paper by Ira Klein.[5]

Population and food supply thus present us with a puzzle. The problem also exists when considered as the relation between agricultural production and population density. It has been argued that agriculture reacts to population growth by technical and institutional changes. One form of this view is the famous involution hypothesis developed by Clifford Geertz, where both society and agriculture are modified by population pressure. Another adjustment hypothesis is that argued by Boserup, where appropriate innovations are the response to pressure.[6] A more

[3] L. G. Reynolds, *Economic Growth in the Third World: An Introduction*, ch. III, New Haven and London, 1986.

[4] T. R. Malthus, *An Essay on the Principle of Population,* vol. I, book 1, London, 1958.

[5] I. Klein, 'Population Growth and Mortality in British India', *The Indian Economic and Social History Review*, vol. XXVI, no. 4 and vol. XXVII, no. 1 (henceforth *IESHR*).

[6] C. Geertz, *Agricultural Involution: The Processes of Ecological Change in Indonesia,* Berkeley, 1963.

specific hypothesis developed by Ishikawa actually links land per head and productivity per unit land by a specific mathematical relation, with the implication that causation runs from the first to the second. This has been done using historical time-series data for Japan, and cross-sectional data for several Asian countries.[7] It is also specifically limited to paddy cultivation. Yet the important paddy region of eastern India does not respond to land scarcity in the way expected by Ishikawa.

Comprehensive agricultural statistics in India emerged from the British Government's efforts to cope with recurring famines and scarcities. The Famine Commission of 1880 recommended the compilation of such data, and comprehensive though often imperfect statistics began to be published from the end of that decade. The reporting system that took shape by the end of the century remained fundamentally unchanged until the Bengal famine of 1943 and continuing food shortages thereafter led to a complete overhaul of the statistical machinery.

The older statistics had been published annually by the Government of India, and the end of the forties saw two scholars R. C. Desai and George Blyn embarking on the formidable task of processing these data into comparable time-series of crop production in British India. Desai, whose chapter on this theme forms the first paper in our collection, was trying to estimate the national income of India for the decade ending 1940–1, but his discussion of the agricultural statistics remains one of the best to date, and it will be difficult to supersede his estimates for that decade. Blyn, on the other hand was solely concerned with agricultural or crop production (the two will be used synonymously throughout this essay), and worked on the much longer period 1891–1947. Preliminary findings were presented in 1951, and a revised version was published in 1966 in a volume entitled *Agricultural Trends in India 1891–1947: Output, Availability and Productivity*. No reader of this book can fail to be struck by the painstaking scholarship and immense labour embodied in it. Its findings were also sufficiently striking, and have been ably presented by Ashwani Saith in his paper included in this volume—complete recapitulation is, therefore, not necessary here. It suffices to say that Blyn presented a fairly grim

[7] S. Ishikawa, *Economic Development in Asian Perspective*, Tokyo, 1967.

picture of twentieth-century India, with food availability failing to match population growth after 1921, and food crops performing worse than commercial crops. The study related to the British-administered territory only—but few would argue that the inclusion of the generally more backward princely states would significantly change the picture. In 1965 S. Sivasubramonian completed a thesis on the national income of undivided India 1901–47, and his findings with regard to the agricultural sector essentially matched those of Blyn.[8]

Other scholars simultaneously approached the historical statistics from a different angle; they were concerned with problems of policy and planning that beset the Government of India before and after Independence. One of them remarked:

> One question in regard to agriculture most frequently asked in recent times is about the magnitude of production increases. It is at the root of the food problem, the problem of allocation of resources to agriculture and within agriculture between competing productive processes, the problem of price rise and inflation, and, if we take the enquiry to its very end, would be concerned with the problem of the pace and pattern of economic growth of the country.[9]

An early study was published by V. G. Panse in 1952.[10] Since the statistics for the permanently settled provinces were deemed unreliable, he confined himself to the remaining parts of British India, and analysed the trends in area and yield of different crops from 1911 to 1945. He found that

> For cash crops the data reveal clear evidence of generally increasing yield rates, and, in respect of sugarcane, an expansion of area as well. In respect of food crops also an expansion of area is perceptible in several cases as also an increase in the proportion of irrigated area. Yield trends are rather heterogeneous, yield showing an increase for certain crops

[8] S. Sivasubramonian, 'The National Income of India 1900–1 to 1946–47', unpublished Ph.D. thesis, Delhi School of Economics, 1965. His estimates for agriculture were published as 'Estimates of Gross Value of Output of Agriculture for Undivided India, 1900–01 to 1946–7', V. K. R. V. Rao et al. (eds), *Papers on National Income and Allied Topics*, vol. I, Bombay, 1960.

[9] M. L. Dantwala, 'Trends in Yields per Acre', N. V. Sovani and V. M. Dandekar (eds), *Changing India: Essays in Honour of Professor D. R. Gadgil*, p. 21, Bombay, 1961.

[10] V. G. Panse, 'Trends in Areas and Yields of Principal Crops', *Agricultural Situation in India*, June 1952.

in certain States, a decline in certain others and the absence of any perceptible change in the remaining.

M. L. Dantwala published a comparison of yields per acre from 1931 to 1959 in 1961. The most striking result was that taking all crops together, yields 'appear to have increased only slightly and insignificantly during 1931–59 . . .', while some important crops, such as rice showed a slight decline in the 1940s which might be related to increased under-reporting in that period. Dantwala tested the hypothesis that the older system of yield reporting underestimated yield by comparison with the crop-cutting surveys that came to be adopted after Independence, but found no evidence of such a tendency.[11]

The passage of time reduced the importance of these problems for policy-making, and the appearance of Blyn and Sivasubramonian's series seemed to provide a sufficiently solid basis for historical study. Both had taken great pains to fill gaps and eliminate inconsistencies in the data, and no one has, as yet thought it necessary or useful to replicate their labours as a whole. Revisions and emendations have either confined themselves to challenging the reliability of the figures themselves, or modifying some aspect of them at the all-India or provincial levels.

The most eloquent proponent of the first approach has been C. J. Dewey.[12] His paper could not, for reasons of space be included here. A few extracts however will give the reader an idea of his line of thought. His discussion concludes:

> Low grade Indian statistics were not just a question of poor organization at the centre. They were also a function of India's poverty. A myriad of good causes pressed on the slender resources of the state. The great majority of producers were illiterate and incapable of appreciating the significance of a statistical return. In a backward economy units of production were small, predominantly rural and dispersed over a huge area; subsistence production complicated the problem of measurement and evaluation; there were few trade or professional associations to act as intermediaries. India's vast size and population—the sheer number of units to be enumerated—was a problem in itself especially when the diversity of conditions made uniform arrangements impossible.

[11] M. L. Dantwala, *passim*.

[12] C. J. Dewey, 'Patwari and Chaukidar: Subordinate Officials and the Reliability of India's Agricultural Statistics', C. J. Dewey and A. G. Hopkins (eds), *The Imperial Impact: Studies in the Economic History of Africa and India*.

For all these reasons, the system through which the Indian agricultural statistics were collected was far more unstable and diverse than the bland prefaces to the published volumes of statistics—with their stereotyped descriptions of uniform procedures rarely operative in practice—would lead one to suppose. It varied from province to province, from district to district, even from official to official; and it changed, also, over time. It contained elements of negligence and incompetence, of subjectivity and conservatism, of corruption and absurdity. And in retrospect it seems impossible to reconstruct the system's vagaries—its advances towards reality and retreats towards convention—in sufficient detail or with sufficient certainty to correct their conflicting biases. Perhaps the only valid generalization about the net margin of error is that the system was inherently conservative. Official indifference and genuine perplexity stereotyped yields, in particular, at levels 'which had no basis in observed reality'. It was because the system was too sluggish to respond to the sowing of improved seeds that Bowley and Robertson—the most distinguished English statisticians to examine the Indian statistics—believed it 'impossible to ascertain whether the quantity of food produced is keeping pace with the population'. This was the opinion, also, of the most distinguished Indian statisticians to consider the problem, Sir John Hubback and P. C. Mahalanobis. We simply cannot know, with anything like the accuracy or the authority that Blyn implicitly assumes, how rapidly Indian agriculture expanded.

These conclusions are preceded by a blistering attack on the quality of the official statistics. Thus the section on area statistics is subtitled 'The Incompetence of the Primary Reporting Agency', and that on crop yields 'The Impossible Average'. Under these heads is assembled a veritable anthology of official denunciation of the agricultural statistics, as for instance a description of the field survey as 'a farce, and the annual papers a fraud'. Patwaris in Bihar and Punjab alike were, according to Dewey (Dewey, p. 287), indisciplined and irresponsible. He adds—

Certainly no Punjab *patwari* was ever dismissed for fabricating agricultural statistics: his official superiors never regarded them as important enough to warrant dismissal. So long as a *patwari* kept his land revenue accounts properly written up, he could fill the returns of agricultural statistics prescribed by an infinitely remote imperial department in any way he chose, frequently repeating the same figures year after year, without fear of reprisal.

As regards yield estimates (Dewey, p. 303), he writes:

The specific decisions were based on no consistent principle, except perhaps the belief that if only a large enough number of estimates was averaged out, however wide off the mark individual estimates might be, the result would turn out to be the right yield, because estimates that were too high would cancel out figures that were too low. A secretariat official exposed this fallacy: 'Put crudely, it amounts to this: that while $0 \times 1 = 0$, $0 \times 1000 = 950$. If very little reliance can be placed upon an individual experiment, the fact that it is repeated a thousand times does not make it any more trustworthy.

This line of thought should result in a complete rejection of the statistics as a whole, and this is where Dewey appears to be heading until seized by misgivings in his very last paragraph. The statistics suddenly become 'an inexhaustible repository of evidence for the historian of Indian agriculture'. In temporarily settled areas the area reports are

hard enough to show changes in cropping pattern which are invaluable evidence of farmers' response to price movements, to irrigation, to railways, to different tenurial systems, to the whole range of factors affecting Indian agriculture . . . the official data—with suitable modifications, and suitable reservations—can still reveal the most rapidly developing and the most disastrously deteriorating agricultural regions . . . all-India averages combine opposing trends—catastrophic deterioration in Bihar with rapid expansion in Punjab—to give an impression of general stagnation. . . .[13]

It seems likely that Dewey did not wholly realize the implications of what he wrote, for these statements amount to an implicit retraction of much of his earlier argument. Having come to curse the patwari he has stayed to bless him. Prices fluctuate considerably from season to season and year to year, and cropping patterns change in various ways in response to these fluctuations. If patwaris were habitually ignorant of the actual state of the fields, being deterred as Dewey eloquently puts it, by 'Snow in the hills, heat in the plains, floods in the river valleys . . .', and even the degree of their ignorance and sloth varied from time to time and place to place, it is impossible to see how the fine micro-regional time-series needed for a study of 'the whole range of factors affecting Indian agriculture' could be extracted from official data. Furthermore, if

[13] C. J. Dewey, pp. 313–14.

the output data are quite undependable, it is surely impossible to compare regions such as Bihar and Punjab with each other; on the other hand, if the performance of agriculture in distinct provinces can be compared over time, then there is no insuperable obstacle to the aggregation of the data to provide an all-India picture. And it is interesting that Dewey is willing to abandon his statistical agnosticism to the extent of assuming that Indian agriculture *expanded*—only Blyn's calculation of its rapidity is challenged. Dewey is an inconsistent Luddite who smashes the statistical machinery only when its products do not suit him.

Even if we disregard Dewey's inconsistencies, any discussion of agricultural statistics has to address the issue that he raises—what was the quality of the area and other statistics supplied by village-level officials? Dewey quotes many denunciations of the latter, but, as S. C. Mishra has pointed out, the same source also contain commendations of their work, so that 'no conclusion can be definitely drawn on the basis of such mixed and partial evidence'.[14] After some two decades of experience in the collection of agricultural statistics in various parts of India, the leading statistician V. G. Panse came out strongly in favour of the patwari agency. Wholesale criticism of the patwari data, he asserted, 'is born of ignorance and is not applicable to several types of agricultural statistics which the patwari produces such as those of land utilization, crop acreages or livestock numbers, but not others like crop yields, has been verified through several carefully conducted checks'.[15] The new crop-cutting surveys in the 1940s selected their fields on the basis of the patwaris' reports, and thus automatically tested the reliability of a well-distributed sample of them. Sukhatme and Panse described their findings in 1948:

In these surveys the fields for harvesting sample plots are selected randomly from a list of the fields shown to be growing a particular crop in the patwari's record, and it seldom happens that the fields so selected are found on inspection to grow something else. Again, the proportion of different categories of a crop, such as irrigated or unirrigated or of different commercial and agricultural varieties observed in the fields

[14] S. C. Mishra, 'On the Reliability of Pre-Independence Agricultural Statistics in Bombay and Punjab', *IESHR*, vol. XX, 2, 1983, p. 182.

[15] V. G. Panse, 'The National Sample Survey, Agricultural Statistics and Planning in India', Sovani and Dandekar (eds), *Changing India*, p. 214.

selected for sample surveys agree closely with the proportions in the area of these categories as enumerated by the revenue staff.'[16]

Since this referred to surveys carried out over several years in Punjab, CP and Berar we may take it as sufficient evidence that the area statistics of temporarily settled provinces were generally reliable—and this has been the opinion of most scholars who have worked in this field. Consequently, it is yield estimates that have borne the brunt of the attacks on the official output statistics for the temporarily settled areas.

The first substantial critique of Blyn's findings was made in a paper published by A. W. Heston in 1973. A rebuttal by A. V. Desai and a rejoinder by Heston appeared in 1978. Heston integrated much of the evidence presented by the agricultural statisticians like Sukhatme, Panse, and Shah but also did a good deal of intelligent and meticulous historical research and he remains, to date, the most solid proponent of what we may term the 'revisionist' school in the present controversy. His 1973 and 1978 papers are included in this volume so I shall only mention their leading points. In 1973, Heston argued that as standard yields in Bombay remained unchanged over the period 1897–1946, variations in yield per acre resulted solely from changes in the condition factors.[17] Trends in these, he argues, resulted from administrative changes, and did not reflect real trends in crop yields. He also felt that this was likely to hold in the temporarily settled parts of India, where there would be similar political pressures for suspension and remission of revenue.

This paper brought forth a response from A. V. Desai, which exposes its author's unfamiliarity with historical material, but nonetheless contains some telling points against Heston's methods and conclusions. The latter's response pointed out a number of Desai's errors, and further widened the scope of his attack on the historical statistics. In addition to arguing that a false trend appeared in the condition factors (CFs), he also added that the standard yields (SYs) themselves were initially too high, both out of ignorance and in order to present rural conditions in more favourable light. They

[16] V. G. Panse and P. V. Sukhatme, 'Crop Surveys in India', *Journal of the Indian Society of Agricultural Statistics*, vol. I, no. 1, 1948, pp. 38–9.

[17] Heston, 1973 in this volume, p. 120. The terms Standard Yield and Condition Factor have been defined and discussed by Heston (pp. 104–7) and Desai (pp. 75–7), in this volume among others.

were then gradually adjusted downwards, towards the real levels, and this contributed to an unreal picture of declining productivity. So both SYs and CFs possess unreal trends, and must be rejected. The best option, he suggests, is the adoption of the yields found around Independence for the whole period, unless there is independent evidence of either improvement or decline. Seasonal fluctuations may be incorporated by applying an index of seasonal deviations from the trend of Revenue Yield (RYs). However, he acknowledges that scholars like K. M. Mukherjee and R. C. Desai could justifiably use the official statistics in their work since the errors in these tend to cancel at the all-India level.[18]

Heston himself adopted a different approach in the chapter on the national income of India that he contributed to the Cambridge Economic History. Here he accepted the official figures for cotton, tea, coffee and sugarcane – official yields rose in all these cases. For seven major foodgrain crops, i.e. rice, wheat, *jowar*, *bajra*, barley, maize and gram, where official statistics show a decline in yield, he substitutes the average yield of the Indian Union for the triennium ending 1954–5, and the same procedure was followed for the remaining crops. Even this optimistic revision does not eliminate the decline in food availability per capita, though it reduces its magnitudes. While Sivasubramonian showed it as falling from 200 kgs in 1901 to 150 kgs in 1946, Heston's estimate shows a fall from 170 to 150 kgs over the same period.

We should also note another slight change in his position from that adopted in his 1978 paper. He now reverts to blaming the condition factor for the downward trend in yields, 'which was due to a secular decline in the condition factor, which was a by-product of the revenue system, and not supported by any rainfall trends. (If there were reasons for a downward trend in official yields, they should have shown up in declines in normal yields per acre, which was not the case.)'.[19] This is quite strange, since in the last table of his 1978 paper he attributes 70 per cent and more of the decline in official yields of three food crops to changes in their standard yields. These various points need to be successively considered.

We may begin with rainfall. While denying that he does so, Heston consistently argues as though total rainfall is the sole deter-

[18] A. W. Heston, 'National Income', Dharma Kumar (ed.), *The Cambridge Economic History of India*, vol. II, Cambridge, 1983, pp. 425–8.

[19] Ibid., p. 390.

minant of variation in crop yields, and that the apparent lack of correspondence between CF and rainfall is proof of the unreliability of the former. In fact a large number of factors determine a harvest, and it is possible to have very different yields with the same total precipitation. Furthermore, even if the relation postulated by Heston in fact held, then the data in his Table 3 indicate that yields in four out of five decades after 1898 should be below those of 1886–97 since the average rainfall was lower. It also washes out his belief that five or ten-year averages successfully neutralize climatic fluctuations. S. R. Sen noted in 1967 that while foodgrain production in India was increasing in the first quarter of the present century, it was characterized by growing instability. In the next quarter, production was stagnant but stable.[20] A careful study by S. K. Ray suggested that 'the relatively stable and unstable periods in past foodgrain production were, in great part, due to rainfall'. The period of higher and lower oscillation were approximately 24 years long.[21] So the rainfall statistics offer no evidence as to the reliability or unreliability of the reported condition factors.

Heston's hypothesis of the presence of an administratively generated downward bias in the CFs has not stood up well to criticism, and Heston himself admits this in his reply to Desai. A cogent refutation is also to be found in Saith (pp. 221ff., in this volume). I have demonstrated elsewhere that CFs in a major part of the Bombay Presidency *rise* after 1907, rather than falling as Heston's hypothesis requires. Furthermore, the revenue and statistical annawari were usually procedurally separate, and after 1920 a change in procedure made revenue suspensions *more* difficult to get.[22] A government that could do this shortly after the Kaira satyagraha, evidently had no intention of sacrificing revenue in order to appease rural agitations.

Coming now to the standard yields, Heston believes that they were initially too high because European yields were projected on India, and because officials desired to exaggerate Indian incomes and minimize the apparent burden of taxation. 'Consequently, a

[20] S. R. Sen, *Growth and Instability in Indian Agriculture,* Calcutta, 1971, pp. 2–3.

[21] S. K. Ray, 'Weather and Reserve Stocks of Foodgrains', Review of Agriculture, *Economic and Political Weekly*, 25 September 1971, pp. A-135 to A-138.

[22] S. Guha, *The Agrarian Economy of the Bombay Deccan 1818–1941*, Delhi, 1985, pp. 92–7.

number of downward revisions were in order and many were made in SYs over the subsequent 60 years.'[23] As regards the first point, by the 1890s crop estimates had been required for revenue settlements in UP, Punjab and Madras for some decades, and crop experiments had been carried out in Bombay for a quarter century. Local estimates had been made for Hunter's *Statistical Accounts* of eastern India as well. It is not likely that European yields would have been adopted in preference to these local sources. And the Bengal official who saw himself amidst the rice fields of Venetia would need to have an exceptionally powerful imagination.

As regards the second point, nationalist criticism of the economic effects of British rule can hardly be said to have died away in the twentieth century—quite the reverse. If this motive had led to the initially high estimation of SYs it should have equally operated to keep them at the earlier levels, if not to increase them further.

Again, if Heston's hypothesis is correct, then yields should start from an initially high level and then decline jerkily as statistical information accumulated. This did not happen. K. L. Datta, who was alive to the defects in the official statistics thought that the crop experiments in the quinquennium ending 1906–7 were 'more numerous, and perhaps more accurate than in any of the preceding periods. . . . In all but two provinces they have justified a modification of the provincial averages accepted as correct, the changes being generally in an upward direction'.[24] And, as Blyn points out, yields in Madras were increased in 1916–17.[25] SYs for individual districts continued to be revised upwards and downwards in subsequent years as well. Heston's argument would require that there be no upward revisions.

Furthermore, the changes did not affect all the crops uniformly. As Panse pointed out (see p. 4), increases were observed in cash crops, and decreases in some food crops in some provinces. Yet there seems to be no reason for officials to have initially underestimated cash crops while overestimating foodgrains.

Quite apart from SY and CF, the distribution of area under various crops would also affect long-run changes in reported yield,

[23] See p. 166, in this volume.

[24] K. L. Datta, *Report on an Enquiry into the Rise of Prices in India*, vol. I, Calcutta, 1914, pp. 73–5.

[25] G. Blyn, *Agricultural Trends in India, 1891–1947: Output, Availability and Productivity,* Philadelphia, 1966, p. 50.

especially if certain crops were displaced from the better lands and regions. This is brought out by a comparison of cotton and jowar in the Bombay Deccan between 1897 and 1937. Over this period the SY of unirrigated jowar decreased in three districts, increased in one, and was unchanged in six. The unweighted mean fell by 10 per cent—from 650 lbs to 585 lbs—but the acreage-weighted mean fell by 24 per cent, from 622 to 470 lbs per acre. On the other hand, the SY of cotton was reduced in seven districts and increased in three; its simple mean rose by 3 per cent and its weighted mean by 12 per cent.[26] K. L. Datta had noticed a tendency for commercial crops to occupy the better lands in the early years of the present century,[27] and these Bombay figures suggest that this tendency persisted.

In support of his contention that official yields did not reflect that real trends, Heston offers improved seeds, implements, dry-farming methods and chemical fertilisers as offsetting soil erosion and the shortage of organic manures.[28] The adoption of dry farming methods and new implements was negligible before Independence, and in any case the innovations that under-financed Departments of Agriculture had to offer were not infrequently of doubtful value. As regards better seed, the Departments had little success apart from cash crops like sugarcane, cotton and wheat.[29] Their officials also had a strong incentive to exaggerate their achievements, particularly in the retrenchment-prone interwar years. It is likely that the coverage of improved strains was exaggerated—at any rate, when such claims were investigated in Bombay in 1950–1, it was found that actual area under better seed was half the claimed area.

Finally, the most important meliorative factor was the 'more intensive use of land due to more workers per acre'.[30] This presumes that the technical and institutional requirements for such intensification were met in rural India: something that can by no means be taken for granted. The only evidence offered in this regard is the well-known inverse relation between farm size and output per acre found in several Farm Management studies of the 1950s. Krishna

[26] *Return of the Yield per Acre of Principal Crops in India, 1896–7 and 1936–7; Season and Crop Reports 1936–40; Reports of the Dept. of Land Records, 1896–1900.*

[27] K. L. Datta, p. 66.

[28] Heston, 'National Income', p. 390.

[29] For a detailed assessment of the working of one of the Agriculture Departments see Guha, *Agrarian Economy*, pp. 114–19.

[30] Heston, 'National Income', p. 390.

Bharadwaj has analysed this body of data, and found that no general relation existed between the yield per acre of specific crops and holding size. The inverse relation, where it exists, is probably due to more intensive cropping on smaller holdings.[31] This suggests that smaller farmers *cannot*, in fact, increase the yield of individual crops by applying more labour: they can only adopt a more intensive cropping pattern. So there is no support for Heston's belief that the yields of individual crops would be kept up by the growth of the agricultural population.

Even if we discount his hypothesis of biases in the revenue yields as being quite unsupported by evidence, it is still necessary to consider the impressive body of data marshalled in his Table 2, where he has compared crop-cutting and revenue yields for each district by seeing whether the former bears a linear relation to the latter. A somewhat similar comparison was made by C. H. Shah who examined the data for Bombay State from 1945 to 1955.[32] He found no statistically significant difference between the two series, and concluded that the revenue series could be used for long-period studies. Heston, reaches the opposite conclusion, even though his period and Shah's overlap for ten years.

Their methods, however, differ. Shah evaluates the revenue and crop-cutting series separately, and tests if the means and variances of the two are significantly different at the 5 per cent and 1 per cent levels. Subsequently he fits separate linear trends to the two series and compares the intercept and trend coefficients—again finding no significant difference for Bombay state as a whole. Heston, on the other hand treats the crop-cutting series as equivalent to the true yield, and any divergence of the revenue series from it is evidence of error in the latter. Now, crop-cutting yields are sample estimates, and subject therefore to sampling error. The *Season and Crop Reports* do not publish these, but Sukhatme has published them for three years in the late 1940s for wheat in major districts—those with more than 200,000 acres under the crop.[33] There were four such districts

[31] K. Bharadwaj, *Production Conditions in Indian Agriculture*, Cambridge, 1974, pp. 13–14.

[32] C. H. Shah, 'Comparison of Yield Estimates Prepared on the Basis of Traditional and Crop-Cutting Methods' and 'A Reply' (to V. G. Panse), *Indian Journal of Agricultural Economics*, vol. XVII and XVIII, 1962 and 1963.

[33] P. V. Sukhatme, *Sample Surveys for the Estimation of the Yield of Food Crops 1944–49*, ICAR, Delhi, 1950, Tables 4.2 and 6.2.

and the sampling error ranged from 5.6 per cent to 18 per cent, the median being 10.2 per cent. It is almost certain that the coarse grains, jowar and bajra would have a larger sampling error. Furthermore, this magnitude of error is for major districts – it would be greater in minor districts where the samples were smaller. This is also suggested by the fact that the s.e. for groups of districts (Divisions) are not much smaller than those for major districts, the range being 3.5 to 12.1 per cent, and the median 4.9. It should be noted that there were only four 'major districts' for wheat, and three for rice. Only 29 out of the 47 districts where Heston compares the five major foodgrains are major districts for those crops. Now the CCY series should be viewed as a band rather than a line, and for jowar, bajra and wheat as a band of ± 20 per cent or more, and much of the divergence between these and the RYs might thus be eliminated.

In any case a comparison of district yields would be relevant if one planned to work with the statistics at that level of disaggregation. The controversy has, however, centred at the level of the provinces and of India as a whole, and Heston himself has made an accross the board adjustment by replacing the historical yields with those of the Indian Union 1952–4. As Desai noted long ago, errors substantially cancel each other at the all-India level, and the discrepancy between official and crop-cutting estimates is much reduced. This is admitted by Heston himself when he accepts Mukherjee's use of the official series. Errors tend to cancel at lower levels of aggregation also: I have calculated the revenue and crop-cutting yields for fourteen districts of Bombay State over the period 1946–60 for wheat and rice, and 1950–60 for rabi jowar, kharif jowar and bajra, and correlated RY and CCY as Heston has done, making the latter the dependent variable. The results are in Table 1.

Comparing the means of RY and CCY, we see that the differences are marginal for rice and bajra, that wheat is considerably overestimated, and kharif and rabi jowar underestimated. The correlations are in all cases significant at the 1 per cent level. The CCYs have a much larger variance than the RYs: from two to eight times as large. This supports the suggestion that the latter underestimated good and overestimated bad harvests. On the whole, there seems to be little basis for a complete rejection of the official series, particularly as Heston's alternative is not without serious drawbacks.

His proposal is to adopt the average Indian yields of 1952–3 to 1954–5 to provide a base yield for the seven major foodgrains, and

Table 1. Correlation between RYs and CCYs

Crop	Mean CCY (lbs/acre)	Mean RY (lbs/acre)	Value of 'r'	Significant at
Rice	892	884	0.77	1%
Wheat	336	403	0.81	1%
Kharif Jowar	457	413	0.92	1%
Rabi Jowar	290	251	0.72	1%
Bajra	249	241	0.84	1%

NOTE: Data for rice and wheat refer to 1945–6 to 1948–9, and 1950–1 to 1959–60. For other crops the period is 1950–1 to 1959–60. The RYs have been calculated by multiplying Standard Yield and Condition Factor for each crop in each district, except in 1957–8. In that year's *Season and Crop Report* the Standard Yield for certain crops was taken as the average of the crop-cutting yield of the previous ten years or so. These new SYs were much lower than the older ones and since there seems to have been no change in the estimation of CFs, the use of the new SYs would result in a dramatic fall in output, and also break the continuity of the series since the official SYs were never intended to be actual average yields (which is why CFs did not average 100 per cent, but remained below it). The Government reverted to the old SYs in 1958–9, and so the output for 1957–8 has been calculated by using the year's CFs in conjunction with the 1958–9 SYs.

SOURCES: For 1945–6 to 1948–9, Sukhatme *Sample Surveys*; for 1950–1 onward, *Season and Crop Reports of Bombay State*, relevant years.

then generate a time-series by multiplying this base yield by the 'deviation of the official yield from the arithmetic trend of that yield over the 1900–47 period'.[34] Quite apart from the fact that the ground for his rejection of the official series is weak, this correction automatically projects Indian yields onto areas that were to be in Pakistan, and this by itself must introduce a considerable degree of inaccuracy. Secondly, fortuitously or otherwise, the triennium chosen by Heston contains one (and in some regions, two) bumper harvests, and the effect of this can be seen by comparing it with the previous and succeeding triennia (Table 2).

If these yields are applied to Sivasubramonian's acreages for the quinquennium ending 1924–5, we get (excluding ragi), an estimate of 41 million tons of foodgrain using the yields of the first triennium, and 49 million using those of the second—not an insigni-

[34] Heston, 'National Income', p. 426.

Table 2. Average Yield per Acre of Crops in India (lbs/acre)

Triennium ended	Rice	Wheat	Jowar	Bajra	Maize	Ragi	Barley
1951–2	640	586	331	250	536	580	660
1954–5	740	690	417	293	706	632	776
1957–8	761	615	395	262	684	689	710

SOURCE: *Area, Production and Yield of Forecast Crops in India* 1949–50 to 1959–60 (GOI, 1961).

ficant difference. It is true that crop-cutting surveys had not covered the whole country in the period covered by Table 2, but if we consider only states where official crop-cutting had started before 1950, such as Bihar and West Bengal, we observe higher yields in the early 1950s than in the previous decade. The same is true if we compare the Punjab data with the results of the ICAR surveys of 1943–9, and Heston notes evidence of an upward movement in Bombay yields as well.[35] Given this, the assumption that the Indian yields of the 1950s can be applied to the undivided India for the preceding fifty years is quite arbitrary and fraught with possibilities of error. Heston's remedy is worse than the disease.

Some scholars have preferred to tackle the statistics at the more manageable provincial level—and the quality of the data, of course, varies widely between provinces. One of the earliest revisions was the one made by M. M. Islam, who attacked one of the most difficult areas—permanently settled Bengal. He recognized the unreliability of the area and yield statistics, but chose to attempt a full-scale revision of only the former. While aware of R. C. Desai's work in this area, he felt that the revision carried out by him was too conservative, and that the official statistics understated area cultivated to a much greater extent than Desai believed, because the degree of understatement was sharply reduced in the early 1940s

[35] See p. 110, fn. 13 of this book. So undependable, however, are the historical statistics of this region that B. B. Chaudhuri in an analysis of power structure and agricultural productivity prefers not to discuss the yield trends at all, and generally makes only approximate estimates of variation in areas. See B. B. Chaudhuri, 'Rural Power Structure and Agricultural Productivity in Eastern India 1757–1947', M. Desai, A. Rudra and S. H. Rudolph (eds), *Agrarian Power and Agricultural Productivity in South Asia,* Delhi, 1984, p. 102.

when independent evidence first becomes available. In 1944–5 a full-scale survey (known as the 'Plot to Plot Enumeration') was carried out, and its findings were promptly published as the official estimates of area in Bengal, so that a comparison of the actual and official areas could not be carried out.

Islam tries to get round this problem by calculating what the official estimate for 1944–5 *would have been* had there been no upward revisions. This he does by projecting reported areas for the 21 years 1920–1 to 1940–1 in order to estimate a hypothetical reported area for 1944–5 for each of the five divisions of Bengal, and then compare this area with that actually ascertained by the survey in that year. The ratio of the two then provides him with a 'revision factor' by which the earlier statistics are multiplied in order to provide a corrected series.[36] This exercise is the core of his book, and most of his other revisions depend upon its soundness. Its assumptions deserve examination.

I have ascertained by recalculation for aman paddy that the projected official figure for 1944–5 is derived by fitting a line of the form 'a + bt' to the 21 years' data ending 1940–1, and much depends, obviously, on how well this line fits the data themselves. I have recalculated and tested the data for the major food crop—winter rice—which covered nearly 21 million acres or over half the cropped area in 1944–5.

Looking at Table 3, we may see that the linear trend is not a particularly good fit, and the $\bar{R}^2$ is low in all five divisions. Secondly, the confidence interval is quite wide, so that the official estimate for 1944–5, on which Islam's statistical edifice rests, could have been anything from 14.3 to 16.6 million acres of winter rice. In other words, the percentage underestimate could range from 31 per cent to 20 per cent: which is to say that Islam would have to revise the 1920–1940 data upwards by anything from 25 per cent to 45 per cent. The revised acreage of winter rice in 1920–1 is given as 20,714,000 acres by Islam—but his method could result in a probable range from 19.2 million to 22.2 million. The higher estimate would imply that the area *fell* by 6 per cent in the next quarter century; and the lower that it *rose* by 8 per cent in the same period. Both lie in the same confidence interval, and it is evident that calculations with such enormous margins of error are of little value, since they

[36] M. M. Islam, *Bengal Agriculture 1920–1946: A Quantitative Study*, Cambridge, 1978, ch. 1.

leave us unable even to say whether the cropped area increased or decreased during the period studied and, since reported yields changed little, also whether aman paddy production increased or decreased over a period of 25 years.

Table 3. Quality of Trend-Fitting: Aman Paddy

Division	$\bar{R}^2$	95% confidence interval (000 acres)	Revision factor 95% interval	Revision factor used by Islam
Rajshahi	0	3075 to 3777	1.39 to 1.70	1.53
Dacca	0.39	4243 to 4569	1.08 to 1.17	1.13
Chittagong	0.09	1902 to 2072	1.11 to 1.21	1.15
Presidency	0.24	2483 to 2933	1.28 to 1.51	1.38
Burdwan	0.22	2610 to 3242	1.41 to 1.75	1.56
Bengal		14313 to 16593	1.45 to 1.25	1.35

SOURCE: Calculated from data in the Appendix to M. M. Islam, *Bengal Agriculture 1920–1946.*

Apart from the statistical difficulties just outlined, Islam tries only to change the level of the official area series. Its trend is apparently found satisfactory. But was this, in fact, the case? Anyone who examines the official statistics for Bengal will be struck by the general absence of any trend in acreage. Thus, the Gross Crop area is reported as 30 million acres in 1890–4, 30 million in 1907–11, 29 in 1916–20, and 30 million in 1936–40, but 39 million in 1944–5.[37] Now, were there 9 million unreported acres in 1890, or did the extent of under-reporting increase over time? By adopting a constant revision factor Islam evidently opts for the first supposition. This implies that acreage, and therefore output remained more or less constant through the first half of the present century, and that production per head therefore fell off sharply after 1920 as a consequence of population growth. For food production per capita Islam's index shows a fall from 100 to 76 over this period, while the official series shows a more moderate decline to 89. If we take the comparison back to 1891 the effect is even more striking:

[37] Area in 1890–4 from K. L. Datta, *Report*, adjusted to exclude Orissa; area in 1907–11, ibid.; 1916–20 from *Season and Crop Reports of Bengal;* 1936–40 from Islam, *Bengal Agriculture,* Appendix and 1944–5 from *Agricultural Statistics of Bengal by Plot to Plot Enumeration*, Govt. of Bengal, 1946. The last is the 'Ishaque Report'.

the then population of 38 million would have the same cultivated area as the 60 million of 1941 – a decline of over a third. Since yields changed little (or, if anything tended to decline) production per head fell from a high level in the late-nineteenth century to an extremely low one in the middle of the twentieth.

There is, however, some evidence that this picture is not wholly accurate – and this is because the assumption of a constant degree of under-reporting is incorrect. The Ishaque report compared the acreage of winter paddy found in 1944–5 with that found in the various district settlement reports, and the former exceeded the latter in a number of districts, and in ten cases the notes to Ishaque's Table 2 explain this as due to the expansion of cultivation since the previous settlement. Such extension would obviously also depend on the availability of land, which varied from district to district, but if we correlate percentage increase in aman area with time elapsed since the last settlement we get a weak, but positive correlation ($r = 0.4$, significant at 5%), between the two. The median increase for districts settled up to 1920 was 11.5 per cent while for those settled in the 1920s it was 10 per cent. Districts settled in the 1930s also show increased aman paddy area; six of these were in western Bengal, and of these five had suffered a decline in population during 1911–21 – recovery from this and the availability of land may account for the growth. The median here was 5.6 per cent, but the highest value, that for Burdwan, was 23.6 per cent. The evidence therefore points to a slow, locally variable, but not insignificant increase in cultivated area in the first half of the present century. Islam's failure to consider this adds another element of uncertainty to his already shaky estimates. In fact, a thorough revision of the agricultural statistics of Eastern India should start from the reliable benchmarks given by the Settlement Reports and use both qualitative and quantitative evidence from the district level. This is obviously not within the scope of the present essay, but scrutiny of the settlement report areas in Ishaque's Table 2 suggests that paddy area might have grown by around 10 per cent in the three decades ending 1945.

Punjab agriculture in the British period has attracted considerable scholarly attention, and two papers on output and yields in this province are reprinted here. While Carl Pray attempts a re-estimation of yield and output levels over 1907–46, M. M. Islam concentrates on an earlier period, 1891–1906, and focuses on possible biases introduced by Blyn in his effort to fill the gaps in the official series. Islam argues that his procedures resulted in overestimation of yield and output growth for the period 1890–1905. Some of the discrepancies observed by Islam are not difficult to explain. For example, he complains that the area and production of wheat in Punjab as given in the *Estimates of Area and Yield* do not match those that appear in the *Season and Crop Reports*. This is simply because the former, down to the 1920s, include the Punjab princely states, and the latter refer solely to British territory, and this is explicitly stated in both. Blyn, incidentally, was aware of, and adjusted for this problem in the *Estimates*.[38]

A more substantial point relates to the reporting of crop areas in Punjab before 1906–7. It was Punjab practice at that time to deduct 'failed area' from sown area, and to report the remnant as 'matured area'. K. L. Datta described the procedure as follows: 'the area of each crop was reduced to a conventional standard called the normal' which was estimated by multiplying sown area by 'a fraction representing the proportion of the crop harvested to a normal crop. . .'.[39] The failed area seems to have been usually about 15 to 20 per cent of the sown area. The sown area for individual crops is unavailable before 1906–7, but is published instead of matured area from that year. The effect obviously, is that a given output being distributed over the (larger) sown area instead of over matured area, the reported yield per acre would fall.

Now, the area of minor foodgrains—barley, maize, gram and bajra—in Punjab would increase sharply from 1906–7, and since Blyn had estimated their yield for the earlier period on the basis of wheat and sesamum whose sown area was available to him from 1893–4, their earlier output is artificially depressed by the fraction: Wheat matured area/Wheat sown area.

Islam evidently estimates this at 0.8, and thus presumably suggests an upward revision of the output figures for the pre-1906 period by 25 per cent. There are grounds, however, for presuming that this is an overestimate. K. L. Datta published a consistent series for matured areas under various crops from 1890–1 to 1911–12 for an area that exactly corresponds to Blyn's Greater Punjab. If we compare these with Blyn's series we can directly estimate the matured area/sown area ratio. This turns out to be much larger

[38] Blyn, *Agricultural Trends*, p. 261, note.
[39] K. L. Datta, *Report*, vol. I, Appendix D, p. 225.

than 0.8; on the aggregate of the years 1893–4 to 1905–6, it is 0.94 for wheat and 0.97 for sugarcane. So the understatement in Blyn would be at most 6.4 per cent for gram and barley, and 3 per cent for bajra. This effect would be swamped by the rapid rise of reported wheat yields in Punjab. The effect of this rise may be seen by the fact that the yield per *matured* acre for the four years ending 1892–3 was 614 lbs, while the yield per sown acre for the five years ending 1910–11 was 747 lbs.[40]

Was the failed area of gram and barley and bajra greater than that of their surrogate crops? In the absence of sown area statistics no definite answer is possible, but it is obvious that irrigation was probably the main protection against total failure. So, Table 4 shows the percentage of irrigated to sown area in the quinquennium ending 1910–11 in British Punjab.

Table 4. Percentage of Sown Area Irrigated, Punjab, Quinquennium ending 1910–11

Crop	Percentage
Wheat	50
Barley	29
Bajra	8
Gram	17
Maize	40
Sugarcane	79
Sesamum	26

SOURCE: BEIP *Agricultural Statistics.*

The lower percentages of irrigated area for barley, gram and bajra would suggest that the failed area in these crops is greater than that of their surrogates. On the other hand, the understatement of area may be neutralized by the rapidly rising trend in yield for gram and barley that results from their association with wheat. The rise in wheat yield is not implausible in view of the vast expansion of its cultivation on virgin lands under canal irrigation, but it is unlikely that the other two crops benefited to the same extent. Thus understatement of area would be offset by overstatement of yield,

[40] Comparing data in *Land Revenue Administration Report of Punjab 1893–94* with *Agricultural Statistics of the Punjab 1901–2 to 1935–6*, Board of Economic Enquiry Punjab, Lahore, 1937.

reducing the error, and leaving its net effect on the statistics indeterminate.

Coming now to Islam's own revised series, it is evident that for the period 1906–7 to 1910–11 the use of the direct estimates from the *Season and Crop Reports* is superior to Blyn's use of surrogate crops to estimate yields, but, on the other hand, he seems to be advocating a complete rejection of the data for 1891–1906, which is rather an extreme solution – many problems in historical statistics can easily be solved by rejecting the statistics. Various devices can be used to get round the problem of comparability: thus K. L. Datta calculated a consistent series of output that can be compared to Blyn, whose appendix tables contain estimates for the output of five major foodgrains in Greater Punjab, but for four of these he estimated yields upto 1910–11 on the basis of the yields of surrogate crops. Only for wheat was he able to get direct estimates for the whole of his first two decades. Datta on the other hand had estimates like Blyn for matured area, but was also able to procure condition factors, and then applied the Standard Yields of 1907 to generate a time-series of production. Blyn and Datta's output estimates are compared for five foodgrains, and for wheat in Figure 1. It is noticeable that Blyn's estimates are well below Datta's till 1904–5; the wheat estimates become practically identical from that year, and the foodgrain estimates from 1905–6. The close match of the fluctuations in yields of the five grains is, incidentally, a tribute to the success of Blyn's use of surrogates to estimate yields. Now, it will also strike the reader that, while Blyn's series shows a strong upward trend, Datta's does not: normal seasons in the early 1890s, then bad years around the turn of the century followed by normalcy again, produce an S-shaped oscillation, but the trend is weak.

Now, the difference between the two series must originate in the adoption of the 1907 SYs by Datta, while Blyn's figures reflect the lower SYs of earlier quinquennia – the upward trend in Punjab output in the first two decades is mainly a result of the revision of Standard Yields. This is, of course, no ground for assuming that that trend is fictitious. It is quite possible, for example, that yields in the canal-irrigated tracts improved from the pioneer levels of the first years and that the rise in the SY of irrigated wheat from 917 lbs in 1897, to 935 in 1902, to 994 in 1907 reflected a genuine improvement. Unirrigated wheat was 576 lbs in the first period, then raised to 642, and subsequently lowered to 619 lbs. Datta, on the other

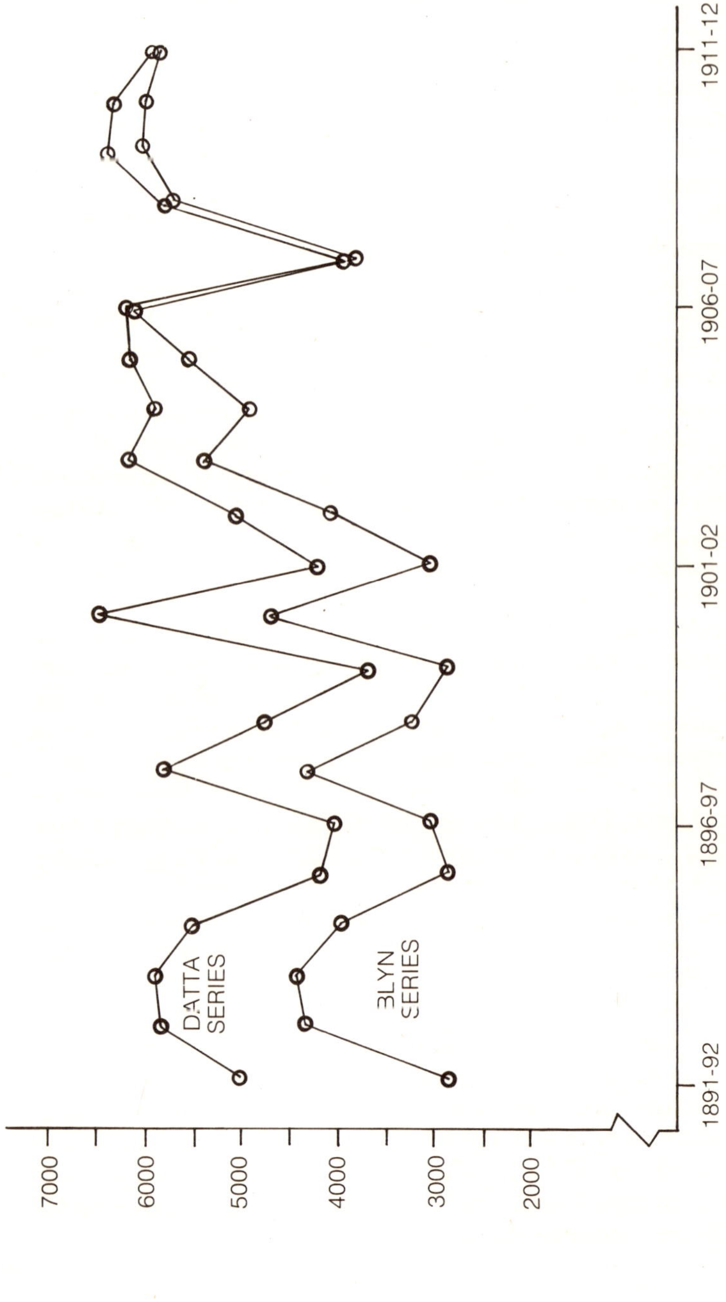

Figure 1. Gross Output of Five Foodgrains, Greater Punjab (000 tonnes)

hand, felt that successive estimates should be viewed as successive approximations to the truth, and that the latest available to him were the most reliable, and thus should be applied to the whole period; such an assumption is not wholly implausible. One strong argument against the immediate adoption of Datta's estimates would be that the earlier CFs were reported against the then existing SYs, and not those of 1907. Use of the latter may inflate the estimates. Further research, perhaps using the assessment reports of this period may be able to settle this point.

This issue of the effect of SY changes on reported yield also sur- faces in the other paper of Punjab by Carl Pray. This author suggests that the fluctuations in reported output were in large measure the consequence of changes in SY. But the presence of sizeable seasonal fluctuations makes this hypothesis almost impossible to prove, nor does Pray test it in any rigorous way.[41]

Islam's paper has implications for British Indian statistics as a whole, and not merely for those of the Punjab inasmuch as he brings to notice the difficulties that Blyn faced in preparing his series up to 1911 and the various adjustments made by him. But we are fortunate in possessing an alternate series prepared by K. L. Datta, who had the advantage of being a contemporary and a senior official. His adjusted series for acreage should certainly be superior to Blyn's in that he was able not only to use all the available official sources but also to clear up doubts and discrepancies by direct reference to the compilers. However, his index of area cultivated shows almost the same changes as a similar series calculated from Blyn's data, which is again evidence of the perspicacity of the latter.

Only one of the papers in this volume attempts a revision on yield statistics at the provincial level: Pray's study of Punjab 1907–47. He argues that the official series are inaccurate, and generally underestimate output. The evidence successively presented is (i) the apparent underestimation of the cotton crop in the 1930s (see his Table 1). This is established by comparing the baled crop *plus* an estimate of extra-factory consumption with the official yield. It will be noticed that the baled or pressed crop comes close to the official estimate: the discrepancy arose mainly from the estimate of home consumption. Now this estimate is derived from a one-time survey carried out by the Indian Central Cotton Committee, where representative villages were selected 'in consultation with local

[41] See Pray, p. 183, in this volume.

revenue officers', and a door-to-door enquiry made.[42] The enquiry did not, therefore use the 'statistically sound sampling techniques' that Pray generally demands. Furthermore, even if the result was accurate at the time, it seems questionable to assume that it remained the same over seven years—surely demand for new quilts or mattresses of home-spun would be affected by economic conditions over the years. Furthermore, the acreage data in Pray's table refer to British territory alone, but cotton moved from the states to British provinces to be ginned and pressed thus inflating the local estimate.

At a more general level, if inaccuracy in cotton statistics is to be used to discredit official crop estimates then the post-Independence data on which Pray relies should also be discarded since, as Table 5 shows, they err as widely as the old revenue yields. In fact, the cotton crop is by its nature uniquely difficult to estimate since the bolls open slowly over several weeks, the yields of successive pickings vary, and, finally the percentage of cotton to seed itself varies between different pickings and over successive seasons. It is thus unwise to totally reject yield estimates because of their failure to attain accuracy for cotton (an error of mine in the past).

The second evidence is the supposed failure to increase yields in line with the spread of improved Coimbatore varieties of cane. The data are culled form an ICAR enquiry that covered 48 purposively selected holdings in each of the three districts, and related to an annual average area of 71 acres in Lyallpur, 32 acres in Jullundur, and 67 in Gurdaspur.

It will be seen that the desi and Coimbatore canes tended to be grown in geographically distinct areas, making comparisons difficult. Furthermore, there is also the problem of the representativeness, as even the sanguine author of the *Marketing Report* (p. 21) admitted:

> As however the above noted three districts are not fully representative of the conditions prevailing in the other sugar growing tracts of the province, no definite conclusions can be arrived at with the available data.

Finally, we should also note that the ICAR study calculated yields on the basis of cane area that came to maturity, and was actually

[42] R. C. Desai, *The Standard of Living in India and Pakistan 1931–32 to 1940–41*, Bombay, 1953, p. 169.

Table 5. A Comparison of Official and Trade Estimates of Cotton Output (lakh bales)

Year	Official Estimate (Revised)	Cotton Committee Estimate II	Percentage Difference
1934–5	48.6	48.0	– 1.1
1935–6	58.7	62.5	+ 6.5
1936–7	62.3	70.9	+ 13.8
1937–8	57.8	63.7	+ 10.2
1938–9	50.5	59.0	+ 16.8
1939–40	49.1	58.1	+ 18.4
1940–1	60.8	70.3	+ 15.6
1941–2	62.2	70.8	+ 13.8
1942–3	47.0	49.6	+ 5.6
1943–4	52.6	57.2	+ 8.8
Aggregate	549.6	610.1	+ 11.0
1948–9	17.7	23.3	+ 32.1
1949–50	26.3	27.4	+ 4.3
1950–1	29.7	31.2	+ 5.1
1951–2	31.3	38.1	+ 21.6
1952–3	31.3	36.0	+ 15.0
1953–4	39.6	43.9	+ 10.8
1954–5	42.3	53.3	+ 26.1
1955–6	40.0	44.6	+ 11.5
1956–7	47.3	42.5	– 10.3
1957–8	47.4	56.5	+ 19.1
Aggregate	352.9	396.8	+ 12.4

SOURCE: M. L. Dantwala, 'Trends in Yields per Acre', Table 3.

crushed for *gur*. This area was always less than the planted area, as the inferior portions of fields were often cut early and fed to cattle.[43] The Provincial estimates, however, relate to the planted (or 'sown' area), and their average yields should be less than the ICAR ones even if the latter represented a proper sample of cane areas in the province.

Again, even if better, i.e. more input-responsive, strains of cane did spread in the 1930s it does not follow that yields would rise by any given percentage; instead, given low prices and a tight credit

[43] This is evident when we look at the disaggregated data, and is commented on in the Report. See ICAR, *Report on the Cost of Production of Crops in the Principal Cotton and Sugarcane Tracts in India*, vol. I, Calcutta 1938, 1940, p. 29.

Table 6. Acreage under Cane: Total of Three Years 1933–6

District	Desi	Improved Coimbatore	Average yield (mds of gur)
Lyallpur	180.6	33.09	23.6
Jullundur	11.14	84.84	39.8
Gurdaspur	200.11	None grown*	17.5

SOURCE: *Cost of Production of Crops*, ICAR, vol. 1, Punjab.

* Pray's statement (Table 2 of his paper) that 'there was no survey in the district that year' is not to be found in his source, the *Marketing Report*. It is his own addition, and it is false.

market, the farmers' response might be to reduce inputs in order to minimize the cost of production.[44] So even if we accept the Agriculture Department's estimates for the spread of new strains we should not expect yields to increase by any specific percentage nor assume under-reporting if they do not. In fact, the official yields in Pray's Table 6 show a decline between the 1920s and 1930s, and then an increase during the Second World War, which is roughly what one would expect.

As regards the remaining crops, mainly foodgrains, Pray compares the results of the sample surveys from 1943–4 to 1945–6 with the official estimates for that period, and finds underestimation. Much of the discrepancy originates in 1945–6, when, as Desai observed 'every provincial unit was interested in stating as low an estimate of its outturn as possible'.[45] And when Sukhatme came to review the results of five years' crop-cutting experiments in Punjab, he noted as a 'remarkable feature' the general overall agreement between the official district normal yields and the averages of the

[44] The Bombay Department of Agriculture recommended this as being the best strategy for sugarcane growers in the 1930s. *Agriculture Department Annual Report 1935–6*, p. 91.

[45] Desai, p. 82, in this volume. Pray writes: 'I am *assuming* that the yield in the beginning period is the same as the end except in crops where there is clear evidence of some change due to new technology, weather, or disease.' Emphasis added. The revision is carried out on this basis, with increased yields for three crops 'due to the introduction of improved crop varieties' — evidence of which is, as we saw, a little shaky. The new aggregate is then disaggregated, and it is hardly surprising that it 'indicates that new varieties of wheat, sugarcane and desi cotton did increase yield per acre and that the introduction of a stream of new varieties of American cotton improved the value of the cropping pattern'. The assumption thus reappears as a conclusion.

survey yields. He suggested that this might be because the former were also based on crop-cutting experiments.[46] In view of this it is somewhat rash to replace the official yields for four decades with the average of three years' crop-cutting yields as Pray suggests we do.

The other evidence for underestimation is also rather dubious. This is a comparison of official yields for east Punjab in 1942–6 with those found in 1952–6 under the assumption that 'there were no major changes in the technology or amount of inputs in these crops. The main cause of differences in yields . . . was the shift from the old method of determining yields to the new technique'. As a matter of fact, this was a period when the consumption of chemical fertiliser in India increased quite sharply, and the Bhakra system began to function. In 1951–2 it irrigated 19,000 acres, and by 1955–6 supplied 960,000 acres in Punjab and 139,000 in PEPSU.[47] These can hardly be regarded as insignificant changes, and the yield of wheat in Punjab in 1952–6 was 8 per cent above the level found by the ICAR in 1943–9. So all the elements of Pray's recalculation are distinctly shaky, and the decomposition of this dubious composite is not likely to produce useful results.

After Punjab we come to UP where Ashwani Saith's paper breaks new ground in a number of directions. First of all it goes back before Blyn, and considers evidence from the early nineteenth century. This material is ably integrated with evidence from later sources in order to construct a coherent description of trends down to the middle of the twentieth century, and the whole is woven into a coherent rebuttal of the major criticisms of Blyn's findings. Material for such a long span, is, however, available for only two districts of UP—Muzaffarnagar and Bareilly. Saith concludes that yields on irrigated and unirrigated land changed little between 1840 and the end of the century, and showed a tendency to drift downwards thereafter. However, the expansion of canal irrigation compensated for this till about 1920, but when this 'shift effect' ceased yields began to move down exactly as depicted by Blyn.

For early nineteenth-century Muzaffarnagar, Saith rejects the average of 14 years' yields extracted by Thornton from *zamindari* accounts in favour of the yield found by appraisement in the rabi season of 1840. The former gave the wheat yield as 653 lbs per acre

[46] Sukhatme, *Sample Surveys*, p. 51.

[47] *Report of the Committee on Fertilisers 1965*, GOI, 1966, p. 4; annual *Reports of the Ministry of Irrigation and Power 1952–3* and *1955–6*.

and the latter as 794 lbs. Saith rejects the lower estimate on the ground that better lands had been misclassified as inferior lands, so that the weighted average yield for all types of soil was shifted downward. If we accept the 1827–40 estimates, then there would appear to have been a slight rise in yield over the middle decades of the nineteenth century, before the decline set in during the second quarter of the twentieth century. The decline may have been understated in the official series. The average yield 1942–9 according to the official estimates was 821 lbs of wheat per acre, but the ICAR crop-cutting survey found the actual to average 740 lbs over 1944–9, or 10 per cent less. Even if we compare it with the lower estimate for 1827–40 i.e. 653 lbs, we observe that an increase in irrigated area from 16.8 per cent of the area under wheat to 64 per cent could only increase yield by 13 per cent overall on the most optimistic estimate (and decrease by 7 per cent by comparison to the single year 1840).

Now, Saith assumes that the 'rent register yields' were aggregated after weighting them according to the distribution of the different types of soil in the district. But I can find no mention of such a procedure in Thornton's report. He merely says that the RR papers were organized according to circle and *mouza* (village) i.e. on a geographical basis.[48] The average yield thus arrived at over 14 years was adopted as the standard, but its distribution over different types of soil was made by assuming that their relative productivity was that found by the estimate (*kankut*) of 1840. The revenue rates for the different soils were then calculated on this basis, and amounts payable by each village and circle worked out from the survey's classification of soils.

Now, it is the tax distribution resulting from this that is the main target of Cadell's criticism in 1878. In particular, he felt that the southern parts of the district where there was a larger area of better soil were under-taxed by comparison with the northern tracts.[49] The quotation in Saith's footnote 32 (p. 239 in this volume) refers to the southern part of the district only. As regards his point (c) the distribution of cash and kind rent at this time was not according to soil but according to crop, so it is not likely that there would be much wheat under the cash rent system. Finally, the year 1840 was

[48] Thornton, *Reports on the Settlement of District of Moozuffurnuggur*, Agra, 1842, p. 21.

[49] Cadell, *Settlement Report on the Ganges Canal Tract in the Muzaffarnagar District*, Allahabad, *1878*, pp. 41–5.

not a notably bad season, and Thornton in fact reports that crops on the poorer soils yielded relatively well that year.[50] There thus seems to be no good reason to reject the average yield of the years 1827–40 in favour of the 1840 yields. The comparative data for certain important crops are given in Table 7.

Table 7. Comparative Data for Average Yields (1827–40 and 1840)

Crop	1827–40		1840	
	Area covered (acres)	Yield (lbs/acre)	Area Covered (acres)	Yield (lbs/acre)
Rice	34,986	531	–	–
Jowar	18,112	421	–	–
Bajra	68,339	355	–	–
Wheat	128,439	653	11,419	793
Gram	35,626	458	2,135	624
Barley	25,749		1,020	897

SOURCE: *Muzaffarnagar S.R.*, Appendices 2 & 3.

Adopting the 1827–40 yield for wheat makes for a sharper increase to 1878 rather than the negligible change that results from single-year comparisons. As regards the terminal period, the 1940s, the ICAR crop-cutting data are obviously superior to the official estimates, and they give the average yield of wheat as 740 lbs in Muzaffarnagar, and 546 in Bareilly,[51] showing a small increase over a hundred years in the former, and a sharp decline in the latter. If we adjust for the spread of irrigation (as Saith suggests), the intrinsic yields will be lower in both cases, so that his conclusions are not affected.

Finally we come to Mohapatra's heroic attempt to provide a definitely rational if not a wholly real series for acreage and output for a permanently settled region—the Chotanagpur division of Bihar. Acreages, condition factors and standard yields all had to be re-cast. The author has given a very full description of the methods used, so they need not be rehearsed here. He breaks new ground by testing his estimates against the consumption figures of nutritional surveys for the decade 1938–47, and the results strongly support his production estimates. It is interesting to observe that per capita production fluctuated upto 1923, and then began to decline

[50] Thornton, *Report*, p. 21.
[51] Sukhatme, *Sample Surveys*, Table 8.4.

as the population grew in the subsequent decades, which is in agreement with Blyn's estimates for British India in these periods. On the other hand, the downward trend visible in the official output series for Chotanagpur is absent in the revised series, where the yield per acre fluctuates, and acreage slowly increases.

This corroborates Blyn's suggestion that the decline in Bihar–Orissa rice yields after the First World War is a statistical aberration, and that the assumption of constant yields for this region is to be preferred. Given the independent confirmation by Mohapatra, it is possible that Blyn's revised series may be preferable to his main one. Its adoption eliminates the downward trend in yields for Greater Bengal in the twentieth century, even though the decline in per capita production of foodgrains persists.

Blyn's alternative estimates were calculated on the assumption that there was no trend in rice yield per acre in Bihar–Orissa after this region was separated from Bengal,[52] and the effects of this revision are best described by Blyn (p. 223) himself:

> The modified trend rates of output, though more favourable, remain less than the population growth rates of about one per cent per year in the last four reference decades. For Greater Bengal the originally negative output trend rates for the last four reference decades are replaced with more credible, rising trends, even though per capita output would still have been falling. For British India the virtually changeless level of foodgrain output in the last part of the period is replaced with a trend which was rising, though relatively slowly. The British India all-crop yield per acre trend is no longer seen as almost at constant level, but rather it pitched upward at a rate which appears beyond the range of that which might have been caused by rainfall alone.

His modified series is reproduced in Table 8. It will be observed

[52] I reproduce Blyn's description of his procedure: '1) annual rice yields per acre reported for the period up to 1911–12 in Greater Bengal were reduced by 22 per cent to make the average of that period equal to the average for 1937–38 – 41–42, 749 pounds; (2) a parabolic trend was fitted to reported rice yields (as given in Appendix Table 3A) for 1912–13 – 1946–47. The relative deviation of each year's reported yield per acre from the trend value for that year was obtained. The yield per acre for each year in the annual series was established 749 plus or minus this relative deviation; this series thus contained annual fluctuation but no trend (given in Appendix Table 9A). (3) Greater Bengal rice output was recomputed by multiplying annual acreage by the yield per acre series established in the manner described above.' *Agricultural Trends*, p. 222, footnote 2.

that, as in the original series, the increase is most rapid upto the First World War, and then slows down so that output per capita would be on the decline from 1921. Foodgrains show the same pattern, but slower growth, and their total output remains almost unchanged over the last twenty-five years of his period.

However, the whole of this effect results from the single assumption that the official rice yields of the late thirties may be substituted for the reported yields of the preceding forty years. Since the later yields were lower than the earlier ones, the effect of this change is to lower rice output by 3 to 4 million tons a year for the years before World War I, and by 1½ to 2 million tons in the two decades after it.

In fact, since acreage was so slow to change, dramatic fluctuations in output can result from changing assumptions about yield levels. Thus K. L. Datta, who, as we saw, used the 1907 Standard Yields for the entire period 1890–1912 produced output estimates that differ significantly from Blyn's original and modified estimates. This is evident from Table 8.

Table 8. Gross Output of Eight Major Foodgrains: Annual Averages (million tons)

Quinquennium ending	Blyn original	Blyn modified	K. L. Datta
1894–5	45.4	41.5	54.4
1899–1900	47.0	43.3	53.3
1904–5	50.0	46.5	57.3
1909–10	48.3	44.9	54.3

NOTE: In the first row, Blyn is averaged over only four years.

SOURCE: Blyn, *Agricultural Trends*, Appendix Tables; K. L. Datta, *Report*, vol. I, pp. 52–6.

Now, if Datta is correct, gross foodgrain output at the end of the last century was as high as in the middle of the present one if not higher, that is, it decreased over time. According go Blyn's original series it stagnated; according to his revised one it grew slowly; it all depends on what assumption we make about the trend in rice yield in eastern India. Mohapatra has found a constant or very slowly rising trend of yield in south Bihar. Before we assume this to hold elsewhere, we should note that in 1940s this Division was, very unexpectedly, found to have the highest rice yields in Bihar[53] which may indicate that it progressed whereas others stagnated. So, in the present state of knowledge it is very difficult to decide the issue of yield trends in Eastern India, but to me it seems safest to accept Blyn's original series rather than any revisions—whether by Datta, Blyn or Heston—that depend on the assumption of a long-run stability in yields. This is for two reasons: first, the CFs were being reported with the then prevailing SYs in mind, and second, the district level data presented below indicate that yields could vary considerably over long periods of time. Hence it follows that the judgements of contemporary observers should not be rejected unless there is strong evidence against them. But the finding of independent evidence must be accorded a high place on the agenda of any historian interested in resolving the controversy that forms the theme of this volume.

Part B: Before Blyn

The reader will observe that the whole discussion so far has centred on the fifty or sixty years after 1890. There is of course good reason for this: it is only from this date that we have even moderately comprehensive series for cropped area in the major provinces of British India and can therefore make comparisons that are not entirely vitiated by changes in coverage. And this is also the beginning of yield estimates made for at least some major crops on an annual basis. The nature of the evidence itself dictates that comprehensive studies of output and productivity must begin in the last decade of the nineteenth century. Yet, when we review the findings of such studies we cannot but be struck by a sense of stasis to find that scholars holding rival views produce with enormous labour, estimates that differ by a fraction of one per cent per year. Indian agriculture seems utterly sluggish and the rhythms of economic change to be dominated by population change—an influenza epidemic can produce a peak in output per capita, and the control of plague can shrink it.

But this seeming agricultural stasis was itself not an inheritance from the remote past—rather it may have set in just before our agricultural statistics commenced in the 1880s. There are evidence that the grand climacteric of Indian agriculture came in some

[53] Sukhatme, *Sample Surveys*.

regions in the middle decades of the nineteenth century, and was followed by a stagnation that ended only after Independence. If this hypothesis is valid then historians need to reach back into the earlier decades of the nineteenth century, and not remain content with an analysis of trends for the last fifty years of British rule. This section therefore cites some of the evidence on this question and offers a few preliminary results in order to emphasize the importance of further work on this period.

Any study that goes back into the nineteenth century must of necessity compile its estimates on the basis of regional and provincial data. Eastern India, as ever, presents the most intractable obstacles in this respect. Colebrooke estimated its population at around 30 million in 1803, and the tilled area at 31 million acres.[54] The Permanent Settlement fixed the land tax at the equivalent of Rs 3 crores. Landlord rents were possibly around Rs 3.5 crores. By 1877 they were returned as Rs 13 crores and by 1900 at Rs 16.8 crores.[55] Meanwhile an estimate of the population in 1822 gave it at nearly 40 million with a density of 259 to the square mile and 1872 at some 68 million by actual census.[56] The increase in landlord income and the evidently growing population indicate an expansion of cultivation. And in areas where there is good evidence of cultivation and population lagging behind—as in western Bengal districts such as Burdwan or Midnapur—the rental also increased by a markedly smaller amount.[57] By the early years of the present century this expansion had run its course and K. L. Datta could state that Bengal and Bihar were fully occupied and cultivated, when he took the total area in tillage at 51 million acres in 1910–11.[58] Further growth was still possible as we saw when discussing Islam's revision of the acreage data, but it was small. Even by encroaching on groves

[54] *Remarks on the Husbandry and Internal Commerce of Bengal*, London, 1806, pp. 19–24.

[55] B. Chaudhuri, 'Agrarian Relations: Eastern India' in *The Cambridge Economic History*, vol. II, p. 135.

[56] R. Montgomery Martin, *British India*, rpt., Delhi, 1983, p. 502; *Report on the Census of Bengal 1872*.

[57] *Census of Bengal 1872*, p. 94; district-wise rent data in M. Finucane, Dy. Collector, Gaya, report of 9 May 1881, printed in *Report of the Government of Bengal on the Proposed Amendment of the Law of Landlord and Tenant*, vol. II, Calcutta, 1883, pp. 396–7.

[58] K. L. Datta, pp. 54–5.

and land for other purposes, paddy land could only grow by a median of 11.7 per cent over twenty-five years.

As regards what was to become the UP, the western districts and Rohilkhand seem to have suffered from the political instability that accompanied the transition to British rule, with a consequent decline in cultivation. Some of this land came under the plough again in the early decades of the nineteenth century. In the East there was clearance and settlement in districts such as Azamgarh and Gorakhpur. The Doab districts suffered a setback as a consequence of the famine of 1837–8, and shortly after this a comprehensive set of statistics for the NWP was published. These were largely based on revenue surveys and therefore fairly reliable. It emerges from this publication that, around 1845 Government land under cultivation amounted to about 21 million acres—fifty years later the same category of land covered nearly 25 million acres.[59] A part of the increase resulted from the lapse or confiscation of tax-free land, and a part from more accurate measurements; the actual increase may have been 10 or 12 per cent over the 1845 level. As regards Awadh, the first figures that I have seen relate to the 1860s, when surveys covering a total of 5.3 million acres in different parts of the province showed 55 per cent of this area to be Government land under cultivation, while returns covering 15.5 million acres in 1894–5 showed 53 per cent.[60] Of course, the first surveys may have concentrated on the more fully cultivated areas, but it still seems likely that cultivation had expanded little, if at all in this region. For the UP as a whole, an increase of some ten per cent seems plausible.

As regards the Central Provinces, we are largely in statistical darkness till the 1860s. However, the kingdom of Nagpur seems to have been as densely populated in 1825 as in 1866, so it seems unlikely that the cultivated area had increased greatly between those dates. Supposing this to hold true for the whole of the CP, then the tilled area early in the century might not be much less than the 12 million acres of 1870.[61] In the adjoining province of Berar,

[59] A. Shakespear, *Memoir on the Statistics of the North Western Provinces of the Bengal Presidency*, Calcutta, 1848, pp. 12–13.

[60] *Parl. Papers (British) 1865, No. 86: Papers relating to the Administration of Oude*, p. 230; *Report on the Administration of NWP and Oudh 1894–95*, Appendices to Report.

[61] R. Jenkins, *Report on the Territories of the Rajah of Nagpore,* Nagpur, 1866; *Report on the Census of the Central Provinces* . . . 1866, Nagpur, 1867?; *Gazetteer of the Central Provinces 1870,* rpt., Delhi, 1984.

however, large areas of land were vacant at mid-century, and cultivated area may well have doubled by 1890 when it reached about 6.5 million acres, while in the CP it grew to 15 million: in the aggregate, an increase of over 40 per cent.[62]

In the Madras Presidency the data are somewhat better. If the stagnant level of revenue collection and various qualitative indicators are dependable, cultivated acreage more or less stagnated from the first to the fifth decade of the nineteenth century, to a large extent due to the combination of heavy taxation and low prices. The Madras government itself noted in 1855 'that less than one-fifth of the whole area of the Presidency is cultivated. The total extent of the ryotwar part of the country is above seventy-seven millions of acres, of which the cultivation of Government land may be computed at 14,670,000 acres, to this 20 per cent may be added for Inam cultivation, making a total 17,500,000 acres. There is no room for doubt that an increase of cultivation would follow reductions of the Government tax'.[63]

This did in fact occur, and when Raghavaiyengar reviewed the progress of the Presidency 1850–90, the cultivated area had increased by 32 per cent, and the irrigated area by 64 per cent. It is striking that almost all the increase in cultivated area is observed between 1852 and 1870, a period when rising prices and revision of the assessment combined to reduce the burden on agriculture.[64]

Bombay, the other peninsular Presidency, shows a similar pattern of growth, also responding to higher prices and lower assessments around the mid-nineteenth century. Its arid Deccan districts saw cultivated area grow by 60 to 70 per cent between the 1830s and 1880s,[65] while the more fully settled districts of Gujarat witnessed slower growth. An early revenue survey of that area covered a total of 3544 square miles between 1810 and 1826, or over half the British territory there. It found 73 per cent of the area classified as 'pro-

[62] *The Report on the Hyderabad Assigned Districts* for 1856–7 gives an estimate of 2,024,000 acres for land under cultivation, but this is described as an understatement. At a surmise, I have taken the true area at 3 million acres. (*Report*, pp. 33, 38). The 1890 figures for both provinces are from K. L. Datta, p. 54–5.

[63] Madras Govt. Consultation, 14 August 1855 quoted in *Selection from the Records of the Madras Government No. 50*, p. 444.

[64] S. Raghavaiyengar, *Memorandum on the Progress of the Madras Presidency during the Last Forty Years of British Administration*, p. xcvii, p. 48.

[65] Guha, *Agrarian Economy*, pp. 54–8; *Admin. Rept. Bombay Presidency* for 1885–6.

ductive' or cultivable to be actually cultivated. The *jamabandi* (revenue) report of 1860–61 referred to 1.9 million acres of assessed government land in the same area: of this 79 per cent was cultivated, representing an increase of only 8 per cent over almost half a century. However the revision of assessments was under way, and the cotton boom of the 1860s was to prove particularly profitable to Gujarat. By the end of that decade, therefore, the percentage of assessed area occupied had risen to 86, or by another 9 per cent. After this there was little scope for growth: occupied area was 89 per cent in 1885,[66] and the more comprehensive series of statistics that commence from that year show little change till Independence. Assuming that Konkan and Kanara followed the Gujarat pattern, and weighting these changes by the relative cropped areas of 1885–6, we may put the overall increase in cultivation in Bombay at about 65 per cent over the period 1825–85.

There remains the Punjab—its cultivated area amounting to 20 million acres in 1868 and 26 million in 1891, with large new areas coming under canal irrigation.[67] If we assume that cultivated area under Sikh rule was only slightly smaller than that under the British, we may hazard a guess of 19 million acres for 1825. These various estimates are put together in Statement I in a format comparable to Blyn's.

Statement I

Province	Estimated Percentage Change in Cultivated Area 1825–90	Average Croped Area 1891–6 (0000)	Estimated Crop Area *c.* 1825 (0000)
Greater Bengal	32	5348	4052
UP	10	3144	2858
Punjab	37	1950	1423
CP	45	1924	1327
Bombay	65	2386	1446
Madras	32	2436	1845
British India	33	17188	12951

SOURCE: See text pp. 35–8.

[66] *Selection from the Records of the Bombay Government (Old Series) No. 11: Reports . . .*, J. Cruikshank, *Revenue Surveyor, Gujarat.* Calculated from Appendix 1; *Jamabandi Reports of the Northern Division of the Bombay Presidency 1861–62 and 1869–70; Admin. Report Bombay 1885–86.*

[67] BEIP, *Agricultural Statistics*, p. 16.

Did the extension of cultivation exceed or fall short of the growth of the population? Unfortunately, estimates for the early nineteenth century are few and shaky, though the 1891 figure of 213 million is reasonably firm. However, most estimates would put the 1825 total between 150 and 200 million, making a 'British India' total of 114 to 152 million in that year. The highest estimate, that by Bhattacharya, would give 170 million.[68] The increase between 1825 and 1891 would, on these various estimates, range from 25 to 87 per cent. Only the very lowest of them, therefore, will show cultivation keeping ahead of population growth. This is not to say that output did not do so: the spread of irrigation, changes in cropping patterns and other factors might have led production to outstrip area cultivated, but on the other hand the shift on to poorer soils may have depressed yields.[69] The question of trends in yields per acre, so important for the twentieth century, is also crucial for our assessment of the nineteenth.

Research on this issue is at a very rudimentary stage. Apart from Ashwani Saith's work and some shaky estimates by Commander,[70] I am only aware of one other comparison of yields in the nineteenth and twentieth centuries, that made by Ratnam for Madras. The subject has not attracted much interest, and easily accessible sources are scarce. I shall therefore merely attempt a quick survey, aiming to provide estimates of changes in yield of a few crops in some regions.

We may begin with cotton—an important commercial crop, for which relatively good estimates are available. (Blyn, incidentally calculated that its yield per acre rose by 66 per cent, from 65 to 108 lbs, between his first and last quinquennia.) The East India Company had acquired south Gujarat in large measure as a source of its China 'investment' of raw cotton, and a tight administration with consequently good statistics existed here from an early date. In 1817–18 the whole of the Broach output of cotton was compulsorily purchased by the Company, and this was calculated to amount to

[68] All these estimates are cited from Visaria, 'Population', *Cambridge Economic History*, vol. II, p. 446.

[69] For a discussion of this, with supporting evidence see Guha, *Agrarian Economy*, pp. 60–2 and 121–4; and Saith, in this volume, pp. 252–3.

[70] Commander's estimates are most casually made. He writes: 'Assuming that cropping shifts did not overly distort the composition of the aggregate agricultural output, it seems that in the Upper Doab between 1807 and 1880 output of all crops increased by around eight times, with the net cropped area

98 lbs per acre. Some small amounts may have been retained for domestic consumption or illicit sale, so the full yield may have been a little higher. This was, however, a very good year. In 1837–40 the Collector of Broach made a careful estimate of the yield of cotton on the basis of yields in villages where crop-sharing had been in force, and reckoned it at 80 lbs. A careful study of the trade and acreage figures of the Broach tract (mainly Broach and Baroda) for 1883–9 found an average export to Bombay of 133,000 bales, which came to 87 lbs per acre. Seventeen thousand bales were assumed to be absorbed locally, making a total yield of 98 lbs.[71] Yields were thus somewhat, though not dramatically, higher than at the beginning of the century. They were to rise further. Using the cotton press and trade returns, the Indian Central Cotton Committee reckoned the yield in Baroda state for the quinquennium ending 1945–6 at 129 lbs.[72] It seems safe to conclude that the yield of cotton rose by 30 to 40 per cent over a century and a half.

An increase in yields is also to be found in Khandesh (north Maharashtra). There yield per acre increased from about 63 lbs to about 100 lbs between the 1870s and the 1930s.[73] Similar increases occurred in the adjoining tracts of Berar, where yields rose from about 50–55 lbs in the 1870s to 108 lbs in the 1920s, before crashing

---

nearly trebling and population quadrupling in the same period.' He has already stated the double-cropped area to be 37 per cent of the cultivated in 1895–1920; if this was true for 1880, and if there was no double-cropping in 1807, then the yield per cropped acre would have to *rise by 95 per cent* for the gross output to increase eight-fold between 1807 and 1880. Commander is, however, blissfully unaware of the implications of his own statement. The very same page we find him saying that 'productivity trends may not in general have been strongly positive'! He then caps it all by agreeing with Saith that 'average physical yields for crops other than sugarcane may have declined by around 10 per cent between 1840 and 1924'. This sort of exercise scarcely merits discussion. S. Commander, 'The Mechanics of Demographic and Economic Growth in Uttar Pradesh: 1800–1900', T. Dyson (ed.), *India's Historical Demography: Studies in Disease, Famine and Society,* London, 1989, pp. 59–60.

[71] Calculated from the following: *Selection from Bombay Government Records (Old Series) No. 3: Memoir of the Zilla of Baroche,* pp. 26–7; J. M. Davies, Collector Broach, 28 January 1847, pp 123–5 in *Report of the Bombay Committee of the Decline of the Cotton Trade 1847, Parl. Papers (Britain) 1847,* Paper 712; 'AFB' *Statistical Tables relating to Indian Cotton,* Bombay, 1889, Estimates for Bombay Presidency.

[72] Indian Central Cotton Committee *Report on the Accuracy of the All India Cotton Forecasts for the Five Seasons ending 1945–46*, Bombay, 1948.

[73] Guha, pp 105–10.

to 70–75 lbs during the 1930s.[74] In both these areas we should note, the increase was in large measure due to a more prolific short-staple cotton supplanting a more delicate medium-staple type. Furthermore, the more secure and fertile districts tended increasingly to specialize in the production of cotton which thus shifted onto better lands. However, while yields rose in the northern parts of Bombay Presidency they either stagnated or declined in the southern cotton belt where yields fell between the 1840s and the 1930s.[75] For the Presidency as a whole (excluding Sind), the calculation was 79 lbs in the 1880s and 104 lbs in the 1940s. For Madras where improved strains achieved notable success, and irrigation was used for cotton, the yield rose from and estimated 46 lbs in the 1880s to 98 lbs in the 1940s.[76] These findings are not greatly different from those to be observed in the official revenue yields though levels sometimes differ. Even the regional rankings were similar. Of course, this is in part because provincial officials were also aware of the trade and consumption data.

The Madras official yields also increased dramatically from 40 lbs, in Blyn's first quinquennium, to 119 lbs in his last one. The general trend for cotton yields seems to have been one of moderate rise in the nineteenth century, and more rapid increase in the twentieth. As regards the other major commercial fibre, jute, Goswami, who was made a careful study of the subject, feels that its yield did not change over the twentieth century.[77]

But what of the food crops? Here we only possess estimates made at one or two points in the nineteenth century and in the 1940s. A variety of paths could connect these points, and much more work is necessary before we can make any inferences as to how the changes occurred. The materials presented here are mainly indicators of what is readily available, and pointers to further research.

The earliest estimates that I have seen are given in Ratnam, and

[74] Calculated by a comparison of rail-borne trade returns and acreage data for the region from: *Administration Report of the Cotton Dept. Hyderabad Assigned Districts, 1881–82*, Appendix A; 'AFB' *Statistical Tables; Bombay Cotton Annual,* 1953–6 to 1939–40.

[75] Guha, pp. 111–14.

[76] Both provinces compared on the basis of 'AFB' *Statistical Tables* and ICCC *Cotton Forecasts* 1945–6.

[77] O. Goswami, 'Agriculture in Slump: The Peasant Economy of East and North Bengal during the 1930s', *IESHR,* XXI, 3, p. 362.

relate to paddy production in Madras at the end of the eighteenth century. One is not altogether confident about the accuracy of land measurement, and there is also the possibility of distortions in the output figures due to the fact that they determined the tax payable. The aggregate of his area and yield data for the four years ending 1798–9 and the single year 1788 for Chingleput district is 1019 lbs of paddy or 673 lbs of rice per acre.[78] A reference to Statement III will show that this is lower than the yield in 1870 and is about the same as that in the 1940s.

The Peshwa's territories were annexed by the British in 1818, and H. D. Robertson, the first Collector of Poona, carried out some crop-cuttings on bajra in 1820,[79] and reckoned the yield on different classes of soil to be as follows:

Statement II

Soil Class	Yield per acre
First Class black soil	1037 lbs
Second Class black soil	691 lbs
Third Class black soil	296 lbs
Distributed according to the soils actually under cultivation	650 lbs
Average yield Pune District (1954–5 to 1963–4)	301 lbs

Too much should not be inferred from data for a few fields in a single year, but there is some supporting evidence from nearby Sholapur district where detailed calculations based on baluta share payments in one village gave an average yield for all foodgrains of 634 lbs per acre in 1829–30, an unfavourable year.[80] The average

[78] R. Ratnam, *Agricultural Development in Madras State Prior to 1900*, Madras, 1966, p. 11. A contemporary official was informed (no doubt by a local vegetarian) that yields in recent years had fallen due to a lack of manure as large numbers of sheep were being consumed by the Europeans in neighbouring Madras.

[79] H. D. Robertson Report dated 10 October 1821, pp. 569–72 in *Selection from the . . . Papers at the East India House . . . Company's Governments in India*, London, 1820–6, vol. IV.

[80] V. D. Divekar, 'Prices and Wages in Pune Region in a Period of Transition, 1805–1830 A.D.', Gokhale Institute Mimeograph Series no. 29, Pune, 1989, pp 76–7; converted to lbs on the basis of pp. 54–7.

yield of wheat, jowar and bajra in the district from 1950–1 to 1959–60 was 480 lbs. Furthermore, some indirect evidence also suggests that nineteenth century yields of at least the common grain crops in the Deccan were higher than in the mid-twentieth century. M. B. McAlpin calculated the percentage of land revenue to total output for certain talukas in the nineteenth century on the assumption that yields were the same then as in the period 1946–54. The result is that 70, 80 and even 89 per cent of the gross produce is shown as being paid in tax in some quinquennia.[81] Since this is an impossibility, we can only infer that yields before 1850 were significantly higher than they were a century later, or the burden of taxation would have been unsustainable.

Lands freshly reclaimed from jungle or grass might produce high initial yields. This is indicated by an early report from the Narbada Valley where W. H. Sleeman recorded in 1824 that in 1807 'land newly broken up in this district yielded from fifteen to twenty returns [times the seed sown]. That after twenty years of uninterrupted tillage the returns of the same land had sunk to from five to eight fold, but that in the adjoining districts belonging to Bhopal and to Scindia, lying on the other side of the Nerbudda the returns were, at the time of his writing equal to those recorded in this district in Sumbut 1863 [1807]. . . .' Landlords' accounts from the 1820s showed wheat to then yield five to six times the seed sown.[82] Finally, we may cite Colebrooke's informed guess that the 'medium produce' of paddy in Bengal was 23 mds or 1880 lbs per acre at the beginning of the nineteenth century.[83]

The tightening of British administrative control over the Indian countryside enabled at least a few officials to make large-scale enquiries into agricultural production in the areas under their charge. Two of the earliest — that by Boulderson in Bareilly 1829–31, and Thornton in Muzaffarnagar 1827–40 — have already been mentioned. Somewhat later, in 1864–5 a Settlement Officer of Hoshangabad district made a number of careful experiments on wheat, and found the yield to be five maunds or 410 lbs to the acre: or about five times the seed sown. This is a little lower than that reported for

[81] McAlpin, p. 126, Table 4.1.

[82] Cited in *Report on the Land Revenue Settlement of the Nursinghpore District*, Nagpur, 1866, p. 48.

[83] Colebrooke, *Husbandry of Bengal*, p. 105. This would amount to about 1200 lbs of rice.

the region in 1824. The officer also commented that earlier 'when uncultivated land was larger in extent, the practice of throwing a field into fallow and breaking up another in its stead was more common than it is now . . .'[84] which might account for the slight decline in yield. The next estimate comes from a prosperous and progressive Punjab district, Ludhiana.[85] The Settlement Officer there:

selected for experiment in each harvest good sized holdings such as would fairly represent the average cultivation. These were put in charge, sometimes of paid watchers, and sometimes of respectable agriculturists, the whole of the crop was cut and stacked according to soils and crops; and the produce weighed in the presence of the owner. . . . Upwards of 50 or 60 holdings, averaging five or six acres in area, were treated in this way in each harvest. . . . The proposed localities were in all cases reported to me for sanction before the experiment was made, and a different village chosen for every harvest, so that the result may be taken as covering the greater part of the District . . . none of the experiments were selected after an inspection of the crop, so that subordinates had no opportunities of picking and choosing; and as the time covered was from the Rabi of 1879 upto that of 1882, inequalities due to seasons above and below the average must have disappeared. . . .

Almost a thousand experiments were made in all, covering an area of more than three thousand acres. The results are in Statement III, and I have taken not the assessment yield assumed for revenue purposes, but the actual results of crop-cuttings given in Appendix III of the *Report*.

Finally, we come to a group of Madras districts where crop-cutting experiments were also carried out as a part of settlement operations in the mid-nineteenth century. Large areas were cut—either half an acre or one acre—and the number of experiments made varied from several hundred to several thousand in each district. In some cases the yields were given for the different classes of soil separately, in which case I have calculated weighted averages for the district in question. Rice is assumed to be two-thirds the weight of paddy, and the Madras Measure to hold 2.6 lbs of the latter.[86]

[84] *Report on the Land Revenue Settlement of the Hoshungabad District*, Nagpore, 1865, pp. 82–3.

[85] *Final Report on the Revision of Settlement of the Ludhiana District 1879–83*, Calcutta, 1884, pp. 194–5, Appendix III.

[86] Data sources are listed after Statement III. Ratnam, *Agricultural Development* consistently assumes that the Madras Measure contained 2.3 lbs of paddy and

These early crop-cutting experiments were not, of course, without their contemporary critics. Auckland Colvin noticed in 1872 that grain was heavier if cut early in the season – presumably because of its moistness at that time – and added that 'a difference of a couple of seers in the produce of 1/10 of an acre comes to a serious amount on the whole'.[87] But this would, of course, not apply where large numbers of cuts were taken throughout the season as must have been done to cover the large areas reported in our sources. Furthermore, in so far as the crop-cuttings were criticized, it was because they were thought to result in *underestimates* of the true yields. Thus Cadell, Thornton's successor in Muzaffarnagar, defended the latter's results by saying that yields in the district were lower than elsewhere due to the large area of low-grade *bhur* soil; when 'the average of irrigated land, the average of dry land and the produce of bhur are stated separately, it is found that the discrepancies between Mr Thornton's estimates and those for other districts are not . . . so great as has been supposed'.[88] These estimates, and the ICAR findings in the 1940s are set forth in Table 9.

Table 9: Estimated Yields of Wheat in UP Districts (lbs/acre)

District	19th Century	1944–9
Aligarh	1400	694
Etawah	1296	639
Muzaffarnagar	794	740
Bareilly	1046	546
Meerut	1464	774
Bulandshahr	1508	820
Agra	1224	652

SOURCE: For the ninteenth century – *Final Report on the Revision of Settlement in the District of Aligarh* (Allahabad 1882), p. 47; for the 1940s – Sukhatme, *Sample Surveys*, Table 8.4.

I have retained this in the Chingleput estimates of the 18th century that I have taken directly from Ratnam. However, the *Report on the Marketing of Rice in India and Burma* Delhi, 1941, reports that the Madras Measure (M.M.) contained, on an average 2.6 lbs of paddy and 3.1 lbs of rice (p. 457). Now, W. H. Bayley, *Memorandum on Weights and Measures in the Madras Presidency*, Madras, 1857, states the M. M. to hold 120 tolas of rice, heaped measure or 3.09 lbs. Hence I infer that the *Marketing Report* is correct, and have converted the Measures given in all the Madras sources at 2.6 lbs of paddy. Paddy is assumed to yield two-thirds its weight in rice.

[87] Cited in *Report of the Economic Enquiry Committee*, Madras, 1931, p. 44.

[88] Cadell, *Report*, p. 22.

Statement III: Yields in Selected Districts of India (lbs/acre)

District/Crop 1	*c.* 1830 2	*c.* 1870 3	1944–9 4	1951–3 5
1. *Bareilly*				
Wheat	1046	928	546	686
Rice	748	750	555	434
Barley	1099	1062	–	627
Bajra	533	549	–	443
2. *Muzaffarnagar*				
Rice	531	642	807	599
Wheat	653	807	740	1022
Barley	606	822	–	36
Jowar	421	528	–	454
3. *Hoshangabad*				
Wheat	–	410	366	
4. *Ludhiana*				
Wheat	–	860	1029	1114
Barley	–	896	–	931
Gram	–	375	–	811
				1955–7
5. *South Arcot*				
Rice	–	1149	893	1362
6. *Trichinopoly*				
Rice	–	1097	1051	1317
7. *East Godavari*				
Rice	–	1526	1044	1347
8. *Tirunelvelli*				
Rice	–	1770	1163	1498
9. *Chingleput*				
Rice	673	919	676	958
10. *North Arcot*				
Rice	–	1776	948	1470
11. *Salem*				
Rice	–	1488	–	1541
12. *Coimbatore*				
Rice	–	2059	–	1589

SOURCES:

Columns 2 and 3

1. Bareilly, 1830 and 1870: *Bareilly Settlement Report*, 1874.
2. Muzaffarnagar: *Settlement Reports*, 1842 and 1878.
3. Hoshangabad: *Settlement Report*, 1865.
4. Ludhiana: *Settlement Report*, 1884.

5. South Arcot: *Selection from Madras Government Records No. 14: Papers relating to the Survey and Settlement of the Chellumbrum and Manargoody Talooks of the South Arcot District*, 1869.
6. Trichinopoly: *Selection from Madras Government Records No. 50: Papers relating to the Survey and Settlement of the Trichinopoly District*, 1876.
7. East Godavari: *Selection from Madras Government Records No. 22: Report on the Survey and Settlement of the Central and Eastern Deltas and Upper Talooks of Godavary District*, 1872.
8. Tirunelvelli: *Settlement Scheme of the Tirunelvelli District* (no t.p.), report by R. K. Puckle, 11 September 1868.
9. Chingleput: *Report on the Revenue Settlement of the Principal Division of the Chingleput District* (no t.p.) and *Report on the Revenue Settlement of the Sub-Division of the Chingleput District*, 1876.
10. North Arcot: Taken from Ratnam *Agricultural Development*, p. 12, who gives it as 2666 lbs of paddy in 1880–1.
11. Salem: Selection from Madras Government Records no 65: *Survey and Assessment of Salem District*.
12. Coimbatore: Ratnam, p. 87, stated as 1200 M. M. paddy per acre in 1878.

Column 4

All the yields are taken from Sukhatme, *Sample Surveys*.

Column 5

All the yields for 1951–2 to 1953–4 are calculated from *Area and Yield of Principal Crops in India*; crop-cutting in Madras officially commenced from 1955–6, and yields for 1955–6 to 1957–8 are from the *Season and Crop Reports of Madras* and *Andhra Pradesh*.

Officials thus found the results of crop-cuttings too low and were often sceptical of their accuracy. In Madras also, G. R. Clerk thought that the cultivators tried to remove portions of the grain so as to understate yields: 'The Tehsildar of Bhimavaram, my uncovenanted Assistants, and my Additional Supervisor reported that they had detected the ryots fraudulently removing some of the bundles of grain . . .'. He tended to doubt the accuracy of experiments made without the presence of a large number of peons and watchmen.[89]

If therefore, we reject the crop-cuttings on the basis of contemporary official criticism of them, then we should, as a corollary accept that the true yields were those in the second column of Table 9, which are about twice as high as the ascertained twentieth century yields.

Assuming then, that the yields in Statement III are reasonably accurate, what conclusions may we draw from them? First of all, of

[89] Cited by *Economic Enquiry Committee*, p. 45.

course, the observations only hold for the points in time at which they are made, and the trends connecting them may be very diverse. And, of course, our geographical coverage is distinctly limited. Nonetheless, the evidence seems to support the tendency to decline that Blyn observed in the official data on foodgrain yields. The assumption of constant yields certainly finds little support.

Improvement as a consequence of irrigation clearly occurred, and this (Saith's 'shift effect') clearly accounts for the upward trend in Ludhiana and Muzaffarnagar. The latter has been fully analysed by Saith, so I shall consider the former. In 1879–82, the average yield of wheat on irrigated land, which comprised 48 per cent of the wheat area, was 1218 lbs; on unirrigated 526 lbs. The average irrigated wheat area in 1944–9 was 68 per cent: if yields had been the same as in the nineteenth century the overall average would have been 997 lbs, where the ICAR found 1029 lbs.[90] The increase in 'intrinsic yield',[91] therefore, was quite negligible; however, unlike Muzaffarnagar, it did not actually decline. Finally, we may note that yields are higher after Independence, and that in several of the south Indian districts they move up towards the nineteenth-century levels.

If we juxtapose these findings with our earlier discussion of the trends in cultivated area which, as we saw, either just kept pace with or lagged behind population growth, we get a rather pessimistic picture of nineteenth-century trends in food availability, especially in areas that did not benefit from the expansion of irrigation. The great famines in the last decade of that century become easier to understand in this context. The first two decades of the present century saw output moving ahead of the near-stagnant population, but the post-1921 population growth once again overtook agricultural production; that is if Blyn is to be believed—and it has been argued in Part A of this essay that he still is our best available guide. Perhaps some reader of this volume will be moved to produce the definitive work that will supersede that begun by George Blyn almost half a century ago.

[90] Calculated from *Ludhiana Settlement Report,* Appendix III and Sukhatme, Table 8.3; irrigated area from 1944–9 *Bulletin of Wheat Statistics*, Government of India, 1972.

[91] I use the term 'intrinsic yield' as defined by Saith on pp. 231–2 of this book.

Select Tables from Blyn, *Agricultural Trends in India, 1891–1947*

Appendix Table 4C: Aggregate annual output, acreage, and yield per acre of All Crops (AC), Foodgrains (FG) and Nonfoodgrain (NFG) crops in British Indiaand Regions, 1891/92–1946/47
(Output Million Rupees; Acres–Millions; Y/A-Rupees)

British India

	AC	FG	NFG	AC	FG	NFG	AC	FG	NFG
		Yield			Acreage			Yield per Acre	
1891/92	7490	5844	1646	168	140	27.9	44.6	41.7	59.0
	8827	6842	2045	177	148	29.2	49.9	46.2	70.0
	9026	7234	1792	178	145	33.0	50.7	49.9	54.3
	9630	7665	1965	186	154	32.0	51.8	49.8	61.4
	9017	6969	2048	176	146	30.1	51.2	47.7	68.0
1896/97	7288	5384	1904	165	137	28.1	44.2	39.3	67.8
	10404	8147	2257	182	153	29.3	57.1	53.2	77.0
	10396	8204	2192	179	151	27.9	58.1	54.3	77.0
	8371	6702	1669	163	137	25.8	51.4	48.9	64.7
	9375	7206	2169	181	151	29.9	51.8	47.7	72.5
1901/02	8900	6716	2184	174	146	28.3	51.1	46.0	77.2
	10426	8128	2298	182	152	29.9	57.3	53.5	76.9
	10112	7765	2347	186	152	34.2	54.4	51.1	68.6
	9453	7142	2311	187	152	34.8	50.6	47.0	66.4
	9001	6788	2213	185	151	33.8	48.7	45.0	65.5
1906/07	10135	7467	2668	193	157	36.3	52.5	47.6	73.5
	8100	5930	2170	180	146	34.0	45.0	40.6	63.8
	9044	6842	2202	186	153	33.4	48.6	44.7	65.9
	11458	8859	2599	195	160	34.7	58.8	55.4	74.9
	11349	8768	2581	196	160	35.7	57.9	54.8	72.3
1911/12	10706	8128	2578	191	153	38.1	56.1	53.1	67.7
	10488	7730	2758	193	157	35.7	54.3	49.2	77.3
	9776	7119	2657	188	151	37.1	52.0	47.1	71.6
	10606	7616	2990	199	161	38.0	53.3	47.3	78.7
	11053	8414	2639	193	160	32.7	57.3	52.6	80.7

Appendix Table 4C (*contd.*)

	AC	FG	NFG	AC	FG	NFG	AC	FG	NFG
		Yield			Acreage			Yield per Acre	
1916/17	11533	8682	2851	200	164	36.5	57.7	52.9	78.1
	11466	8646	2820	201	163	38.1	57.0	53.0	74.0
	8188	5869	2319	172	140	31.6	47.6	41.9	73.4
	11284	8283	3001	196	158	37.5	57.6	52.4	80.0
	8742	6449	2293	178	146	32.4	49.1	44.2	70.8
1921/22	10668	8252	2416	194	162	31.5	55.0	50.9	76.7
	10937	8276	2661	196	162	34.2	55.8	51.1	77.8
	10148	7211	2937	192	155	37.2	52.9	46.5	79.0
	10273	7318	2955	199	158	41.4	54.6	46.3	71.4
	10245	7188	3057	194	154	39.7	52.8	46.7	77.0
1926/27	10249	7106	3143	190	152	38.2	53.9	46.8	82.3
	9936	6695	3241	192	154	38.5	51.8	43.5	84.2
	10668	7376	3292	198	157	41.2	53.9	47.0	79.9
	10849	7590	3259	196	156	40.3	53.4	48.7	80.9
	10948	7604	3344	198	159	38.8	55.3	47.8	86.2
1931/32	10616	7705	2911	198	161	36.8	53.6	47.9	79.1
	10720	7313	3407	194	157	37.0	55.3	46.6	92.1
	11280	7752	3528	200	161	38.7	56.4	48.1	91.1
	10558	7218	3340	191	155	35.9	55.3	46.6	93.0
	10406	6776	3630	192	158	34.4	54.2	42.9	105.5
1936/37	11355	7550	3805	200	160	40.2	56.8	47.2	94.7
	11128	7338	3790	199	157	42.0	55.9	46.7	90.2
	9823	6666	3157	197	158	39.2	49.9	42.2	80.5
	10831	7176	3655	197	158	39.4	54.9	45.4	92.8
	10883	6578	4305	203	159	44.3	53.6	41.4	97.2
1941/42	10420	7009	3411	201	162	38.6	51.8	43.3	88.3
	10833	7195	3638	205	168	37.4	52.8	42.8	97.3
	11708	7988	3720	207	170	37.1	56.6	47.0	100.3
	10930	7671	3259	210	175	35.0	52.0	43.8	93.1
	10499	7093	3406	206	172	34.3	51.0	41.2	99.3
1946/47	10526	7127	3399	203	169	34.2	51.9	42.2	99.4
				Greater Bengal					
1891/92	3258	2650	608	53.9	46.5	7.36	60.4	57.0	82.6
	3995	3138	857	53.3	44.9	8.42	75.0	69.9	101.8
	4260	3454	806	53.5	45.1	8.45	79.6	76.6	95.3
	4673	3866	807	54.1	45.9	8.19	86.4	84.2	98.5
	3674	2943	731	52.6	44.6	7.96	69.8	66.0	91.8

Appendix Table 4C (*contd.*)

	AC	FG Yield	NFG	AC	FG Acreage	NFG	AC	FG Yield per Acre	NFG
1896/97	2487	1759	728	50.6	43.2	7.43	49.2	40.7	98.0
	4640	3714	926	55.1	47.2	7.85	84.2	78.7	118.0
	4588	3781	807	54.3	47.2	7.10	84.5	80.1	113.7
	4069	3332	737	53.5	46.4	7.13	76.1	71.8	103.4
	3716	2934	782	50.5	43.2	7.31	73.6	67.9	107.0
1901/02	3409	2584	825	49.0	41.9	7.09	69.6	61.7	116.4
	4111	3343	768	51.7	44.8	6.93	79.5	74.6	110.8
	3809	2991	818	49.2	42.0	7.21	77.4	71.2	113.5
	4046	3241	805	53.4	45.6	7.81	75.8	71.1	103.1
	3670	2870	800	52.0	44.2	7.82	70.6	64.9	102.3
1905/07	3641	2775	866	52.1	43.8	8.25	69.9	63.4	105.0
	3174	2319	855	50.6	42.4	8.24	62.7	54.7	103.8
	3250	2386	864	47.1	40.0	7.14	69.0	59.7	121.0
	4469	3683	786	53.1	45.6	7.53	84.2	80.8	104.4
	4587	3731	856	53.0	45.5	7.50	86.5	82.0	114.1
1911/12	4165	3311	854	52.4	44.8	7.59	79.5	73.9	112.5
	3677	2741	936	51.1	43.7	7.39	72.0	62.7	126.7
	3815	2950	865	50.6	43.3	7.34	75.4	68.1	117.8
	3291	2350	941	51.1	43.5	7.63	64.4	54.0	123.3
	4027	3218	809	51.5	44.6	6.89	78.2	72.2	117.4
1916/17	4067	3203	864	51.7	44.5	7.16	78.7	72.0	120.7
	4202	3325	877	51.2	44.1	7.07	82.1	75.4	124.0
	3005	2237	768	49.8	43.1	6.68	60.3	51.9	115.0
	3804	2924	880	50.6	43.6	6.98	75.2	67.1	126.1
	3222	2542	680	49.2	42.8	6.38	65.5	59.4	106.6
1921/22	3641	3032	609	50.0	44.4	5.64	72.8	68.3	108.0
	3729	3076	653	50.2	44.4	5.77	74.3	69.3	113.2
	3215	2405	810	48.0	41.4	6.64	67.0	58.1	122.0
	3388	2595	793	49.0	42.4	6.59	69.1	61.2	120.3
	3339	2513	826	49.2	42.3	6.87	67.9	59.4	120.2
1926/27	3346	2356	990	48.2	40.7	7.50	69.4	57.9	132.0
	3028	2117	911	45.9	38.9	6.96	66.0	54.4	130.9
	3778	2881	897	49.3	42.5	6.75	76.6	67.8	132.9
	3685	2740	945	48.6	41.6	6.96	75.8	65.9	92.7
	3793	2828	965	48.6	41.6	7.04	78.0	68.0	137.1

Appendix Table 4C (*contd.*)

	AC	FG Yield	NFG	AC	FG Acreage	NFG	AC	FG Yield per Acre	NFG
1931/32	3575	2893	682	48.9	43.3	5.61	73.1	66.8	121.6
	3460	2618	842	48.2	42.4	5.76	71.8	61.7	146.2
	3404	2488	916	48.2	42.1	6.14	70.6	59.1	149.1
	3493	2506	987	48.1	41.7	6.38	72.6	60.0	154.7
	2937	2037	900	46.9	41.0	5.86	62.6	49.7	153.6
1936/37	3711	2690	1021	48.5	41.9	6.60	76.5	64.2	154.7
	3426	2513	913	48.2	41.7	6.47	71.1	60.3	141.1
	2931	2140	791	48.5	41.8	6.65	60.4	51.2	118.9
	3313	2339	974	48.5	41.8	6.69	68.3	56.0	145.6
	2907	1761	1146	49.1	39.9	9.20	59.2	44.1	124.6
1941/42	3216	2497	719	48.5	42.9	5.60	66.3	58.3	128.4
	3052	2106	946	49.8	42.8	6.95	61.3	49.2	136.1
	3782	2915	867	53.5	46.9	5.58	70.7	62.2	153.5
	3376	2654	722	55.1	49.7	5.35	61.3	53.4	135.0
	3289	2427	862	51.5	46.5	4.97	63.9	52.2	173.4
1946/47	3214	2527	687	52.4	47.4	5.01	61.3	53.3	137.1
					United Provinces				
1891/92	1323	928	395	28.5	22.6	5.87	46.4	41.1	67.3
	1436	1026	410	28.2	23.0	5.16	50.9	44.6	79.5
	1450	976	474	29.2	23.1	6.13	49.7	42.3	77.3
	1489	1104	385	36.9	30.7	6.23	40.4	36.0	61.8
	1689	1185	504	34.4	28.8	5.56	49.1	41.1	90.6
1896/97	1412	1051	361	30.9	25.4	5.46	45.7	41.4	66.1
	1792	1289	503	34.1	28.6	5.45	52.6	45.1	92.3
	1771	1263	508	34.4	28.8	5.56	51.5	43.9	91.4
	1638	1217	421	31.5	26.2	5.26	52.0	46.4	80.0
	1859	1357	502	35.7	30.1	5.63	52.1	45.1	89.2
1901/02	1819	1329	490	36.0	30.2	5.75	50.5	44.0	85.2
	1983	1480	503	37.4	30.3	7.13	53.0	48.8	70.6
	1909	1440	469	38.2	31.2	7.03	50.0	46.1	66.7
	1507	1024	483	38.3	31.0	7.32	39.3	33.0	66.0
	1608	1143	465	35.5	38.9	6.63	45.3	40.0	70.1
1906/07	1991	1364	627	39.4	32.1	7.32	50.3	42.5	85.7
	1304	943	361	32.3	25.8	6.51	40.4	36.6	55.5
	1742	1275	467	36.1	29.2	6.87	48.3	43.7	68.0
	2004	1487	517	37.9	30.8	7.09	52.9	48.3	72.9
	2009	1443	566	39.1	31.6	7.47	51.4	45.7	75.8

Appendix Table 4C (*contd.*)

	AC	FG Yield	NFG	AC	FG Acreage	NFG	AC	FG Yield per Acre	NFG
1911/12	2093	1481	612	39.7	31.5	8.16	52.7	47.0	75.0
	2081	1452	629	39.0	31.5	7.53	53.4	46.1	83.5
	1386	919	467	33.8	26.6	7.17	41.0	34.5	65.1
	2117	1479	638	38.8	31.2	7.63	54.6	47.4	83.6
	2105	1549	556	39.3	32.2	7.11	53.6	48.1	78.2
1916/17	2215	1636	579	40.3	32.9	7.42	55.0	49.7	78.0
	2074	1538	536	40.8	32.8	7.95	50.8	46.9	67.4
	1339	980	359	31.5	25.6	5.94	42.5	38.3	60.4
	2098	1494	604	37.8	30.5	7.27	55.5	49.0	83.1
	1531	1092	439	34.8	28.3	6.48	44.0	38.6	67.7
1921/22	1969	1485	484	38.3	31.8	6.52	51.4	46.7	74.2
	1961	1431	530	38.9	32.1	6.78	50.4	44.6	78.2
	2003	1402	601	38.7	31.6	7.13	51.8	44.4	84.3
	1790	1305	485	38.5	31.2	7.28	46.5	41.8	66.6
	1794	1266	528	37.5	30.4	7.09	47.8	41.6	74.5
1926/27	1928	1337	591	37.0	30.1	6.89	52.1	44.4	85.8
	1731	1229	502	38.5	31.4	7.14	45.0	39.1	70.3
	1442	989	453	37.5	30.4	7.10	38.5	32.5	63.8
	1785	1252	533	36.5	29.6	6.86	48.9	42.3	77.7
	1815	1231	584	38.7	30.8	7.92	46.9	40.0	73.7
1931/32	1970	1270	700	38.7	31.2	7.47	50.9	40.7	93.7
	1922	1141	781	37.2	29.9	7.31	51.7	38.2	106.8
	1939	1178	761	38.6	31.0	7.60	50.2	38.0	100.1
	2035	1251	784	37.6	30.3	7.25	54.1	41.3	108.1
	2203	1274	929	37.6	30.1	7.48	58.6	42.3	124.2
1936/37	2246	1232	1014	39.0	30.9	8.10	57.6	39.9	125.1
	2173	1252	921	42.6	34.7	7.92	51.0	36.1	116.3
	1730	1198	532	39.8	32.3	7.51	43.5	37.1	70.8
	2130	1414	716	39.7	32.1	7.55	53.7	44.0	94.8
	2128	1268	860	39.0	31.0	8.00	54.6	40.9	107.5
1941/42	1731	1107	624	38.7	31.0	7.68	44.7	35.7	81.3
	2116	1341	775	40.3	33.0	7.31	52.5	40.6	106.0
	2054	1239	815	41.0	33.3	7.65	50.1	37.2	106.5
	1986	1242	744	40.5	33.0	7.47	49.0	37.6	99.6
	1903	1223	680	41.0	33.7	7.27	46.4	36.3	93.5
1946/47	1913	1189	724	40.5	33.1	7.41	47.2	35.9	97.7

Appendix Table 4C (*contd.*)

	AC	FG Yield	NFG	AC	FG Acreage	NFG	AC	FG Yield per Acre	NFG
					Madras				
1891/92	869	729	140	22.2	19.3	2.93	39.1	37.8	47.8
	931	749	182	24.3	20.8	3.51	38.3	36.0	51.9
	1078	875	203	25.4	21.1	4.30	42.4	41.5	47.2
	1032	843	189	24.5	20.5	3.96	42.1	41.1	47.7
	1413	1200	213	25.4	21.1	4.30	55.6	56.8	49.5
1896/97	1290	1100	190	24.6	21.0	3.58	52.4	52.4	53.1
	1286	1082	204	25.0	21.2	3.77	51.4	51.0	54.1
	1448	1242	206	25.4	22.1	3.25	57.0	56.2	56.3
	1090	923	167	23.3	20.0	3.29	46.8	46.2	50.8
	1254	1075	179	25.1	21.4	3.71	49.9	50.2	48.2
1901/02	1457	1216	241	26.1	22.5	3.63	55.8	54.0	66.4
	1515	1261	254	27.3	23.2	4.06	55.5	54.3	62.6
	1498	1247	251	26.9	22.6	4.27	55.7	55.2	58.8
	1219	994	225	24.6	20.7	3.94	49.6	48.0	57.1
	1306	1062	244	25.4	21.5	3.86	51.4	49.4	63.2
1906/07	1413	1157	256	26.2	22.2	4.00	53.9	52.1	64.0
	1396	1142	254	26.4	22.2	4.22	52.9	51.4	60.2
	1268	1014	254	26.3	22.2	4.07	48.2	45.7	62.4
	1462	1200	262	26.3	22.1	4.21	55.6	54.3	62.2
	1631	1334	297	26.9	22.6	4.28	60.6	59.0	69.4
1911/12	1731	1434	297	26.3	21.5	4.77	65.8	66.7	62.3
	1545	1263	282	27.0	22.5	4.50	57.2	56.1	62.7
	1537	1231	306	28.1	22.6	5.47	54.7	54.5	55.9
	1630	1308	321	27.4	22.2	5.19	59.5	58.9	61.8
	1755	1405	350	27.8	23.2	4.56	63.1	60.6	76.8
1916/17	1868	1465	403	27.9	22.4	5.52	67.0	65.4	73.0
	1806	1371	435	28.1	22.6	5.61	64.3	60.7	77.5
	1465	1088	377	26.5	21.2	5.31	55.3	51.3	71.0
	1694	1344	350	27.9	23.1	4.78	60.7	58.2	73.2
	1647	1275	372	26.9	22.0	4.88	61.2	60.0	76.2
1921/22	1692	1322	370	27.3	22.8	4.54	62.0	58.0	81.5
	1751	1321	430	27.8	22.5	5.28	63.0	58.7	81.4
	1556	1143	413	26.1	20.5	5.57	59.6	55.8	74.1
	1751	1260	491	27.4	21.4	6.01	63.9	58.9	81.7
	1861	1307	554	28.1	21.4	6.72	66.2	61.1	82.4

Appendix Table 4C (*contd.*)

	AC	FG Yield	NFG	AC	FG Acreage	NFG	AC	FG Yield per Acre	NFG
1926/27	1663	1178	485	27.1	21.1	5.95	61.4	55.8	81.5
	1879	1265	614	28.2	21.5	6.70	66.6	58.8	91.6
	1938	1288	650	28.5	21.2	7.31	68.0	60.8	88.9
	1893	1303	590	28.8	21.9	6.87	65.7	59.5	85.9
	1911	1296	615	28.7	21.9	6.77	66.6	59.2	90.8
1931/32	1826	1308	518	27.6	21.6	6.02	66.2	60.6	86.0
	1934	1308	626	27.9	21.2	6.74	69.3	61.7	92.9
	1918	1274	644	27.2	21.0	7.18	70.5	60.7	89.7
	1662	1192	470	27.1	21.3	5.77	61.3	56.0	81.5
	1780	1241	539	27.7	21.3	6.38	64.3	58.3	84.5
1936/37	1907	1272	635	29.0	21.7	7.28	65.8	58.6	87.2
	1956	1237	719	29.4	20.9	8.50	66.5	59.2	84.6
	1696	1105	591	28.2	21.1	7.12	60.1	52.4	83.0
	1861	1200	661	28.5	21.4	7.11	65.3	56.1	93.0
	2064	1319	745	29.5	21.7	7.75	70.0	60.8	96.1
1941/42	1797	1246	551	27.6	21.0	6.59	65.1	59.3	83.6
	1724	1169	555	28.7	21.7	6.98	60.1	53.9	79.5
	1862	1233	629	29.2	22.2	6.95	63.8	55.5	90.5
	1962	1254	708	28.9	21.7	7.20	67.9	57.8	98.3
	1651	1038	613	27.2	20.2	7.04	60.7	51.4	87.1
1946/47	1916	1262	654	28.4	21.4	6.98	67.5	59.0	93.7
				Greater Punjab					
1891/92	540	432	108	17.2	15.6	1.60	31.4	27.7	67.5
	770	645	125	22.1	20.0	2.05	34.8	32.3	61.0
	792	655	137	21.6	19.2	2.44	36.7	34.1	56.1
	745	601	144	21.0	18.4	2.59	35.5	32.7	55.6
	554	439	115	15.6	13.4	2.18	35.5	32.8	52.8
1896/97	587	457	130	15.2	13.0	2.20	38.6	35.2	59.1
	792	641	151	22.3	19.6	2.72	35.5	32.7	55.5
	573	481	92	17.5	15.5	2.02	32.7	31.0	45.5
	499	398	101	12.8	11.0	1.81	39.0	36.2	55.8
	873	692	181	24.6	21.2	3.40	35.5	32.6	53.2
1901/02	592	458	134	17.2	14.8	2.35	34.4	30.9	57.0
	737	594	143	19.4	16.6	2.82	38.0	35.8	50.7
	970	792	178	21.6	18.6	2.97	44.9	42.6	59.9
	890	711	179	21.0	17.8	3.22	42.4	40.0	55.6
	904	793	111	20.5	17.6	2.90	44.1	45.1	38.2

Appendix Table 4C (*contd.*)

	AC	FG Yield	NFG	AC	FG Acreage	NFG	AC	FG Yield per Acre	NFG
1906/07	1059	868	191	26.8	23.4	3.44	39.5	37.1	55.5
	745	572	173	21.4	18.5	2.94	34.8	30.9	58.8
	1032	823	209	26.6	23.0	3.57	38.8	35.8	58.5
	1111	875	236	26.3	22.8	3.48	42.2	38.4	67.8
	1064	874	190	25.6	22.4	3.14	41.6	39.1	60.5
1911/12	993	826	167	24.3	20.7	3.56	40.9	39.9	46.9
	939	738	201	24.2	21.1	3.10	38.8	35.0	64.8
	1006	750	256	24.4	20.7	3.67	41.2	36.2	69.8
	1143	904	239	28.7	25.1	3.60	39.8	36.0	63.8
	762	602	160	23.4	20.7	2.67	32.6	29.1	59.9
1916/17	1000	786	214	28.3	25.3	3.04	35.3	31.1	70.4
	1122	892	230	29.4	25.6	3.80	38.2	34.8	60.5
	864	645	219	20.7	17.9	2.81	41.7	36.0	77.9
	1141	858	283	26.2	22.4	3.78	43.5	38.3	74.9
	762	529	233	21.2	17.9	3.28	35.9	29.6	71.0
1921/22	1172	947	225	27.8	24.3	3.50	42.2	39.0	64.3
	1201	939	262	28.5	25.0	3.50	42.1	37.6	74.9
	1213	914	299	27.2	23.4	3.78	44.6	39.1	79.1
	1074	747	327	28.2	23.8	4.40	38.1	31.4	74.3
	1064	752	312	26.2	21.9	4.28	40.6	34.3	72.9
1926/27	1077	817	260	26.8	22.6	4.24	40.2	36.2	61.3
	952	686	266	25.9	22.2	3.68	36.8	30.9	72.3
	1015	764	251	28.5	23.4	5.06	35.6	32.6	49.6
	1160	888	272	27.2	23.2	3.99	42.6	38.3	68.2
	1097	812	285	26.4	22.5	3.85	41.6	36.1	74.0
1931/32	1058	776	282	26.9	22.7	4.23	39.3	34.2	66.7
	1031	745	286	26.1	22.1	4.04	39.5	33.7	70.8
	1150	807	343	30.3	25.9	4.36	38.0	31.2	78.7
	1132	787	345	23.4	19.6	3.83	48.4	40.2	90.1
	1226	805	421	27.4	23.0	4.35	44.7	35.0	96.8
1936/37	1376	871	505	27.0	22.2	4.83	51.0	39.2	104.6
	1247	859	388	27.2	22.4	4.78	45.8	38.3	81.2
	1095	735	360	25.5	21.2	4.28	42.9	34.7	84.1
	1213	837	376	25.2	20.6	4.56	48.1	40.6	82.5
	1307	847	460	28.3	23.3	4.97	46.2	36.4	92.6

Appendix Table 4C (*contd.*)

	AC	FG Yield	NFG	AC	FG Acreage	NFG	AC	FG Yield per Acre	NFG
1941/42	1347	904	443	27.9	23.2	4.70	48.3	39.0	94.3
	1478	1071	407	29.5	25.5	4.02	50.1	42.0	101.2
	1315	902	413	28.2	24.2	4.04	46.6	37.3	102.2
	1446	1011	435	31.3	27.0	4.29	46.2	37.4	101.4
	1382	930	452	31.0	26.9	4.06	44.6	34.6	111.3
1946/47	1318	868	450	26.9	23.0	3.89	49.0	37.7	115.7
				Bombay–Sind					
1891/92	698	531	167	24.0	20.3	3.73	29.1	26.2	44.7
	856	634	222	24.3	20.3	3.97	35.2	31.2	55.9
	941	619	322	23.8	19.2	4.62	39.5	32.2	69.7
	851	633	218	24.1	19.6	4.47	35.3	32.3	48.8
	721	509	212	23.1	18.7	4.40	31.2	27.2	48.2
1896/97	593	432	161	19.6	16.0	3.64	30.3	27.0	44.2
	872	678	194	23.9	20.3	3.58	36.5	33.4	54.2
	895	649	246	23.4	19.5	3.88	38.2	33.3	63.4
	418	234	184	19.2	16.3	2.93	21.8	14.4	62.8
	655	478	177	21.4	18.0	3.42	30.6	26.6	51.8
1901/02	530	390	140	22.8	18.7	4.11	23.2	20.9	34.1
	825	593	232	23.4	19.2	4.24	36.8	30.9	54.7
	852	578	274	23.7	18.4	5.30	35.9	31.4	51.7
	597	435	162	23.4	18.4	4.95	25.5	23.6	32.7
	752	521	231	22.6	17.6	5.04	33.3	29.6	45.8
1906/07	885	564	321	24.4	18.9	5.50	36.3	29.8	58.4
	680	468	212	23.9	18.7	5.22	28.5	25.0	40.6
	808	578	230	25.3	20.4	4.87	31.9	28.3	47.2
	977	639	338	25.1	19.9	5.20	38.9	32.1	65.0
	936	631	305	25.5	19.7	5.83	36.7	32.0	52.3
1911/12	620	412	208	22.4	16.8	5.57	27.7	24.5	37.3
	954	652	302	25.0	19.8	5.24	38.2	32.9	57.6
	954	633	321	25.4	19.7	5.71	37.6	32.1	56.2
	1075	725	350	25.9	20.0	5.93	41.5	36.3	59.0
	995	728	267	24.6	20.3	4.33	40.4	35.9	61.7
1916/17	1100	742	358	26.5	20.8	5.70	41.5	35.7	62.8
	967	647	320	26.4	20.4	6.05	36.6	31.7	52.9
	522	344	178	21.8	16.9	4.86	23.9	20.4	36.6
	1040	719	321	25.6	20.4	5.21	40.6	35.2	61.6
	675	466	209	23.2	18.5	4.65	29.1	25.2	44.9

Appendix Table 4C (*contd.*)

	AC	FG Yield	NFG	AC	FG Acreage	NFG	AC	FG Yield per Acre	NFG
1921/22	904	649	255	25.3	21.1	4.15	35.7	30.8	61.4
	949	650	299	25.4	20.3	5.10	37.4	32.0	58.6
	833	526	307	25.3	19.3	5.99	32.9	27.3	51.3
	989	642	347	26.5	19.9	6.56	37.3	32.3	52.9
	913	558	355	25.8	19.0	6.75	35.4	29.4	52.6
1926/27	900	600	300	25.9	20.0	5.90	34.7	30.0	50.8
	1025	648	377	26.4	20.1	6.35	38.8	32.2	59.4
	1090	659	431	26.7	19.7	6.97	40.8	33.4	61.8
	946	603	343	27.5	20.7	6.81	34.4	29.1	50.4
	1012	668	344	27.2	21.6	5.59	37.2	30.9	61.5
1931/32	986	635	351	26.5	20.4	6.06	37.2	31.1	57.9
	1060	661	399	27.1	20.9	6.22	39.1	31.6	64.1
	1054	646	408	27.5	21.2	6.27	38.3	30.5	65.1
	985	647	338	26.9	21.0	5.89	36.6	30.8	57.4
	1050	631	419	27.3	20.8	6.53	38.5	30.3	64.2
1936/37	1004	582	422	27.1	20.8	6.30	37.0	28.0	34.9
	1051	614	437	28.4	21.5	6.91	37.0	28.6	63.2
	1038	618	420	28.0	21.2	6.77	37.1	29.2	62.0
	968	548	420	28.0	21.1	6.93	34.8	26.0	60.6
	1133	608	525	28.8	21.6	7.21	39.3	28.1	72.8
1941/42	1051	562	489	28.6	21.5	7.09	36.7	26.1	68.9
	1079	643	436	27.5	21.8	5.72	39.2	29.5	76.2
	1194	706	488	28.2	22.2	5.97	42.3	31.8	81.7
	1011	616	395	27.3	22.8	4.49	37.0	27.0	88.0
	930	574	356	26.4	22.2	4.17	35.2	25.9	85.4
1946/47	933	564	369	27.2	22.7	4.47	34.3	24.8	82.5
				Central Provinces					
1891/92	543	400	143	19.1	13.6	5.50	28.4	29.4	26.0
	551	416	135	19.8	14.4	5.35	29.6	28.9	25.2
	564	424	140	20.1	14.1	6.03	28.1	30.0	23.2
	518	407	111	18.5	13.2	5.32	28.0	30.8	20.9
	638	468	170	18.7	14.1	4.62	34.1	33.2	36.8
1896/97	499	375	124	17.6	13.0	4.60	28.4	28.8	27.0
	647	474	173	17.6	12.9	4.65	36.8	36.7	37.2
	732	516	216	18.8	13.8	5.02	38.9	37.4	43.0
	432	358	74	16.3	12.1	4.23	26.5	29.6	17.5
	693	430	263	18.1	12.7	5.39	38.3	33.9	48.8

Appendix Table 4C (*contd.*)

	AC	FG Yield	NFG	AC	FG Acreage	NFG	AC	FG Yield per Acre	NFG
1900/01	745	516	229	19.0	13.6	5.39	39.2	37.9	42.5
	849	583	266	19.5	13.7	5.81	43.5	42.6	45.8
	677	455	222	19.2	12.9	6.30	35.3	35.3	35.2
	806	488	318	19.9	13.4	6.48	40.5	36.4	49.1
	664	438	226	19.9	13.3	6.64	33.4	32.9	34.0
1906/07	783	533	250	20.4	13.7	6.74	38.4	38.9	37.1
	493	331	162	19.0	13.0	5.99	25.9	25.5	27.1
	713	498	215	19.6	13.6	6.02	36.4	36.6	35.7
	915	622	293	20.4	14.3	6.13	44.9	43.5	47.8
	719	522	197	20.7	14.1	6.56	34.7	37.0	30.0
1911/12	803	543	260	20.9	13.4	7.50	38.4	40.5	34.7
	793	534	259	20.7	13.8	6.88	38.3	38.7	37.6
	639	385	254	20.0	13.3	6.65	32.0	28.9	38.2
	878	582	296	20.6	13.7	6.91	42.6	42.5	42.8
	981	680	301	21.0	14.8	6.15	46.7	45.9	48.9
1916/17	773	572	201	20.8	14.3	6.45	37.2	40.0	31.2
	691	518	173	20.5	14.0	6.46	33.7	37.0	26.8
	541	341	200	18.9	13.7	5.19	28.6	24.9	38.5
	922	597	325	19.9	13.7	6.16	46.3	43.6	52.8
	405	267	138	18.8	13.1	5.69	21.5	20.4	24.3
1921/22	883	584	299	19.6	13.5	6.05	45.1	43.3	49.4
	870	590	280	20.3	13.7	6.57	42.9	43.1	42.6
	824	556	268	21.1	14.2	6.91	39.1	39.2	38.8
	796	518	278	21.1	14.0	7.12	37.7	37.0	39.0
	766	512	254	21.1	14.0	7.13	36.3	36.6	35.6
1926/27	796	540	256	21.0	14.5	6.45	37.9	37.2	39.7
	830	507	323	21.3	14.8	6.45	39.0	34.3	50.1
	839	493	346	21.3	14.4	6.86	39.4	34.2	50.4
	881	557	324	21.0	14.3	6.66	42.0	39.0	48.6
	818	517	301	21.2	14.9	6.32	38.6	34.7	47.6
1931/32	683	538	145	21.2	14.9	6.34	32.2	36.1	22.9
	773	538	235	21.0	15.1	5.92	36.8	35.6	40.0
	772	549	223	20.9	14.8	6.07	36.9	37.1	36.7
	754	569	185	20.9	15.0	5.81	36.1	37.9	31.8
	683	497	186	20.9	15.0	5.87	32.7	33.1	31.7

Appendix Table 4C (*contd.*)

	AC	FG Yield	NFG	AC	FG Acreage	NFG	AC	FG Yield per Acre	NFG
1936/37	812	567	245	21.2	15.3	5.87	38.3	37.1	41.7
	767	549	218	21.4	15.2	6.18	35.8	36.1	35.3
	733	553	180	21.0	15.2	5.80	34.9	36.4	31.0
	747	528	219	20.9	15.5	5.40	35.7	34.1	40.6
	711	450	261	21.0	15.4	5.63	33.9	29.2	46.4
1941/42	637	370	267	20.7	15.1	5.59	30.8	24.5	47.8
	759	568	173	20.3	15.2	5.10	37.4	37.4	33.9
	771	574	197	21.3	16.1	5.17	36.2	35.7	38.1
	723	546	177	21.0	16.0	5.03	34.4	34.1	35.2
	707	513	194	21.7	16.7	4.96	32.6	30.7	39.1
1946/47	565	399	166	21.0	16.0	4.95	26.9	24.9	33.5

SOURCES: Computed from adjusted crop data, as in Appendix 3A, and average 1924/25/–28/29 prices given in Appendix Table 4A, as explained in Chapter IV, 1. For British India and Greater Bengal, see also modified series in Appendix Tables 9B and 9C.

Appendix Table 9C: Modified Annual Series of British India All-Crop and Foodgrain Output and Yield per Acre Based on Modified Greater Bengal Rice Yield per Acre Series (Output in Million Rupees, Y/A in Rupees)

	Output		Yield per Acre	
	All-Crop	Foodgrain	All-Crop	Foodgrain
1891/92	6947	5301	41.4	37.9
	8193	6208	46.3	41.9
	8315	6523	46.7	45.0
	8838	6873	47.5	44.6
	8415	6367	47.8	43.6
1896/97	6947	5043	42.1	36.8
	9646	7389	53.0	48.3
	9625	7433	53.7	49.2
	7691	6022	47.2	44.0
	8783	6614	48.5	43.8
1901/02	8383	6199	48.2	42.5
	9744	7446	53.5	49.0
	9510	7163	51.1	47.1
	8793	6482	47.0	42.6
	8424	6211	45.5	41.1
1906/07	9579	6911	49.6	44.0
	7636	5466	42.4	37.4
	8561	6359	46.0	41.6
	10705	8106	54.8	50.7
	10588	8007	54.0	50.0
1911/12	10039	7461	52.6	48.8
	10086	7328	52.3	46.7
	9335	6678	49.7	44.2
	10244	7254	51.5	45.1
	10554	7915	54.7	49.5
1916/17	11009	8188	55.0	49.9
	10939	8119	54.4	49.8
	7842	5523	45.6	39.5
	10834	7833	55.3	49.6
	8357	6064	46.9	41.5
1921/22	10205	7789	52.6	48.1
	10462	7801	53.4	48.2
	9788	6851	51.0	44.2
	9885	6930	49.7	43.9
	9881	6824	50.9	44.3

Appendix Table 9C (*contd.*)

	Output		Yield per Acre	
	All-Crop	Foodgrain	All-Crop	Foodgrain
1926/27	9918	6775	52.2	44.6
	9649	6408	50.3	41.6
	10276	6984	51.9	44.5
	10498	7239	53.5	46.4
	10597	7253	53.5	45.6
1931/32	10278	7367	51.9	45.8
	10439	7032	53.8	44.8
	11025	7497	55.1	46.6
	10322	6982	54.0	45.0
	10225	6595	53.3	41.7
1936/37	11141	7336	55.7	45.9
	10958	7168	55.1	45.7
	9704	6547	49.3	41.4
	10727	7072	54.5	44.8
	10828	6523	53.3	41.0
1941/42	10379	6968	51.6	43.0
	10827	7189	52.8	42.8
	11752	8032	56.8	47.2
	11019	7760	52.5	44.3
	10630	7224	51.6	42.0
1946/47	10716	7317	52.8	43.3

SOURCE: See Chapter IX, 1.3.

Chapter 1

Crop Production

[1953]

R. C. DESAI

This Chapter describes the sources of and the methods by which outturn of agricultural crops was estimated. The observations relate to the following crops the outturn of which was directly helpful in estimating consumer purchase.

Grains and Pulses: Rice, wheat, barley, *jowar*, *bajra*, *ragi*, maize, gram, other foodgrains including pulses.

Oilseeds: Linseed, sesamum, rape and mustard, groundnut, coconuts, castor, other oilseeds.

Sugar: Sugarcane, others.

Fruits and vegetables including rootcrops.
Condiments and spices.
Miscellaneous foodcrops.

Beverages: Tea, coffee.
Tobacco.

Sources

The basic publication on agricultural statistics in India and Pakistan was the *Season and Crop Report* issued by the Department of Agriculture or Land Records in each Provincial Administration. This gave information for each district which remains the basic unit of published agricultural statistics. For the period covered by this study, the Director General of Commercial Intelligence and Statistics[1] at Calcutta issued annually two central publications: *Agricultural Statistics of India*, Volume 1 (British India) and Volume 2 (Indian States) and *Estimates of Area and Yield of Principal Crops in India*.[2] The latter was issued soon after the harvest and set out the figures published in the

[1] Hereafter referred to as DGCIS.
[2] Hereafter abbreviated the *Ag. Stats.* and the *Estimates*.

Final Forecasts. From among the crops above, forecasts were prepared for rice, wheat, sugarcane, linseed, rape and mustard, sesamum, castorseed, and groundnut. It also included estimates of area and outturn of tea, coffee, barley, *jowar*, *bajra*, maize, gram and tobacco. The *Ag. Stats.* was a later publication and gave area estimates only. The aggregates of area given here differed from those in the *Estimates*.

The reasons were:

1. Certain tracts for which forecasts were not published were excluded from the aggregate for British India in the *Estimates*. Figures for these tracts were, however, included in the *Agricultural Statistics*.
2. In the districts of Almora and Garhwal and in the hill tracts of the Nainital District of the United Provinces there was no agency for the collection of statistics and no figures for these were included in the *Estimates*, but rough estimates for these areas were included in the *Agricultural Statistics*.
3. In some cases the figures given in the *Estimates* were revised before being included in the *Agricultural Statistics*.[3]

The *Estimates* on the other hand contained estimates of area and outturn for a great many of Bombay, Rajputana and central India states for a few crops information in respect of which was not available in the *Ag. Stats*. Inclusion in the latter was merited only if a complete classification of all cultivated soil was available, while in case of the *Estimates* the approach was on the basis of individual crops and thus some of these states which could only furnish information in respect of a few of the major crops were included. Inclusion in the *Estimates* on the other hand required statistics both of area and outturn. The *Ag. Stats*. did not require outturn estimates and hence its coverage generally was greater than that of the *Estimates* except in the case of one or two major crops.

A further source of information was *The Food Statistics of India*, a

[3] *Guide to Current Official Statistics*, Volume I (Third Edition) p. 10.

Area under Rice for the year 1935–6		(000 acres)
Estimates		79,035
Punjab, N.W.F.P. & Ajmer-Merwara,		1,011
Almora, Garhwal and Nainital,		122
Revision Orissa.	deduct	–280
Ag. Stats.		79,888

publication issued in 1946 by the Department of Food.[4] This publication incorporated information on the area and outturn of rice, wheat, *jowar*, *bajra*, maize and barley received from the hitherto 'non-reporting' areas for the years 1936–7 onwards.[5]

A source of frequent check on official statistics and in some cases the only source of information was the long series of the *Marketing Reports* issued by the Agricultural Marketing Adviser to the Government of India. From among the commodities or groups listed above there are separate *Marketing Reports* on rice, wheat, barley, gram, linseed, groundnut, coconuts, sugar, potatoes, grapes, bananas, cashewnuts, citrus fruits, coffee and tobacco. The *Reports* provide good descriptive material and specific instances being the product of 'inquiries'. The dignified term 'survey' (e.g. market survey) often indicates a member of the marketing staff going to a town market and inquiring from one or two 'prominent' merchants the volume of produce coming to the market or from a couple of 'typical' shopkeepers the prices obtained for it. In preference to a total black out such information was often used, but its statistical value can only be exaggerated.

Comprehensiveness of Statistical Information

The publications noted on the previous page differed in their coverage and hence any general statement on the coverage of official statistics is likely to be misleading. The total bloc area of India and Pakistan by Professional Survey[6] was customarily classified into the following four administrative divisions for which the area of reporting and non-reporting units as in the *Ag. Stats.* was separately stated.

[4] Hereafter abbreviated *Food Statistics*.

[5] 'Non-reporting' areas were defined as those areas which did not report agricultural statistics to the DGCIS. Since some of the states only reported area and not yield, the 'area-non-reporting' units had to be distinguished from a larger number of the 'yield-non-reporting' units. The term 'non-reporting' had been loosely used in official publications and at times it was not clear in which sense it was mentioned. The term will be used in this essay only for area-non-reporting units which, of course, did not report yields as well.

[6] 'The area covered by "Professional Survey" is that carried out by the survey of India in northern India, and by the corresponding departments in the southern provinces. The agricultural statistics are, however, prepared in a number of provinces or parts of provinces from "Village Papers", i.e. papers, prepared by the village accountants for the purpose of assessment and collection of land revenue' (Introductory Note. *Ag. Stats.*). According to the 'Village

Table 1. Comprehensiveness of Agricultural Statistics
(000 Acres)

	Reporting	Non-reporting	Total
1. British Provinces (including Indian States within the political jurisdiction of the Government of Assam)	512,664	7,891	520,555
2. Indian States having direct political relations with the Crown Representative	147,822[7]	288,926	436,748
3. Certain specially administered territories in the N.W.F.P. (Tribal areas etc.) not included under 1		14,536	14,536
4. British Baluchistan (including administered areas)		34,706	34,706
Total	660,486	346,059	1,006,545

Thus of the 1,007 million acres of the geographical area of India and Pakistan complete crop-classification of cultivated soils was not available for about one-third. The coverage from the point of view of the individual crops lacked uniformity and it was not often possible to total up the bloc area of units in respect of which information was obtained by DGCIS and published in the *Estimates*. Thus if a crop was reported, for instance, in 'Bombay States' it was not possible to ascertain whether all the Bombay states were

Papers' the reporting area for the year 1938–9 was 511,877 (British India) and 151,161 (States) 000 acres instead of 512,664 and 147,822 ,000 acres according to 'Professional Survey'. 'The causes of this difference are: (a) While the surveyed area is calculated in bloc, the area by village papers represents the added total of field and village areas, and (b) the system followed as regards the inclusion or exclusion of areas covered by water, buildings, roads, and railroads is not uniform in the two sets of returns.' Ibid. The bloc total area of India and Pakistan also differed slightly in the various publications. The latest Survey estimate as available in the Census of 1941 was 1,581,640 square miles, i.e. 1,012,102 ,000 acres. According to the 1938–9 issues of the *Ag.Stats*. the bloc total was 1,006,545,000 acres. According to the *Food Stats*. the figure was 1,008,572,000 acres. It was not generally possible to revise all the details in respect of which a table was prepared from any of the publications and hence the bloc totals slightly differ in different tables.

[7] The gross area of these states is 257,959 ,000 acres. Of these no returns were available for 110,137,000 acres comprising chiefly of unsurveyed areas and lands held on *jagirs* and other privileged tenures.

included or a few, and whether the same states were included in respect of all the crops mentioned in the publication. The labours of the Food Department succeeded in getting a few more units to submit 'estimates' (official term for guesses) of area and yield of cereals from the year 1936–7 onwards. The results are stated in Table 2.[8]

Table 2. Comprehensiveness of Statistics by Crops (Agricultural) (000 Acres)

Cereals	Bloc area of the Yield-reporting Units in the *Estimates*	Bloc area of units from which information was obtained by Food Deptt.	Bloc area of units still under black-out	Area under Crop as published by DGCIS in the *Estimates* (Average ending of 7 years 1942–3)	Additional area under Crop Covered by Food Deptt. (Average ending of 7 years 1942–3)	Column 6 per cent of Column 5
(1)	(2)	(3)	(4)	(5)	(6)	(7)
Wheat	669,292	264,893	74,387	34,516	898	2.6
Rice	640,304	283,760	84,508	73,933	3,821	6.8
Jowar	592,997	317,326	98,249	34,517	3,533	10.2
Bajra	592,997	319,669	95,906	18,159	3,094	17.0
Maize	552,351	325,472	130,749	6,387	1,841	28.8
Barley	556,184	317,355	135,033	6,351	931	14.6

It is obvious from the above table that the cultivation was very small in the area for which information was not available. The increase in outturn was also of the same order as the increase in acreage. Subject to the observations in the next paragraph a 40 per cent increase in the coverage of wheat gave only 2.6 per cent increase in the actual acreage under the crop or in its yield. A 59 per cent increase in the coverage of maize increased the area under the crop by 28.8 per cent and the yield by 29.4 per cent.[9] This was primarily

[8] *Food Statistics*, p. 66. It appeared that in the table gross area of the states was included and no deduction appeared to have been made for unsurveyed areas, etc., mentioned in the footnote on page 21.

[9] 'The total addition to be made to the estimated production of foodgrains from the (yield) reporting areas on account of the inclusion of nearly 70 per cent of the (yield) non-reporting area was only 8.4 per cent of the estimated yield of cereals from the reporting areas.' *Food Statistics*, p. 3.

due to the fact that in many of the yield-non-reporting areas there was either no production at all or that it was negligible.

The value which could be placed on the statistics obtained by the Food Department was doubtful. The Report of the Inter-Departmental Committee on Official Statistics mentioned that a detailed examination of the reliability of these figures was being undertaken by the then Department of Education, Health and Lands. An inquiry from the Statistician to the Department as to the degree of accuracy he attached to these figures, elicited the reply: 'These figures are provisional and are under scrutiny.'[10] Meanwhile, the Department of Food saw it fit to publish these. In absence of any official indication suspicion attaches to the accuracy of these figures. They were all obtained during the War after the creation of the Food Department and the tragedies of the Bengal Famine. When a general scarcity was feared and when Food Department with its power to requisition food supplies had called out information mostly from princely states, these were very likely to be biassed. Every unit whether deficit or surplus was interested in the underestimation of its supplies, either in order to secure more supplies from outside or part with as little of its own supplies as possible. The *Food Statistics* was alive to the general unreliability of these estimates. It commented, 'It is true that the estimates provided for by the administrations of the non-reporting areas are even more in the nature of guess-work than the statistics furnished by the reporting areas'.[11] It would have been more helpful if while incorporating the information thus obtained the Food Department had indicated the 'planks' on which this guesswork was based and if it could justify any suspicion of reliability. Since there was no further information to check these figures the comments that follow refer to the statistics supplied by the DGCIS in the *Ag.Stats.* and the *Estimates*.

Determination of Outturn

The framing of estimates of outturn of agricultural crops in India and Pakistan involved a consideration of three factors, viz. area, standard or normal yield, and seasonal or crop condition factor. The estimate of outturn of a crop in a district was a product of the area under the crop and the standard yield deflated for the current seasonal or crop condition factor. The area was normally available to the nearest

[10] D.O. no. D.3436-St/46 dated New Delhi, 7 June 1946.

[11] *Food Statistics*, pp. 2–3. But it seems that the Food Department had failed to realise that this guesswork also involved a strong unilateral bias.

100 acres, the standard yield was expressed separately for irrigated and unirrigated soil in pounds or Indian maunds (82 2/7 lbs.), and the crop condition factor was expressed as per cent or annas in a rupee of the standard or normal or average yield. If in a district the area under a crop was 1,000 acres, the standard yield was 12 maunds and the condition factor was 12 annas or 75 per cent, the outturn of the crop would be 9,000 maunds.

Area Under Crops

The reliability of statistics from the 'reporting' areas in British India was broadly a function of the prevailing system of land tenure. The Temporary Land Revenue Settlement areas had a permanent revenue agency in different villages which kept records of area cultivated, classification of crops, estimates of yield, revenue assessed and collected, etc. On the other hand in the Permanently Settled Areas the revenue had been fixed once and for all and no permanent staff existed for the purpose.* This classification was not very strict and much depended on whether a province was predominantly under Permanent Settlement or not. Thus Bengal had no permanent re-

* Permanently and Temporarily settled Area in British India (000 acres)

Province	Year	Permanently Settled	Temporarily Settled	Total
(1)	(2)	(3)	(4)	(5)
Ajmer-Merwara	1938–9	778	784	1,562
Assam	1938–9	3,919	31,566	35,485
Bengal	1937–8	39,158	10,100	49,258
Bihar	1936–7	39,694	4,630	44,324
Bombay	1935–6		48,653	48,653
C.P. and Berar	1938–9		63,112	63,112
Coorg	1937–8		1,012	1,012
Delhi	1938–9		368	368
Madras	1938–9	21,246	58,515	79,761
N.W.F.P.	1938–9		8,579	8,579
Orissa	1936–7	9,861	10,745	20,606
Punjab	1938–9		60,176	60,176
Sind	1935–6		30,180	30,180
United Provinces	1936–7	7,306	60,660 + 1	67,966 + 1
		121,962	389,081	511,043

SOURCE: *Agricultural Statistics*, 1938–9, vol. 1, p. 10.

venue agency in temporarily settled areas, while in the United Provinces the Permanently Settled areas fell in line with other areas in having a permanent revenue agency. Thus the reliability varied province-wise rather than on the basis of total area under Permanent or Temporary Settlement.

In case of areas where there was a permanent revenue agency the basic unit of information was the village, and the official supplying the information was known as the *Patwari*. He was described as 'well-paid literate, drawn from men of social standing . . . and trained in his duties'. He made a field-to-field inspection of the villages under his charge, and had an adequate number of senior officers above him to supervise his work. It was hence commonly acknowledged that where the *Patwari* system obtained the reporting of area and classification by crops was fairly accurate.[12]

The statistics of area under predominantly Permanently Settled Provinces hardly compared in accuracy with those in which the Patwaris were employed. The returns here were made by the village *chowkidar* (policeman), who had many police duties, who was 'ill-paid and illiterate, and there were no persons corresponding to the circle officers connecting the village officials with the district officials'. The village agency was too ill-equipped and untrained for field-to-field inspection and hence the sub-divisional officials roughly ascertained the proportion the area under the crop was to the normal average for the crop and passed on these estimates to the district officials. Through these the reports finally reached the Director of Agriculture and at every stage the several officials allowed the weight of their subjective estimation of the situation to bear on the primary figures. The acreage estimates, hence, could not be accurate[13] and they generally erred on the side of underestimation. The attention to this aspect was specially drawn after the Bengal Famine. The Famine Inquiry Commission found that whereas the area under rice as reported by the Director of Agriculture was 22.39 million acres the area under rice compiled from the Settlement Reports totalled 25.54

[12] Hubback, however, remarked: 'It is usually believed that the estimate of cropped area is sufficiently accurate. It may be, but the belief is intuitive, rather than rational', and he observed: 'It would certainly be a great advantage if the harvested area could be obtained by some form of sampling'. 'Sampling of Rice Yields in Bihar', reprinted in *Sankhya*, vol. 7, pt. 3.

[13] 'For these tracts, the acreage as well as the outturn cannot be more than a rough estimate. Such estimates of areas, once formed, are liable to become stereotyped and repeated year after year without regard to the influence of exceptional seasons or changes in the economic conditions of the tracts.'

million acres.[14] The random sample surveys of acreage carried out by

Table 3. Estimates of Effective Area under Crops by Random Sampling Method in Bengal and Bihar

BENGAL

Crop	Year	Number of Districts surveyed	Size of Grids[15] Acres	Estimated effective Area under the crop 000 Acres	Standard Error of Estimate in Col 5 000 Acres	Corresponding Official Estimate 000 Acres
(1)	(2)	(3)	(4)	(5)	(6)	(7)
Jute	1941	21	1,2,2,5,3, 4,6,9	1,573		1,533
	1942	21	1,2,2,5,3, 4,6,9,16	2,996		2,704
	1943	25	2.25	2,755	78.2	2,146
	1944	25	2.25	2,106	24.3	1,694
	1945	25	2.25	2,520	17.3	2,018
	1946	25	2.25	2,273		1,490
Autumn rice	1944	25	2.25	7,873	63.8	8,084
	1945	25	2.25	6,884	32.1	6,671
	1946	25	2.25	6,262		6,699
Winter rice	1944	25	2.25	22,201	275.5	207,98[16]
	1945	25	2.25	21,087	51.4	19,471
	1946	25	2.25			19,909

Estimates, Appendix 1. 'In 1936 the agricultural authorities in Bihar were confronted with an inexplicable fall of some 100,000 acres under rice in a certain district but no explanation has ever been forthcoming. In another case an actual survey of the jute area in an important district in Bihar revealed the real acreage to be nearer 300,000 than the stereotyped figure of 120,000 which had been appearing in the official estimates year after year without change. A third example is revealed by a recent examination by the marketing staff of the Indian Central Jute Committee of statistics relating to jute grown in Bengal. This disclosed that the official estimates were liable to fall short of the probable area sown by as much as 45 per cent.' *Report on the Marketing of Rice in India and Burma* (1941), p. 13. Of course, the error should be much smaller for a large unit like the province.

[14] Not much reliance, however, can be placed on Settlement Reports either. It may be mentioned, however, that there was no evidence of a fall in area under rice since before the beginning of this century to which period these Settlement Reports probably related.

[15] 'Grid' is the technical term used for the sample unit.

[16] Revised figure after plot-to-plot enumeration.

Table 3. (*contd.*)

BIHAR
(000 Acres)

Crop	Survey Estimate	Settlement[17] Report	Forecast[18] 1943–4
(1)	(2)	(3)	(4)
	District Shahabad.	(Area 2,798,000 acres)	
Wheat	300.35 ± 19.87	227.9	263.8
Barley	78.40 ± 9.51	105.4	102.5
Gram	337.33 ± 26.86	339.5	282.8
Arhar	58.60 ± 12.59	51.4	41.0
	774.68 ± 68.63	724.2	689.6
	District Monghyr.	(Area 2,370,000 acres)	
Wheat	284.08 ± 31.62	144.9	219.8
Barley	66.90 ± 5.32	81.4	81.9
Gram	193.43 ± 26.86	210.5	210.5
Arhar	103.71 ± 23.22	42.5[19]	81.0
	648.12 ± 87.02		593.2

Professor Mahalanobis at the instance of the Bengal Government showed the official returns of the area under rice to contain an underestimation of about 3.5 million acres. The underestimation was also established by a plot-to-plot enumeration which was carried out by the Bengal Government in 1944–5 which gave a figure of area under rice 2 million in excess of corresponding official figure. The significance of these could be ascertained from the footnote to the Final Forecast of the Rice Crop 1944–5.

The figures arrived at by 'usual procedure' were 18,592,000 acres and 6,775,000 tons of the winter crop of rice in Bengal. 'Alternative methods, however, indicate a larger figure for winter crop acreage. The area, according to plot-to-plot enumeration is 20.6 million acres, while by a sample survey it is found to be 22.1 million acres. The corresponding yield figures are 7.50 million tons and 8.05 million tons respectively.'[20]

[17] Settlement period: Shahabad 1907–16, Monghyr 1905–12.

[18] Forecast for Rabi crops dated 26 April 1944 and Fourth Wheat Forecast issued by Director of Agriculture, Bihar.

[19] Figure for North Monghyr alone.

[20] *Indian Trade Journal*, vol., CLVIII, no. 2049, dated 27 Sept. 1945, p. 532.

The results of Professor Mahalanobis' Area Surveys in Bengal and Bihar are given in Table 3.[21]

Practically in every instance official estimates are below sample estimates, except Autumn rice in 1944 in Bengal and barley crop in Bihar. The latter only shows that the barley acreage estimates remained stationary since the Settlement Period and did not reflect the fall it had taken since.

The statistics of area related to area actually sown and not area successfully cropped. 'The general rule is that the returns should exhibit the areas actually sown whether the crop comes to maturity or not, the principle underlying his rule being that the failure of a crop should affect not its area but outturn. An exception to this rule is, however, made when fields, owing to the failure of the first sowing have been devoted to other crops.'[22] In this case the area first sown was omitted. It was difficult to ascertain how far errors of eye estimation in this respect led to faulty estimates of the area under the crop. So far as there was any crop at all the crop condition factor would be affected. When there was a total failure of crops it should be fairly easy for the district officer to ascertain the extent in a rapid survey by a motor car. A perusal of Hubback's note seemed to suggest that this factor tended to overestimate the actual area under the crop. This might not be correct. His suggestion, however, is quite helpful. A sample-survey random over time as well as space would give a fair approximation of total outturn and hence of partial or complete failure of crops. The first might not decrease the area but give a low outturn in crop-cutting experiments, the latter would give reduced area under crops.

Another product of irregular information was the estimation of the area under mixed crops. There was some ambiguity in the term 'mixed'. Mixed crops might have two different meanings. In one plot of land one portion might be sown with one crop, another with another crop and so on with two or more crops. In this case there is no ambiguity in the area under each individual crop. But the usual form of mixed crop sowing is to sow the plot with a mixture of two or more crops over the whole plot. The problem then was to estimate the net or effective proportion of land under each crop in the mixed

[21] *Sources*: Bengal, through the courtesy of the Superintendent of Crop Surveys, Government of Bengal, D.O. no. 154/3/47 dated 18 March 1947, and Bihar, 'Report on the Bihar Crop Survey: Rabi Season 1943–4', *Sankhya*, vol. 7, pt. 1, p. 47.

[22] *Estimates* Appendix 1.

plot. A further complication was added by the fact that the relative composition of land under each crop and the number of crops vary from field to field. 'The areas covered by the several crops in a mixed field are estimated in various ways in the different provinces, and the estimates are based on formulae prescribed by the provincial authorities in individual cases, as it has not been found practicable to prescribe one uniform method of calculation.'[23] The main item affected was oilseeds. In the *Ag. Stats*. 'in case of the United Provinces areas reported for oilseeds represent areas under "pure" crop, i.e. seeds sown unmixed with any other crop and exclude oilseeds which are thinly sown in combination with wheat, barley, gram, and other foodcrops'.[24] For the purposes of the forecasts and hence in the *Estimates* the statistics of acreage refer to 'net' or 'effective' area under the crop. 'The estimates for the mixed crop in the United Provinces', however, 'are highly conjectural'[25] and were kept separate. The significance of this inaccuracy can be gauged from the following figures for 1937–8.

Table 4. Area under Oilseeds, 1937–8
(000 Acres)

Crop	United Provinces		India and Pakistan Crop excluding the Mixed Crop in the United Provinces
	'Pure' Crop	Mixed Crop[26]	
(1)	(2)	(3)	(4)
Linseed	2,480	632	3,258
Rape & Mustard	209	2,375	3,086
Sesamum	368	955	3,495

In the case of Bihar, of the plots examined by Mahalanobis in the two districts, 6.2 and 8.0 per cent only were under pure crop. He inquired about the way in which the Department of Agriculture was arriving at figures for area under each crop when sown in mixed condition. 'No definite information could be secured but I was given to understand that the Agricultural Department was not using

[23] *Estimates*, Appendix 1.
[24] Note to the Table on Area under Crops, *Ag. Stats.*, vol. 1.
[25] *Estimates*, Footnote to the Table on Linseed, Rape & Mustard and Sesamum.
[26] The above footnote in the *Estimates* applies to the figures in this column. In case of castor seed even this daring attempt is given up and the figures 'exclude estimates for the mixed crop for which there are no reliable data at present'.

any standard method for the purpose. The area figures for individual *mauzas* are supposed to be supplied by local officers, and nothing was known as to how the acreage for individual crops was estimated.'[27] In Delhi 'it was found that the annual forecasts of yield were based on the area devoted solely to wheat and that mixed crop areas on which wheat is sown along with barley or gram were not taken into consideration'.[28]

Standard Yield

Standard Yield has been defined as 'that crop which past experience has shown to be the most generally recurring crop in a series of years; the typical crop of the local area; the crop which the cultivator has a right (as it were) to expect, and with which he is (or should be) content, while if he gets more he has reason to rejoice, and if less he has reason to complain'; or in other words, it is the 'figure which in existing circumstances might be expected to be attained in the year if the rainfall and the season were of a character ordinary for the tract under consideration, that is, neither very favourable nor the reverse'. Briefly, it is stated to be 'the average yield on an average soil in a year of average character'.[29] The Standard (it is also called 'normal' or 'average') yield was generally obtained by crop-cutting experiments over a number of years on plots selected by district officers or officials (belonging to the category 'responsible') of the Provincial Agricultural Departments on the basis of what they considered to be average or standard for that locality. No objective procedure was laid down for the selection of the plots. It depended entirely for its accuracy 'on the ability of the officer to select'.[30] On the basis of the yields obtained by these crop-cutting experiments annually for major crops, every five years a revision was supposed to be made by the Director of Agriculture or Land Records at the Provincial

[27] *Sankhya*, vol. 7, pt. 1, p. 66.

[28] *Report on the Marketing of Wheat in India and Burma* (1937), p. 9.

[29] *Estimates*, Appendix 1. The wording is the same as in a circular dated 1897.

[30] Hubback, 'Sampling of Rice Yields in Bihar', *Sankhya*, vol. 7, pt. 3. He continues: 'The method is comparable to estimating the average income of the population of a town by watching the streets for a few days and then picking out a man, who looked to be in average circumstances and discovering what his income is.' He also observed: 'There is no possible way (in the official method) of estimating what is the probability that the result of such selections is within a given range from the true mean yield.'

Centre, who revised these in the light of his own intuition or further inquiries. Till the next revision a list was maintained by these agricultural Departments of the standard yield of each crop in each district for irrigated and unirrigated soil separately, and on the basis of this the current outturn per acre was determined. In actual practice these standard yields in quite a number of cases had been going on without revision for a series of quinquennial periods.

Another possible source of error lay in the different sizes of sample cuts in different provinces. Thus the size of the cut was 1/10 of an acre in Madras, the Central Provinces, Bengal, Sind and the United Provinces; between 1/3 and 1/5 of an acre in the Punjab and between 1/20 and 1/80 of an acre in the North-West Frontier Province. Smaller sizes generally tended to overestimate the yield. The accuracy of the results also depended on the number of cuts taken per unit of survey and these also varied from place to place and in the same place from time to time. Lack of uniformity in these respects, as also the personal bias involved in the selection of the plots, involved unjustifiable elements in experiments intended to secure unbiassed estimates of yield.

Condition Factor

The height of subjectivity was reached in the estimation of the seasonal or crop condition factor. The *Patwari* sent his subjective estimation of the current yield as a proportion of the normal to the Circle Officer. The Circle Officer checked the figures from personal experience and intuition. The Subdivisional Officer added his own personal experience. And finally the District Collector and then the Director of Agriculture at the top pulled their weight of personal intuition, knowledge, experience and inspection on the figures received by them. The methods were not uniform. In Madras correction was only made by the Director of Agriculture, all others reporting the arithmetic average of the reports of their sub ordinate officers. In other cases the correction proceeded at the district level. This game of successive guessing stands condemned on account of bias. In the Permanently Settled Provinces the primary agency was the *Chowkidar*, but there was no superior agency corresponding to the circle officers checking the primary figures.

That the system tended to underestimate the outturn had been maintained for a long time past. The errors arising from this subjective reporting instead of cancelling out tended to be systematic in the direction of underestimation. Various reasons were mentioned for this. The one that was persistently given was the pessimism of the *Patwari* or *Chowkidar* who underrated good seasons and exaggerated bad seasons.[31] The incidence of the *Patwaris*' pessimism on official statistics of outturn is, however, exaggerated. Firstly, the results as available involved the correction of preliminary reports by circle officers or revenue officers, and this reduced the inaccuracy. But so far as correction was supposed to be involved in the process of averaging it might be mentioned that no amount of averaging would wipe out an error which was not random but systematic. Second, in some cases the underestimation was corrected for by adopting a lower anna equivalent for the normal. Thus a 10 anna condition report was adjusted to a 12 anna normal instead of 16 annas. In his inquiries the author often queried the grounds on which this lower anna normal was adopted, but did not succeed in getting an unambiguous reply. Sometimes the Director concerned intuitively considered the standard yield as too high and ruled a lower anna equivalent for the normal and in this case the primary purpose was not to correct the underestimation of the *Patwari*, but to correct the overestimation in the results of selective crop-cutting experiments. Since, however, taken over a long period the average of the condition factors was lower than the corresponding anna equivalent of the normal, a priori it may be said that the condition estimates were underestimates. On the other hand Hubback strongly maintained[32] and other evidence available from the results of the crop-cutting experiments by the random sampling method went to support the conclusion that the normals themselves were very highly pitched. Thus on these grounds alone the direction or the extent of bias could not be determined.[33]

[31] The *Patwari* or the *Chowkidar* 'being generally untrained and pessimistic by nature is hardly able to form a correct estimate of outturn in terms of the normal crop. His idea of a normal crop is that which he longs to see but rarely sees and the result is that the standard with which he compares a crop is really something above the normal. Consequently, his estimates generally fall below the mark.' Dr Meek in Evidence before the Royal Commission of Agriculture, *Evidence*, vol. 1, pt. II, p. 358.

[32] 'Sampling of Rice Yields in Bihar,' ibid.

[33] The suspicion that the official estimates were underestimates was particularly strong among commercial classes. Thus with regard to the outturn of wheat the Season and Crop Report of the Punjab noted in 1922–3: 'The principal exporting firms get fairly good results by assuming that the outturn is 33 per cent greater than the official estimates.' (The exaggeration

Crop-Cutting Experiments by Random Sampling

The only confirmation lay in a scientific system of crop-cutting experiments which could get rid of all subjective elements in crop estimation. The earliest crop-cutting experiments by random sampling were carried out by Hubback during 1923–5 in Bihar and Orissa. Deshmukh and Rau also made experiments in the Central Provinces in 1929 and 1930. But these early experiments failed to make any impression on the Government. The reason probably was the inevitable tendency to resent any innovation in the departmental routine, particularly if it involved heavy additional expenditure as well. While the Government were marking time, at the instance of

---

in this figure of 33 per cent is reduced if it is intended only to refer to the outturn that is marketed). The Punjab Marketing Report in 1935–6 referring to this quotation observed that there was no reason to suppose that conditions had changed since then. There was also a parallel discrepancy between the Trade estimates of cotton and jute. The latter also have defects of their own, still the disparity is significant.

Divergence of Official Forecasts from Trade Estimates of Jute & Cotton (000 bales of 400 lbs. each)

Year	Jute			Cotton (Indian)	
	Exports, Mill Consumption and other Consumption	Exports, Mill Purchases and Extra-factory Consumption	Official Forecast Estimate	Exports, Mill Consumption and Extra-factory Consumption	Official Forecast Estimate
(1)	(2)	(3)	(4)	(5)	(6)
1931–2	7,883	6,704	5,542	4,369	4,003
1932–3	8,381	8,878	7,072	5,670	4,618
1933–4	9,068	8,853	7,987	6,183	5,057
1934–5	9,466	9,966	8,500	6,166	4,797
1935–6	9,657	8,670	7,215	6,526	5,867
1936–7	11,443	10,932	9,611	7,340	6,234
1937–8	10,914	10,132	8,656	5,544	5,722
1938–9	10,609	9,920	6,819	6,875	5,051
1939–40	10,595	10,500	9,738	5,812	4,909
1940–1	7,367	9,696	13,172	*n.a.*	6,080

Revised

NOTE: The figures are taken from the *Estimates* with the only change in Column 5 where consumption of Burma of the order of 9–11,000 bales was excluded. Before 1936–7, since when the Indian Central Cotton Committee

the Indian Central Jute Committee the Indian Statistical Institute,[34] under the direction of Professor Mahalanobis, took up a five year scheme to estimate the area and outturn of jute crop in Bengal. While this was being carried out the Imperial Council of Agricultural Research[35] proposed a scheme using the same *Patwari* agency and demonstrating the practicability of technique of a suitable random sampling method so that the Provinces could take it up as departmental routine on a permanent basis. The first series of experiments planned on these lines were carried out by the Indian Central Cotton Committee under the direction of Dr V. G. Panse covering the cotton crop in the Akola district in the Central Provinces and Berar. It was extended to another district in 1943–4 and finally covered the whole cotton belt of the Central Provinces and Berar in 1944–5, and was being since repeated. The result for 1944–5 showed that the official estimate was lower than the survey estimate by about 10 per cent for the province as a whole, while the discrepancy was larger for individual districts.

War conditions generally and the Famine in Bengal immediately impressed upon the Government the necessity of obtaining accurate information on the outturn of food. There were three inquiries in connection with the area under rice in Bengal.[36] All the three showed underestimation which averaged about 10 per cent. Another inquiry for the two districts of Shahabad and Monghyr in Bihar was undertaken on behalf of the Government by ISI. The yield per acre in the inquiry was lower than corresponding official estimate as harvesting had progressed to some extent before the inquiry started and hence the results could not be compared with official statistics.

---

has after a survey (pp. 226–7) revised extra-factory consumption of cotton at 450 instead of the conventional 750,000 bales, adjustments included a deduction of 300,000 bales. No other changes were made as the purpose of this table was only to indicate what the commercial estimate corresponding to the official estimate was and not to revise these estimates. Corrections would involve deduction, from trade estimates of jute consumption, of the quantities of jute imported from Nepal of the order of about 50,000 bales and changes in the stocks of cotton and jute, statistics for which were available for a few years only. After deducting the Burma consumption, exports to Burma should be added up to the Trade estimate. The adjustments are small in magnitude and the main conclusion is not affected.

[34] Hereafter referred to as ISI.

[35] Hereafter referred to as ICAR.

[36] By the Famine Commission into Settlement Records, by ISS through random sample survey, and by the Government by plot-to-plot enumeration.

Table 5. Estimates of Yield per Acre obtained from Crop-Cutting Experiments by Random Sampling Method and Corresponding Official Estimates

Province and Crop	Year	Crop-Cutting Expt. Yield per acre lbs.	Standard Error of Estimate Col. 3 per cent lb.	Official estimate of current Yield per Acre lbs.	Col.5 as per cent of Col. 3
(1)	(2)	(3)	(4)	(5)	(6)
Jute	1942*	1,522	1.51	–	–
Bengal	1943	1,251	2.56	1,136	90.8
	1944	1,267	4.025	1,465	115.6
	1945	1,254	2.20	1,251	101.4
	1946	930		1,210	130.1
Wheat					
U.P.	1943–4	569		735	129.2
	1944–5	681		750	110.1
	1945–6	635		639	100.6
Punjab	1943–4	829		795	95.9
	1944–5	918		867	94.4
	1945–6	851		712	83.7
C.P. & Berar	1944–5	388		403	103.9
	1945–6	418		365	87.3
Sind	1944–5	538		572	106.3
	1945–6	662		572	86.4
N.W.F.P.	1945–6	619		547	88.4
	1946–7	521		526	100.95
Autumn Rice					
Bengal	1944–5	773	4.15	732	94.6
	1945–6	617		691	112.0
	1946–7	576		658	114.2
Orissa	1945–6	448		445	99.3
	1946–7	412			
Bihar	1945–6	453			
	1946–7	447			
Winter Rice					
Bengal	1943–4	732	1.24	815	111.3
	1944–5	708	1.74	839	118.5
	1945–6			856	
U.P.	1945–6	532		576	108.3

Orissa	1944–5	743	556	74.8
	1945–6	788	565	71.7
C.P.	1944–5 +	713	650	91.2
	1945–6	676	603	89.2
	1946–7§	663		
Bombay	1944–5¶	1080	1043	96.6
	1945–6	933	924	99.0
Madras	1944–5 ‖	901		
	1945–6 + +	927	918	99.0
Bihar	1945–6	663		

NOTE: The yield of jute is in terms of dry fibre and of rice in terms of cleaned rice.

* 9 districts only
15 districts only
+ Raipur District only
§ Preliminary estimate
¶ Kolaba District only
‖ Tanjore District only
+ + 7 districts only

The Government of India finally adopted the scheme prepared by ICAR and under the guidance of its author, Dr P. V. Sukhatme, the first experiments were carried out in the Punjab and the United Provinces in 1943–4. The scheme was extended to the whole wheat belt comprising of the Central Provinces, the United Provinces, the Punjab and the North-West Frontier Province, and was repeated in 1944–5 when Bihar was also included. Experiments were carried out on rice in 1944–5 in the Central Provinces, Bombay, Madras and Orissa and in 1945–6 the scheme was extended to all rice growing districts of the United Provinces, the Central Provinces, Bombay, Madras, Bihar and Orissa. Experiments were also carried out on gram and *masur* (red lentils) on a full provincial scale but results of these were not available. Bengal continued being tackled by ISI.

The author was able to obtain a few results of crop-cutting experiments from ISI and ICAR. The standard error in ICAR estimates was not available but it varied from 1 (the United Provinces, Punjab) to 3 per cent (the North-West Frontier Province). The results do not show a unilateral bias all over the country. Whatever the *Patwaris'* mood the official statistics overestimate the outturn of crop in the United Provinces. The same appears to be true for the *Chowkidar* in Bengal. A greater fault, it appears, lay not with the *Patwaris* or *Chowkidars* but with the Directors who in their offices maintained out of date and unscientific schedules of 'normal' area and 'normal' yields. Bombay and Madras came very near to random sample estimates. The underestimating provinces are Punjab, and Orissa.

Orissa was the worse, and while comparable results were not available Bihar was very much the same.[37] In case of the Central Provinces, there is generally an underestimation but in 1944–5 the wheat crop was overestimated. Sind also overestimated its wheat crop in 1944–5 and underestimated the 1945–6 crop. On the basis of these figures the total outturn of rice and wheat would be affected somewhat as shown in Table 6.

Thus it does appear that on the balance rice and wheat involved an underestimation of 3.5 and 1.1 per cent. It certainly is not so large as one inferred from the indirect evidence available so far. But the results are not conclusive. The official statistics for the year 1945–6 were rather biassed. In February 1946 the Food Department had come out with a statement on the threat of an impending famine involving possibly even a break–down of the rationing system. Thus every provincial unit was interested in stating as low an estimate of its outturn as possible. How far that affected the official statistics of yield for the year 1945–6 will perhaps never be known. But from the above figures a tendency to that effect is noticeable, specially in respect of wheat for which an acute shortage was feared. The United Provinces hastened to correct its usual overestimation and ran close with the ICAR estimate. Under-estimation in the case of the Punjab (the only province with an exportable surplus) increased from about 5 per cent to 16 per cent of its outturn. Sind and Central Provinces which had overestimated their outturn the previous year by 6.3 and 3.9 per cent underestimated this time by 13.6 and 12.7 per cent respectively. The North-West Frontier Province alone was an exception, but its outturn was insignificant.

If, therefore, the results for 1945–6 are taken out observations are left for a very short period to justify any definite conclusion on the direction or the magnitude of bias involved in the official statistics prepared by the usual methods before the war.[38] And

[37] Bihar seemed to be particularly an unfortunate province. 'It was pointed out' at its first meeting by the Wheat Committee appointed by ICAR 'that in the case of Bihar . . . the crop forecast figures were most unreliable. A 10 per cent check made there recently on the estimates for sugarcane disclosed a serious understatement which amounted to a 100 per cent disparity.' *Report on the Marketing of Wheat*, pp. 9–10. Possibly in exaggeration.

[38] It also emerged from a personal discussion with Dr. Sukhatme that the comparison of ICAR estimates with official estimates was impaired by the fact that in many cases the former were available to the Provincial Government before the issue of the Final Forecast and thus the Forecasts were not entirely

Table 6. Outturn of Rice and Wheat Corrected according to the Estimates of Yield by Random Sampling Method (000 Tons)

Province and Crop	Official Estimate of Yield[39]	Corrected Yield	Rough basis of correction Col. 2 per cent of Col. 8
(1)	(2)	(3)	(4)
Rice			
Bengal	9,034	8,213	10% overestimation
U.P	2,024	1,874	8% "
Orissa	1,575	2,100	25% underestimation
Bihar	3,144	4,192	"
C.P.	1,569	1,743	10% "
Bombay	887	896	1% "
Madras	4,850	4,899	
	23,083	23,917	3.5% *Underestimation*
Wheat			
U.P.	2,780	2,460	13% overestimation
Punjab	3,724	4,092	9% underestimation
C.P.	673	708	5% "
Sind	368	368	
N.W.F.P.	250	266	6% underestimation
	7,795	7,894	1.1% *Underestimation*

Total outturn: Br. India: Rice 25,363 Coverage 91 per cent
Wheat 8,607 " 90 "

even in these instances the discrepancy was rather small. It was, therefore, not felt justifiable to tamper with the pre-war statistics of yield per acre. This was, of course, no approval of all the guesswork that was involved in the preparation of agricultural statistics so far. The fact that for such a large unit as the country as a whole these guesses were not so wrong as was feared did not make them any more scientific. For any particular province they might be and were very wrong.

independent of the results of crop-cutting experiments. It was not possible to gauge the influence of this factor but it ruled out consideration of any mark up or down on the pre-war official estimates on the basis of the results of these experiments.

[39] Figures in Col. 2 are from the *Estimates* for the crop year 1937–8.

Mixed Crops

The irregularities in connection with the ascertaining of the 'net' area under mixed crops were noted on page 10. An equally significant problem was that of estimating the yield per acre under mixed crops. The procedure was not described anywhere. The general practice was to multiply the total 'net' acreage under the crop by the standard yield for the district and then deflate it for the condition factor for the current year. This rested on an assumption that the output of a crop per unit of soil actually under the crop sown in a mixed condition, would be the same as from an equal area in a field 'purely' devoted to its cultivation. Mahalanobis in his Bihar inquiry had observed that this was not the case as thinner compositions gave proportionately higher yields and that this was the probable reason for the popularity of mixed crops in Bihar. Thus the total yield of wheat was 4.32 maunds per acre with only 1–2 anna proportion under wheat while for a field devoted 15–16 anna to wheat gave a total of 7.4 maunds per acre. The difference in the total outturn of wheat in the two districts was considerable. Converting the net acreage in the sample into gross acreages for the districts and multiplying by rates of yield appropriate to different compositions the total outturn of wheat increased from 1,947 to 3,860,000 maunds for Shahabad and from 1,832 to 4,486,000 maunds for Monghyr districts, an increase of 123.7 and 108.6 per cent.[40]

This was a surprisingly high figure. Mahalanobis himself did not attach much importance to the results he obtained as they were based on insufficient data. While this isolated example would not be taken as conclusive it certainly pointed out the need for further studies on these lines. Work could be undertaken along with other crop-cutting work to determine (i) the actual area by studying the composition pattern of mixed crops and (ii) yield per unit of area for a crop under various different compositions. On the basis of such work alone, accurate forecasting of crops in 'mixed' sowings could be made.

Estimation of Net Outturn

The estimation of net outturn in the case of grains involved deductions on account of driage, husk, etc. The husk content is quite

[40] *Sankhya* vol. 7, pt. 1, pp. 67–8.

significant in case of rice. It had been noticed that the yield of paddy[41] was deflated to obtain rice out of husk by a conversion factor, which was lower than that adopted in common trade practice and confirmed from actual hulling and commercial milling trials by the Agricultural Marketing Adviser to the Government of India. According to his *Report* 'the approximate discrepancy which exists between the published official estimates of production and the probable actual outturn . . . on the basis of data relating to eleven major provinces and states . . . works out at 2.16 million tons or an underestimation of 9.9 per cent'.[42] But this did not seem to be the case or was offset by errors in the opposite direction in official statistics which were compared with the results of the crop-cutting experiments. The Marketing Report observations and experiments hardly possessed any sampling value, and there was no other evidence to adjust the official estimation of outturn on the basis of the new conversion factors suggested by the Marketing Adviser in respect of each province and some of the states. No evidence could be obtained either, that the official conversion factors had been changed since the defects were pointed out by the Marketing Adviser in 1941.

Notes on Major Adjustments

The threads in the discussion might be gathered in so far as these necessitated adjustments.

(a) *Non-Reporting Areas.* Adjustments for non-reporting units involved tackling all the general and specific sources for each unit and in respect of each crop. Apart from the general sources described above, publications on specific crops like the *Marketing Reports*, *Indian Tea Statistics*, *Indian Coffee Statistics*, *Annual Review of Sugar Industry in India*, etc. or on specific units like *Season and Crop Reports* for the major provinces or *Administration Reports* for Centrally Administered Provinces and for individual states like Hyderabad and Mysore were referred to. By adopting the most comprehensive estimates in respect of each unit and each crop the scope of the non-reporting areas was considerably narrowed down. The gaps still left

[41] The term is used throughout this study to indicate rice in husk, and the term 'rice' is confined only to rice out of husk.

[42] *Report on the Marketing of Rice* (1941), p. 15.

were filled up primarily by guesses, which were based mainly on the extent and significance of the crop concerned in surrounding regions for which statistics were available.

(b) *Years for which Reports were not available.* The official statistics related to the 'crop year' which ended on 30th June. In Assam, however, the crop year ended on 31st March and in the Central Provinces it ended on 31st May. The 'crop' year relevant to a given 'consumption' year depended on the harvest time of the produce and the time it took in subsequent processing and distribution. Crops which were harvested in autumn or in the early months of winter were assumed to be consumed in the same consumption year ending on 31st March. The crops so considered were rice, *jowar*, *bajra*, maize, *ragi*, pulses other than gram, small millets, unclassified foodgrains and pulses and miscellaneous foodcrops. The rest of the crops were assumed to be consumed in the following year, either because these were harvested late in the crop year (wheat, for instance, in May) or had to be processed before they were available for consumption (oilseeds, tobacco). Rice in Assam, Bengal, Bihar and Orissa was raised in three sowings, autumn, winter and, to a very small extent, in spring or summer. Small adjustments were therefore necessitated for spring and summer crops. Thus the estimation for the consumption year 1937–8 in the case of Bengal involved a total of 1936–7 summer crop and 1937–8 autumn and winter sowings. The relevant period of agricultural statistics for the study covered the eleven crop years 1930–1 to 1940–1. Of the above publications the *Estimates* covered the entire period. The *Ag. Stats.* covered the period only in respect of British India, and up to 1938–9 only in respect of the princely states. The *Food Statistics* covered only the years beginning with 1936–7 in respect of the additional information obtained by it. *Marketing Reports* dealt with the three to four years preceding publication and were spread over the entire period. Most of the gaps were filled up by 'grafting' of the various available estimates, and thus the discrepancy for years common to two or more publications was narrowed down. The discrepancy was then inter-or-extrapolated by linear regression if a good fit could be obtained, or by simple inspection where the quantities concerned were very small.

(c) *Area Underestimation in Permanently Settled Areas.* While there was a general evidence as to the underestimation of acreage in Bengal it was not easy to determine the magnitude in respect of each crop. In Bengal the two most important crops are rice and jute. With jute this study is not concerned. The area under rice was marked up by 10 per cent. A small mark up of 25,000 acres was made on the reported acreage under gram. In Bihar and Orissa underestimation was corrected for by the marking up by 10 per cent the reported acreage under rice, wheat, gram, and unclassified foodgrains and pulses. The mark ups are indeed arbitrary. No mark down was adopted in respect of barley crop in Bihar as was observed in Mahalanobis' survey for two districts as the *Marketing Report on Barley* observed that these districts were relatively unimportant in respect of barley cultivation in the Province and hence the conditions there might not be representative of the Province.

(d) *Acreage Under Mixed Crops in the United Provinces.* It was noticed on page 10 that the area under oilseeds in mixed sowings in the United Provinces was included entirely under food-grains, and thus the reported acreage in the *Ag. Stats.* exaggerated the net area under foodgrains and pulses and underestimated the acreage under oilseeds by about 4 million acres. Oilseeds are generally mixed with wheat, barley, gram, small millets and pulses in varying proportions. Since no one (not even the Director of Agriculture in the United Provinces) knew the extent of mixed area under each crop arbitrary mark downs were resorted to. The reported acreage and outturn of wheat in the United Provinces were marked down by 5 per cent, barley by 10 per cent, gram and small millets by 20 per cent, other pulses by 40 per cent and unclassified foodgrains and pulses by 35 per cent. The acreage was allocated to linseed, rape and mustard, and sesamum as 'estimated' in the *Estimates*, 20,000 acres were uniformly allocated to castor, and the residual were allocated to 'Other Oilseeds'. The adjustments are given in Table 7.

(e) *Yield Adjustments.* It was decided not to tamper with the estimates of yield per acre generally, and hence the only adjustments in the outturn as published were caused by corresponding area adjustments. The general principle was to assume the same per acre yield on adjusted figures as on the previous estimates. Where for a few years only acreage, and not the outturn, was available the yield was obtained by regression on area or on the total outturn or on the outturn of neighbouring regions. In units with smaller significance

Table 7. Adjustments of Area under Mixed Crop in the United Provinces (000 Acres)

	1930-1	1931-2	1932-3	1933-4	1934-5	1935-6	1936-7	1937-8	1938-9	1939-40	Notes
Deduct											
Wheat	394	411	397	436	391	366	388	404	433	412	5% of reported total
Barley	437	418	398	441	422	392	420	388	402	386	10% " acreage "
Gram	1,040	1,150	1,092	1,070	1,112	1,150	1,304	1,164	1,118	1,090	20% " " "
Sm. mill		326	353	344	371	384	336	352	291	318	20% " " "
Pulse	3,000	1,860	1,860	1,860	1,860	1,860	1,920	1,920	1,865	1,933	40% " " "
Others		127	167	171	128	99	128	133	121	86	35% " " "
	4,871	4,292	4,267	4,322	4,284	4,251	4,496	4,361	4,230	4,225	Total
Add											
Linseed	644	589	624	593	622	650	600	632	643	630	'Estimates'
Rape & Mustard	3,230	2,659	2,484	2,594	2,444	2,330	2,499	2,375	2,485	2,502	'Estimates'
Sesamum	847	882	839	902	805	921	774	955	979	979	'Estimates'
Castor	20	20	20	20	20	20	20	20	20	20	Guess
Others	130	142	300	213	393	330	603	379	103	94	Residual
Total	4,871	4,292	4,267	4,322	4,284	4,251	4,496	4,361	4,230	4,225	

simple averages of per acre yield for at least more than five consecutive years were adopted.

Notes on Individual Crops

It would be impossible within the scope of this study to describe in detail the specific changes made in the various estimates. A few illustrative instances only are given to indicate the nature of revision and the adjustments made in the case of practically each of the commodities. Adjustments in case of Hyderabad were necessitated as outward exports from the State often continuously exceeded reported production. In the case of Mysore the acreage under gram was reported in the *Ag. Stats.* at about 8,00,000 acres and by the *Estimates*, the *Food Statistics* and the *Marketing Report* at about 40,000 acres. It appeared that some variety of pulses was being mistakenly reported as gram in the *Ag. Stats.* The adjustments, therefore, were made as follows:

In the case of coconuts the sudden variations in the reported area in the *Ag. Stats.* were indicative of errors in reporting. Owing to the long term nature of the crop acreage could not fluctuate widely from year to year. The *Marketing Report* was the only source for ascertaining the yield of nuts. The yield varied with the density of growth, the proportion of bearing trees and the average yield of nuts per tree. All these factors had been considered by the *Marketing Report* in terms of an average of a few years. A constant yield for the entire period except for 1932–3 and 1936–7 was adopted. For 1932–3 there was evidence of a low yield, and hence the yield was marked down by 10 per cent. Similarly the yield was marked up by 10 per cent for 1936–7, which was a bumper year.

In the case of sugarcane the DGCIS published as supplement to the *Indian Trade Journal*, *Review of the Sugar Industry in India* for the sugar years ending on 31 October. Production estimates were issued by the Directors of Agriculture and were available in the *Forecasts* and the *Estimates* not in terms of sugarcane, but in terms of one of its products, viz. *gur*.[43] This was due to the fact that prior to the phenomenal growth of the sugar industry during the thirties

[43] Unrefined sugar.

Table 8. Adjustments for Acreage under Gram and Pulses in Mysore
(000 Acres)

Publication	1931-2	1932-3	1933-4	1934-5	1935-6	1936-7	1937-8	1938-9
Gram *Ag. Stats.*	801	824	1173	740	819	821	821	772
Other Pulses *Ag. Stats.*	821	838	515	804	791	760	702	813
	1,621	1,662	1,688	1,544	1,610	1,581	1,522	1,585
Gram *Marketing Report*	48	44	43	45	54	38	38	35
Pulses[44] *Food Statistics*	943	981	960	888	945	965	897	963
Others Residual	630	637	685	611	611	578	587	587
	1,621	1,662	1,688	1,544	1,610	1,581	1,522	1,585

[44] Excluding gram, avarer, and cow peas.

practically the whole crop was devoted to the production of *gur*. While *gur* still is the most important single product of sugarcane, about 40 per cent of the cane supply is devoted to direct consumption and manufacture of crystalline sugar. Production statistics of *gur* should have referred only to the quantity of *gur* produced and not to the gur equivalent of the total crop of sugarcane. Adjusted gur outturns were, therefore, converted into corresponding sugarcane figures on the basis of conversion ratios given in the *Marketing Report*.[45] The reported acreage in the *Ag. Stats.* under 'Sugar yielding crops other than sugarcane' referred to palm trees. The position with respect to the area under these trees was uncertain. Thus Bihar and Orissa did not report any acreage the reason being that palm juice was not utilised to any appreciable extent for producing *gur*. On the other hand Travancore, an important *gur* producing state, did not report any area either. There was another complication. Some provinces reported acreage, irrespective of whether the whole area was tapped or not. In other cases only trees that were tapped were reported. The trees were tapped for two products – fermented juice, such as toddy, etc., and unfermented juice which was consumed by itself or was used for producing *gur* or sugar. The number of trees tapped for sweet juice, and the product obtained in terms of gur were taken from the *Marketing Report*. Toddy is considered in a later section along with other alcoholic drinks.

In the case of tea and coffee estimates of acreage and production were directly obtained from planters and published in the *Indian Tea Statistics* and the *Indian Coffee Statistics*, and subsequently in the *Estimates*. In many cases especially in South India the returns were incomplete and inaccurate. In the case of coffee, plantations of less than 10 acres were omitted prior to 1931–2 and less than 5 acres since. The acreage estimates, therefore, were revised with reference to returns filled in by village *Patwaris* in the *Ag. Stats.* A significant revision of yields was also necessitated for coffee in light of the revisions suggested by the *Marketing Report* for holdings of 10 acres and above.

And such was the procedure practically for every crop.

[45] The *Review of Sugar Industry* also gave cane equivalent by reconverting *gur* estimates in the Forecasts, but these were based on antiquated ratios, and were misleading.

Table 9. Area under Crops, Crop Year 1937-8
(000 Acres)

Crop	*Ag. Stats.*	*Estimates*	*Food Statistics*	Adjusted Acreage Total	Markups	
					Non-reporting Areas	Permanent Settlement Areas
(1)	(2)	(3)	(4)	(5)	(6)	(7)
Rice	77,148	72,568	77,535	84,485	1,000	3,686
Wheat	34,144	85,640	36,610	36,847	250	110
Jowar	34,634	33,489	36,634	37,697	500	
Bajara	18,735	17,242	19,811	20,446	250	
Barley	7,134	6,245	7,155	6,902		
Maize	7,920	6,276	8,052	8,655	500	
Ragi	5,792		5,690	6,442	500	
Gram	19,058	15,742	14,995	18,176		163
Small Millets			8,352	7,292		
Pulses (ex. Gram)	34,814		20,050	22,218		
Foodgrains and Pulses Unclassified				9,899	1,500	446
Linseed	3,434	3,890		4,410		
Rape & Mustard	3,449	5,461		6,033	200	
Sesamum	4,296	4,450		5,782	300	
Groundnuts	8,360	8,898		9,375		

Coconuts	1,482			1,503		
Castor	1,335	1,148		1,551	150	
Other Oilseeds	2,855			3,431	100	
Sugarcane	4,029	3,869		4,191		70
Other Sugar	178			178*		
Condiments & Spices	2,354			2,413	50	
Potatoes				446		
Bananas				399		
Grapes	4,597			4		
Cashewnuts				*n.a.*		
Citrus Fruits				108		
Other Fruits & Vegetables				4,587		
Miscellaneous Foodcrops	2,515			2,638	100	
Tea	824	834		834		
Coffee	209	182		209		
Tobacco	1,033	1,288		1,460	25	

NOTE: Col. 5 includes figures given in Col. 6 and 7.
* Unadjusted acreage as in the *Ag. Stats.*
Calendar Year 1937.

Adjusted Estimates

In Tables 9 and 10 adjusted area and outturn estimates in respect of each crop for the crop year 1937–8 are set off against corresponding estimates in major official publications to indicate the magnitude of adjustments. The mark ups in respect of non-reporting areas and Permanently Settled areas in so far as they involved guesswork are separately stated. The adjusted overall estimates over the entire period are given in Tables 11 and 12.

Table 10. Outturn of Crops, Crop Year 1937–8
(000 Tons except coconuts 000,000 and Tea and Coffee 000,000 lbs.)

Crop	Estimates	Food Statistics	Adjusted Total Outturn	Markups	
				Non-Reporting Units	Units under Permanent Settlement
(1)	(2)	(3)	(4)	(5)	(6)
Rice	26,699	28,834	31,525	500	1,375
Wheat	10,764	11,072	11,274	200	43
Jowar	6,506	7,249	7,450	100	
Bajra	2,625	3,143	3,223	50	
Barley	2,088	2,408	2,459		
Maize	2,117	2,,717	2,961	200	
Ragi		1,801	2,074	200	
Gram	3,525	3,449	4,100		57
Small Millets		1,515	1,355		
Pulses (ex. Gram)		4,116	3,516		
Linseed	461		526		
Rape and Mustard	1,021		1,068	20	
Sesamum	465		574	30	
Groundnuts	3,501		3,681		
Coconuts			2996		
Castor	104		138	10	
Sugarcane			57,435		850
Sugarcane (Gur equivalent)	5,403		5,774		85
Other sugar (")			167		
Potatoes			1,792		
Bananas			3,997		
Grapes			14		
Cashewnuts			40		
Citrus Fruits			401		
Tea*	430		430		
Coffee	34		60		
Tobacco	505		638	10	

NOTE: Col. 4 includes figures in Col. (5) and (6).

The outturn of the rest of the crops could not be determined and valuation of these is made on acreage basis.

* Calendar Year 1937.

Table 11. Adjusted Area under crops, Crop years 1930-1 to 1940-1
(000 Acres)

Crops	1930-1	1931-2	1932-3	1933-4	1934-5	1935-6	1936-7	1937-8	1938-9	1939-40	1940-1
Rice		82,780	81,062	81,284	80,303	81,499	83,739	84,485	84,967	84,912	82,986
Wheat	33,193	34,750	33,862	36,921	35,324	34,629	34,279	36,847	36,400	34,968	
Jowar		38,398	37,827	37,529	37,665	36,998	41,644	37,797	38,913	38,690	38,707
Bajra		22,009	22,282	21,069	20,283	20,300	19,323	20,446	20,743	20,977	22,136
Barley	7,360	7,129	7,068	7,367	7,162	6,807	7,127	6,902	6,707	6,641	
Maize		8,890	8,905	8,782	8,833	8,841	8,782	8,655	8,800	8,940	8,814
Ragi		7,395	7,253	7,059	6,971	6,624	6,645	6,642	6,443	6,392	6,502
Gram	17,803	20,719	17,960	21,861	17,901	20,683	20,221	18,176	15,131	15,117	
Small Millets		7,418	7,745	7,630	7,308	7,288	7,352	7,292	7,779	7,515	7,395
Pulses (ex. Gram)		24,011	23,632	23,695	23,481	23,313	22,427	22,218	22,995	23,363	22,757
Foodgrains & Pulses—Others		10,877	11,588	11,664	11,165	10,905	10,595	9,899	9,999	10,221	10,237
Linseed	3,506	3,816	3,711	3,657	3,850	3,902	4,169	4,410	4,352	4,247	
Rape and Mustard	7,221	6,843	6,713	6,587	5,799	5,907	6,519	6,033	6,034	6,693	
Sesamum	5,941	5,583	6,024	5,607	4,861	5,250	5,397	5,782	5,646	5,366	
Groundnuts	6,489	5,490	7,086	7,768	5,336	5,459	7,115	9,375	9,066	8,996	
Coconuts	1,418	1,403	1,446	1,454	1,480	1,485	1,490	1,503	1,506	1,519	
Castor	1,687	1,804	1,840	1,768	1,687	1,654	1,667	1,551	1,649	1,460	
Other Oilseeds	2,656	2,802	3,163	2,923	2,915	2,995	3,587	3,431	2,884	2,834	
Sugarcane	3,043	3,235	3,600	3,571	3,754	4,324	4,777	4,191	3,415	3,938	
Crops	1930-1	1931-2	1932-3	1933-4	1934-5	1935-6	1936-7	1937-8	1938-9	1939-40	1940-1

Other Sugar*	154	164	152	153	149	147	160	178	167	165	
Condi. & Spices	2,328	2,561	2,551	2,406	2,933	2,856	2,531	2,413	2,607	2,726	
Potatoes	419	421	430	432	448	440	441	446	469	470	
Bananas		393	401	427	429	405	391	399	407	404	405
Grapes	4	4	4	4	4	4	4	4	4	4	
Citrus Fruits		50	55	61	71	81	95	108	124	135	150
Other Fruits, Veg.		4,584	4,610	4,382	4,638	4,686	4,770	4,587	4,597	4,661	4,617
Misc. Foodcrops		3,309	2,764	3,314	3,125	3,076	2,990	2,638	2,043	1,980	2,200
Tea		803	809	815	826	830	833	834	833	833	835
Coffee	199	200	204	205	207	213	214	209	204	211	
Tobacco	1,320	1,367	1,328	1,289	1,493	1,456	1,368	1,460	1,478	1,505	

* Unadjusted acreage as given in the *Ag. Stats.*
Calendar Years 1931 to 1940.

Table 12. Adjusted Outturn of Crops, Crop years 1930-1 to 1940-1
(000 Tons except coconuts 000,000 and tea and coffee 000,000 lbs.)

Crops	1930-1	1931-2	1932-3	1933-4	1934-5	1935-6	1936-7	1937-8	1938-9	1939-40	1940-1
Rice		33,419	30,711	30,238	30,015	26,962	32,665	31,525	28,543	30,128	25,670
Wheat	9,750	9,471	9,881	9,800	10,150	9,897	10,228	11,274	10,392	11,167	
Jowar		7,144	7,380	7,361	7,195	7,093	8,058	7,450	7,545	7,602	8,200
Bajra		3,555	3,484	3,300	3,186	3,339	2,981	3,223	3,140	2,977	3,795
Barley	2,804	2,801	2,748	2,813	2,899	2,723	2,700	2,459	2,198	2,347	
Maize		3,135	2,992	2,773	3,027	3,019	2,801	2,961	2,757	3,120	3,119
Ragi		2,434	2,541	2,448	2,094	2,164	2,242	2,074	1,882	2,059	2;180
Gram	4,237	4,763	4,206	4,900	4,250	4,643	4,766	4,100	3,332	3,815	
Small Millets		1,591	1,706	1,560	1,388	1,509	1,425	1,355	1,475	1,434	1,590
Pulses (ex. Gram)		3,843	3,647	3,767	3,695	3,726	3,569	3,516	3,673	3,687	3,454
Linseed	446	482	503	450	487	477	481	526	502	530	
Rape and Mustard	1,059	1,078	1,095	995	942	1,001	1,013	1,068	966	1,163	
Sesamum	567	544	606	592	424	504	547	574	501	520	
Groundnuts	2,789	2,317	3,071	3,379	1,990	2,319	2,855	3,681	3,417	3,485	
Coconuts	2,818	2,785	2,600	2,890	2,945	2,966	3,265	2,996	3,002	3,015	
Castor	140	166	174	161	123	138	149	138	151	134	
Sugarcane	34,417	42,181	49,550	51,894	54,770	62,570	68,284	57,435	36,404	49,227	
" (Gur eqt.)	3,503	4,267	5,003	5,242	5,496	6,303	6,862	5,774	3,707	4,997	
Other sugar (Gur eqt.)	175	175	175	178	177	168	178	167	182	180	

Potatoes	1,716	1,723	1,754	1,759	1,835	1,784	1,779	1,792	1,894	(2,000)	
Bananas		3,980	4,049	4,315	4,328	4,051	3,908	3,997	4,061	4,231	4,035
Grapes		14	14	14	14	14	14	14	15	14	14
Cashewnuts	21	23	26	29	32	34	37	40	43	45	
Citrus Fruits		174	194	217	256	294	351	401	465	512	574
Tea*		393	433	383	399	394	395	430	452	452	465
Coffee	56	54	55	58	70	79	65	60	69	62	
Tobacco	552	567	582	522	653	600	559	633	619	613	

* Calendar Years 1931 to 1940.

Chapter 2

Official Yields per Acre in India, 1886–1947: Some Questions of Interpretation*

[1973]

ALAN W. HESTON

A main concern of historical studies of agriculture has been the trend in simple welfare measures like total and per capita production. These welfare measures are of particular importance for interpreting the economic history of India since 1880 because of the dominance of the agricultural sector. Over half the value of total output consisted of agricultural crops; further, output per worker in agriculture is often taken as an approximation for trends in output per worker in other sectors, particularly services.

Total and per capita production are affected by changes in acreage in all crops, change in acreage from lower to higher yielding crops, and changes in the yield of each crop. In this paper our concern is only with yields per acre in various crops, and not with changes in total acreage or crop composition, even though these latter two factors may be quantitatively more important in affecting agricultural output. However, the effects of acreage increases and changes in cropping patterns are in turn dependent on what yields per acre are assumed for the changed acreage, and cannot be properly assessed without knowledge of yield changes.

It is generally accepted that yields per acre as well as total availability of food grains declined under the British during the period 1890–1947. Blyn (1966) has demonstrated that acceptance of

* The research underlying this paper was done as a fellow of the American Institute of Indian Studies during the year 1965–6. The author is indebted to the Record Office of the State of Maharashtra and the libraries of the University of Bombay and the Asia Society of Bombay for use of their resources. I would like to thank M. D. Morris and Tom Kessinger for comments on an earlier draft of this paper.

official statistics on acreage and output in India means acceptance of a declining per capita availability of foodgrains. Blyn (1966, p. 151) found the trend in yields to be –0.18 per cent per year for foodgrains during the period 1891–1946. This overall trend includes a gentle rise into the 1920s and then a fairly marked decline of 12 per cent until Independence. K. Mukherji (1965) and Sivasubramoniam (1969) have also examined the basic data making somewhat different assumptions about coverage and crops, with substantially the same results as Blyn.

One general point about the statistics prior to 1947 is that they were collected for revenue purposes. Total production in an area was meant to be the product of the areas planted to a crop times the standard yield per acre times the condition factor. The area cropped was generated by the land revenue settlements, and in principle modified for year to year changes. Areas cropped, though generated by the revenue system, were thought to be fairly objective and accurate.[1] The remaining two figures, the standard yield and the condition factor, jointly gave an estimate of actual yield (or revenue yield) per acre of a crop. However, as we will describe below both of these statistics were generated by revenue officials, and were both inherently subjective. But what is crucial in our understanding of agricultural trends is precisely these estimated yields per acre, which are essentially byproducts of the land revenue system, and it is to the question of the validity of these yield estimates we now turn.

In the present paper we will argue that in the period 1886–1947 there were biases in the official yields per acre—particularly an upward bias from 1886 to 1897 and downward bias from about 1937 to 1946—in several areas of India. The evidence of this paper is drawn mainly from the Bombay Presidency, but as we will discuss below, the logic of the argument extends to at least some other areas of the subcontinent. The study begins with the crop year 1885–6 because this is the first year that the ingredients of yield estimation are available for the Bombay Presidency. As

[1] F. Noyce (1919, p. 23), for example, says, 'It is universally admitted that the Indian figures (on acreage) are hard to beat in the matter of accuracy.' While others might put it less extravagantly, later writers such as Panse (1961, p. 216) who reports on patwari records of cotton acreage against national sample survey estimates, suggest that the acreage statistics are relatively reliable. Descriptions of the collection of agricultural statistics in Bombay are given by Anderson (1948 and 1929), among others.

mentioned above, the official statistics for British India begin in 1891. However, they could have been put together earlier for some areas, and most of the early problems with the statistics in the period 1886–97, are also in the British India figures for the 1891–7 period.

The paper first discusses the method of yield estimation in Bombay during the period beginning with the standard yield per acre, and including the relation of crop cutting yields to revenue yields (standard yield times condition factor). The second section analyses trends in the condition factor, and in total rainfall, and presents data on yields during the whole period 1886–1946. The concluding section considers the implications of these results for estimates of crop production in Bombay during the period, and the extent these generalizations may apply to other parts of India. Some of the materials included in Sections 1 and 2 have been better described in other sources, but at the cost of some repetition a conscious attempt has been made to make the present argument self-contained.

Standard Yields and the Methods of Yield Estimation in Bombay

The estimate of the yield per acre of a particular crop in a district was the product of the standard yield per acre times the condition factor. For example, if the standard yield of rice in a district were 1200 pounds, this was meant to be the yield in a typical year, when the condition factor was normal. If the condition factor were say 75 per cent of normal, then the actual yield would be estimated at 3/4 of the standard yield, or 900 pounds per acre. In broad terms, this was the method of estimating the actual yield per acre of a crop in a district; when this yield was multiplied by the acreage in that crop it gave the total production.

Three general points need to be made about yield estimation. First the above method is the traditional, subjective, or revenue method of estimation. This is to contrast it with yield estimation by crop cutting experiments, which is the method adopted in India after Independence. We will deal below with the defects of the traditional method, but suffice it to say that crop cutting in most of the world is the currently accepted method of estimating yields—the error of measurement from crop cutting in an Indian state is of the order of 2 or 3 per cent, and for a district, somewhat larger, perhaps 5 or 10 per cent. I don't believe anyone would argue today on scientific grounds that revenue methods of yield estimation are comparable in accuracy to crop cutting yields, though traditional methods of estimation still play a role in South Asia.[2]

One reason the traditional method of yield estimation is known as the revenue method, is that both parts of the yield estimation are generated by the revenue officials. The standard yield per acre of a crop for a district was a guide to the burden of land taxes and was continually used in illustrative calculations. If a land settlement called for Rs 3.00 per acre for paddy land, the British could cite the standard yield of 1000 pounds per acre in the districts, and the gross income of say, Rs 30 per acre circa 1900, which was then said to be quite enough to pay the revenue.[3] The condition factor, which perhaps in the early 1800s was viewed as simply a guide to the nature of the season, and for forecast crops, and especially cotton, a commercially most valuable guide, later became involved with the land revenue system in many parts of India, when it determined remissions of revenue.

A final general point to be made about traditional yield estimation is that the two components, the standard yield per acre, and the condition factor, are independent. The persons compiling these two measures were different; the condition factor was estimated by village officers who were not asked to calibrate their judge-

[2] The two important aspects of the traditional system in India are that for certain minor crops, where crop cutting has not been introduced, the revenue method is still used; and the condition factor, even for crops where crop cutting is used to estimate final yields, the revenue estimate of the condition factor, is used for preliminary estimates of crop output, which for purposes of policy like deciding surplus and deficit states, can be important. The minor crops are some pulses, millets, minor fibres, fruits, vegetables and the like. In Pakistan, to my knowledge, crop estimation is still by revenue methods, even though crop cutting has been carried out for 20 years. See *Final Report of the National Income Commission* (1965).

[3] William Digby (1901) was especially fond of pointing out the differences between the standard yields and the revenue yields per acre. He particularly took to task Lord Cromer and Sir David Barbour who prepared estimates of the income of various parts of India using the standard yields as the average yield. Digby cites the fact that in the Central Provinces the average yield in the 1890s was about 370 pounds whereas the standard yields were 600 to 1000 pounds (pp. 496–7), and in Berar where the standard yield was 754 pounds and the average revenue yield in the 1890s was 145 pounds (p. 487). There are numerous instances throughout the period from 1880 to 1900, when standard yields were generally introduced, that British officials used them for illustrations of the prosperity of rural India as though they were average yields, so it was administratively convenient that standard yields were pitched high.

ments on the season with a particular standard yield per acre. With these general comments out of the way, we can turn to a discussion of the standard yield, the condition factor, and the resulting actual yields.

Standard Yield per Acre

Unfortunately, officials were more willing to publish standard yields than to make clear what the term actually meant, though most sources suggest, and it is consistent with revenue estimation procedure that it is the average yield for a district.[4]

Others now argued that the standard yield was above the average crop cutting yield, and in 1963, the Annewari Commission asked the government of Maharashtra to accept a definition of a standard yield as the average of the best three years in the previous decade.[5] However, to make our argument the definition of the standard yield is less important than its trends over the period, which we describe below.[6]

[4] A quotation defining standard yield is given by Panse (1946, p. 99) who describes the procedure that was supposed to be carried out in the various provinces, namely a quinquennial revision of standard yields on the basis of crop cutting experiments where an attempt was made to survey he says, 'an average crop on an average soil for experimental harvesting.' In fact, Panse explains that this procedure was only carried out systematically in Punjab, which is again why there are so few changes in standard yields between 1897 and 1961 in Table 1.

In his usual colourful way F. G. H. Anderson who came to India about 1890 and worked over 20 years in Bombay, describes his difficulty in understanding the nature of a 16 anna crop, which in the quotation below is the same as a standard yield. Anderson says, 'We then come back to the first difficulty. What is a 16 anna crop? My answer is "I do not know." It is very sad that a Settlement Officer of many years experience should not know. But it is a fact . . . And I know also that the last three Directors of Agriculture have assured me that they did not know' (1929, p. 132).

[5] *Report of the Annewari Committee for the Determination of Standard Yields*, Revenue and Forests Department, Government of Maharashtra, Government Press and Printing, Nagpur, 1966. While I do not accept the definition of standard yield as used in the Annewari report, this paper draws heavily on the excellent work of its authors, V. M. Joshi, Chairman, M. A. Telang, and D. S. Ranga Rao.

[6] For all of India standard yields are published in *Average Yield Per Acre of Principal Crops in India*, and earlier in *Quinquennial Report on Average Yields of Principal Crops in India*, and in *Agricultural Statistics in India*. Often standard yields are termed 'normal' or 'standard normal' or as in the above title simply 'average' yields but following the practice of the Annewari Report, we will only use the term standard yield to refer to these yields.

Collection of agricultural data on acreage began systematically in Bombay in the 1800s, and by 1869–70 the Collectors had been asked to frame estimates of outturn of the principal crops for each of the districts.[7] During the 1870s officials conducted a number of experiments in Bombay and the great variation in yields was noted in the response of Mr J. N. Peile to the Famine Commission of 1880 (no date, vol. 3, pp. 64–8). These experiments, settlement reports, and other information formed the basis of the estimates of standard yields adopted in 1884.

Standard yields were also framed for 1892, but the next major revision took place in 1897 with some marked reductions from the 1884 yields being the rule. Mr Mollison, author of the widely used, *Textbook on Indian Agriculture* (1910) was in part responsible for these standard yields which for the first time made 'allowance' for the low yields of poor soils. The experiments on which these standard yields were based were often conducted very casually, and by people untutored in agriculture. Though the publication *Agricultural Statistics* of the Government of India seemed pleased with the care bestowed in framing the 1897 Bombay yields, P. C. Patil, of the Agricultural College Poona remarked in 1921, 'These yields are said to have been fixed without elaborate and careful tests and the same handed down with slight modifications made at revisions conducted every five years' (Patil, 1922, p. 50). These 1897 standard yields were retained for many crops till 1964, and are the first column in Table 1 for each crop, while column 3 gives the 1945 standard yield. The remaining figures in Table 1 include the average of 1906–20 revenue yields in column 2, the average revenue and crop cutting yields between the inception of crop cutting (1945–6 at the earliest) and 1953–4 in columns 4 and 5.

The marked stability of standard yields shown between columns 1 and 3 is unfortunately not an indication of their accuracy, but rather a reflection of the 'state of neglect' of agricultural statistics. A decade after the standard yields of 1897 were set, the government discontinued crop cutting experiments, one reason given being that the model farms in Poona, Surat and other centers could provide as good data as deputy and assistant collectors had been collecting. About this contention, there seems little doubt. However, it is also true that crop cutting experiments, properly carried

[7] These estimates were used by D. Naoroji in forming his estimate of agricultural income in Bombay (1901, pp. 15–20).

out, could have provided much more than did the model farms where yields were anything but typical. The result, in any event, was that Bombay went without crop cutting experiments of any general applicability from 1909 to 1945–6, which is the reason for the stability of standard yields exhibited in Table 1.[8] It is well established that standard yields have exceeded actual yields and were probably meant to exceed the average of actual yields. The evidence in Table 1 certainly demonstrates this for Bombay.[9] In column 6 of Table 1, the average yields for the nine years from 1946–54 for each district given in column 1 are divided by the standard yields for 1945 as given in column 3. As may be seen all 59 figures in column 6 are less than 1.0, meaning that standard yields were greater than crop cutting yields. Further, since 1897 standard yields are usually the same or higher than 1961 standard yields, crop cutting yields are also less than 1897 standard yields.

Our first conclusion about standard yields is, therefore, that their stability in Bombay was not an agricultural, but an administrative phenomenon. An important corollary of the stability of standard yields is that trends in actual yields over the period of estimation cannot be due to changes in standard yields—they can only result from changes in the condition factor. A second conclusion (from

[8] The initial failure of crop cutting in Bombay seems to be the result of the lower level personnel having little knowledge of agriculture and little direction from above. Mr Anderson points out, for example, that in Bombay revenue settlements all soils receive an anna classification, usually running from 1 to 16 annas, so that dry crop land in a particular taluka which is rated 12 annas would, in a normal year, pay land revenue equal to 3/4 the maximum dry crop rate in that taluka. This system meant that by just noting the survey number of land on which crops were cut, the crop cutting surveys could have at once provided a check on whether output is a function of the anna classification of the soil. In addition, since the proportions of land of different classifications was known, the surveys, even if they, say, oversampled from good lands, could have been useful since output from average land could be inferred with some reliability from knowledge of output in any particular type of land. However, extraordinary as it may seem, as the crop cutting experiments were carried out, from 1884–1909, the quality of the land was never noted, and if experiments agreed with past standard yields they tended to be judged well chosen experiments, and if not. The experiment with anna classification of the soils was done in connection with the Annewari Report (1966, Ch. VII) where it was found that output per acre of the 2½ anna soil was 3/4 or more of 6 anna soil, so there was no simple linear relation between soil type and productivity as assumed in assessments.

[9] Panse (1952, p. 146) says, 'It is well known that the normal yields were initially pitched too high.'

column 6 of Table 1) is that actual yields in the districts of the former Bombay Presidency during all or parts of the period 1946–54 were below standard yields in all 59 cases, and between 50 per cent and 70 per cent of standard yields in 26 cases.[10] Some implications of these findings will be developed below.

The Condition Factor

The other ingredient in the yield estimation is the condition factor. To obtain the outturn, an early administrator says, '. . . we must form an estimate of how the current crop differs from the normal average. In Madras such an estimate is framed by each village accountant . . . a weighted average is struck and this is then reduced to a percentage, taking 12 as equal to 100 per cent.'[11] The condition factor is thus essentially a subjective judgement on how a given year compares with a typical year.

For purposes of discussing the condition factor we present two related sets of data. Table 2 presents ratios derived for the districts in Table 1. Column 4 gives the ratio of the condition factor for 1946–54 to the period 1906–20.[12] In only six of the 59 cases in

[10] One question that might be raised about the post-1947 yields is whether they were affected by changes in the areas of the districts due to integration of the Princely States in the period 1948 to 1950. Since there were no crop cutting yields for the Princely areas, no direct comparison for British and Princely areas could be made. A comparison of crop-cutting in British areas for 1946 to 1949 with crop cutting yields in British plus Princely areas after 1949–50 could be made, but the only conclusion was that seasonal effects on yields swamped any differences that might have existed in yields in British and adjacent Princely areas.

[11] The source is G. A. D. Stuart (1919, p. 276) who was a Director of Agriculture in Madras, and whose suggestions (in the above source) for interpreting the condition factor were widely adopted.

[12] P. C. Patil (1922, pp. 55–6). Patil (1932) also produced a type of study similar to the Farm Management Studies of independent India, coming to the same conclusion that if small farmers value their own labour at going wages, they will make an accounting loss. Patil, who was a government servant, had these results published as a study of the Bombay government, though the latter did 'not accept responsibility' for the study (Patil, 1932, 'Introduction' by T. E. Main), which I interpret to reflect a heightened sensitivity of British administrators during this period. This point is explored further below.

The condition factor in column 1 of Table 2 for 1906–20 will be column 2 divided by column 1 of Table 1, unless the standard yield changed between 1897 and 1906–20, as for example, groundnuts in Jalgaon district, where it declined from 3000 to 2900 pounds in 1916, and later to 900 pounds as given in column 3 of Table 1.

Table 1. Comparisons of Standard Yields (SY), Crop Cutting Yields (CCY) and Revenue Yields (RY) for Bombay Districts, 1886–1954

Crop/District	1897 SY	1916–20 RY	1945 SY	1945–53 RY	1946–54 CCY	CCY/SY (5)/(3)
	(1)	(2)	(3)	(4)	(5)	(6)
Rice						
Ahmedabad	1440	951	1440	839	458	.318
Kaira	1320	1135	1320	577	553	.420
Panch Mahals	1200	1029	1200	336	245	.204
Surat	1560	1297	1560	964	783	.502
Nasik	1080	824	1000	688	639	.592
Thana	1200	1073	1200	1050	1138	.949
Kolaba	1320	1255	1250	1115	1161	.929
Ratnagiri	1020	830	950	799	880	.927
N. Kanara	1320	1007	1100	788	1094	.995
Belgaum	1140	850	1140	641	915	.803
Dharwar	1140	784	1140	707	856	.752
Kharif Jowar						
Ahmedabad	1080	601	600	251	94	.157
Surat	1160	861	760	475	510	.671
Dhulia	720	471	720	402	286	.398
Jalgaon	720	615	720	432	593	.825
Nasik	520	281	520	279	410	.790
N. Satara	720	532	700	436	545	.780
Belgaum	800	588	800	389	588	.735
Bijapur	540	365	540	260	300	.557
Dharwar	900	678	1000	495	511	.511
Rabi Jowar						
Broach	1020	725	820	464	375	.458
Jalgaon	520	615	575	277	324	.565
Nasik	520	281	520	276	152	.294
Ahmednagar	540	311	300	186	217	.725
Poona	500	309	400	215	192	.481
Sholapur	540	345	350	188	233	.667
Bijapur	540	365	540	272	212	.393
Wheat						
Ahmedabad	560	385	600	361	341	.569
Broach	600	438	600	351	292	.488
Dhulia	600	418	600	428	337	.562
Jalgaon	600	460	600	426	344	.575
Nasik	460	317	460	359	295	.642
Ahmednagar	460	263	460	350	224	.488
Belgaum	560	383	560	230	158	.284

Bijapur	400	278	400	149	140	.351
Dharwar	600	398	500	206	147	.296
Bajra						
Ahmedabad	840	518	750	384	203	.272
Kaira	970	551	970	526	409	.422
Dhulia	500	322	500	291	288	.577
Jalgaon	380	318	380	237	195	.515
Nasik	360	236	360	229	223	.622
Ahmednagar	340	209	340	182	186	.549
Poona	340	217	340	181	248	.731
Sholapur	320	137	320	123	81	.255
N. Satara	360	228	360	215	242	.674
Belgaum	400	249	400	200	211	.529
Bijapur	320	184	320	144	142	.446
Cotton						
Ahmedabad	125	84	140	69	75	.541
Broach	130	100	135	81	93	.691
Surat	120	90	135	82	93	.694
Dhulia	90	83	130	71	75	.584
Jalgaon	90	77	130	84	93	.720
Belgaum	100	69	92	41	48	.523
Bijapur	90	, 58	83	38	42	.514
Dharwar	100	89	90	50	60	.669
Ragi						
Ratnagiri	680	493	770	428	518	.673
Maize						
Panchmahals	1190	852	1000	620	753	.753
Gram						
Nasik	350	235	350	338	234	.671
Groundnut						
Jalgaon	3000	2633	900	558	520	.578

SOURCE: The basic data on the condition factor, and the revenue yields are from the *Season and Crop Reports* of the Bombay Presidency from 1886 to 1947, the *Season and Crop Reports* the Bombay State from 1947 to 1960, of Mysore from 1950–6, of Maharashtra and Gujarat after 1960. For the crops discussed in this paper, crop cutting estimates were introduced officially in 1950 in the *Season and Crop Reports*. For the period 1946–50, the crop cutting yields were presented by Khosal (1950). The revenue yields for the period 1906–20 are from P. C. Patil (1922). During the period 1885–6 to 1896–7, the condition factor was reported in annas, and converted on the basis of 16 annas = 100. From 1897–8 to 1904–5, the annas were converted on the basis of 12 annas = 100, after which date the condition factor was reported on an index basis. The standard yields were published in *Agricultural Statistics of India* and have been presented in the *Annewari Report*, and after 1950, were published in the *Season and Crop Reports*.

column 4 is this ratio greater than one. This means that for the vast majority of the important crops in the Bombay Presidency, a secular decline in the condition of crops relative to normal was reported over the first fifty years of the century; and as previously noted, because there has been no change in standard yields, this secular decline in the condition factor implies a secular decline in the estimated yield per acre by the revenue method.

Another striking feature of Table 2 is that the condition factors in columns 2 and 3 are with one exception less than 1.0, as an average value respectively for a nine and a fifteen year period.[13] Over such a long time, the seasons average out, so one must conclude that the reporting system in Bombay produced condition factors well below 100 per cent. Two points need to be made. First, the fact that the condition factor was always 'too low' during the 1906–20 period, does not mean that estimated yields (column 2 of Table 1) are necessarily too low, because, as we have shown, the standard yields were too high. But—and this is the second point—even if the below average condition factors in fact tended to offset the excessive standard yields, it was a spurious result, because officials responsible for the judgement on the nature of the crop in a particular year, were not necessarily aware of the standard yield assumed for a normal year.

We can now develop the initial point illustrated in column 4 of Table 2, the finding that the condition factor apparently declined over a substantial portion of the period 1900 to 1947. A time series analysis of the condition factor for the four major cereals of Bombay and cotton over 6 periods of roughly a decade in length provide a somewhat different perspective on this finding. In the analysis we

[13] One might question this assertion for the period 1946–51, which may be thought too short to iron out the seasons. However, the revenue yields have been computed for the 15 year period 1946–61 for most of the crops in Table 2, and the same results are obtained. It is relevant to point out, though that the yields from crop cutting from 1946–61 were higher than crop cutting yields 1946–54 in 49 of the 59 cases. Because there has been an increase in yields since Independence, the period for which we computed average yields after 1947 to compare with earlier revenue yields was cut short. However, this would not make any difference in our results. One might also wonder why there were revenue yields after crop cutting was introduced, and the answer is simply that revenue yields were needed to assess revenue; crop-cutting yields were used to estimate output, and in theory to set standard yields after a certain period, which was the raison d'etre of the Annewari Report.

have weighted the condition factor in each of the districts of the Presidency by its acreage in the crop. The periods were chosen as follows.

For a number of years prior to the published estimates beginning in 1886 estimates of the condition of crops were in the form of annas as part of a 16 anna rupee. From 1886 to 1897 this was continued and 16 annas was taken as normal or 100 per cent. However, during this period it became clear that the reported anna valuations took a 16 anna crop, not as a typical crop, but one to be encountered infrequently, if at all.[14] Beginning with the crop year 1897–8, 12 annas was taken as the normal crop in Bombay. I have therefore taken the period 1886 to 1897 as a unit. Parenthetically it is obvious that the effect of the 'devaluation' of normal conditions from 16 annas to 12 annas, is to make the condition of agriculture look better, and the burden of revenue assessments on the rural population appear less. In other words, if the village reporters set a crop at 8 annas, and the standard yield is 900 pounds, then prior to 1898, the yield would be 450 pounds (8 as/16as 900), and after 1898, it would be 600 pounds (8 as/12as 900). Naturally, it was hoped that of the transition would not be as discontinuous as the above example suggests, but in some ways the logic of the situation suggests this of it.[15] However, in Bombay still another change, the

[14] To again quote from Stuart (1919, p. 276) referring to the case when a 12 anna crop was normal, 'Now the village accountant, like most farmers, is a pessimist and thinks poorly of most crops. He is told that 12 as. represents a normal crop, but to him a normal crop is the crop he would like to see, but rarely does see. Consequently the final integration of the estimates of the large number of village accountants always works out at very much below 100 per cent—it is usually nearer 75 per cent.' It should be added that this type of bias of the village accountants operated in favour of agriculturists, as will be noted below.

[15] By this I mean that according to writers like Stuart, the culprit in the matter was the accountant who was inherently pessimistic. If he always reported the condition as 75 per cent of what it was, then, in order to use his estimates, you do not want to inform him that standards in annas of a normal yield are different, or he would adjust his evaluations downward. Rather you work with his estimates and change the normal annas to 75 per cent of the previous norm, or from 16 to 12. The logic of this, suggests, that previous estimates ought to have been adjusted upward, but no one suggested this. However, Stuart did suggest that the normal level of the condition factor ought to be the average level reported by the village accountants (he assumed that the standard yields were correct for the districts so that an estimate of yield using the average condition factor as the standard yield, would give the correct actual

Table 2. Ratios of Condition Factors (CF), Crop Cutting Yields and Revenue Yields Various Period from 1886–1954

Crop/District	CCY 1946–54 SY/1945	CF 1946–54	CF 1906–20	CCY/RY 1946–54	RY 1946–54/RY 1906–20
	(1)	(2)	(3)	(4)	(5)
Rice					
Ahmedabad	.318	.583	.660	.545	.883
Kaira	.420	.437	.860	.960	.508
Panch Mahals	.204	.280	.857	.729	.327
Surat	.502	.618	.831	.812	.744
Nasik	.592	.677	.763	.929	.835
Thana	.949	.875	.894	1.084	.979
Kolaba	.929	.892	.951	1.041	.938
Ratnagiri	.927	.842	.814	1.101	1.034
N. Kanara	.995	.716	.762	1.389	.940
Belgaum	.803	.562	.746	1.428	.754
Dharwar	.752	.620	.688	1.212	.902
Kharif Jowar					
Ahmedabad	.157	.419	.556	.376	.754
Surat	.671	.626	.742	1.073	.844
Dhulia	.398	.559	.654	.713	.854
Jalgaon	.825	.601	.854	1.374	.703
Nasik	.790	.538	.540	1.468	.996
N. Satara	.780	.623	.739	1.251	.843
Belgaum	.735	.487	.722	1.509	.674
Bijapur	.557	.483	.676	1.154	.714
Dharwar	.511	.495	.678	1.032	.731
Rabi Jowar					
Broach	.458	.567	.884	809	.641
Jalgaon	.565	.483	.946	1.169	.511
Nasik	.294	.532	.540	.553	.984
Ahmednagar	.725	.622	.576	1.165	1.080
Poona	.481	.539	.618	.891	.872
Sholapur	.667	.538	.639	1.240	.842
Bijapur	.393	.504	.676	.778	.746
Wheat					
Ahmedabad	.569	.602	.687	.945	.876
Broach	.488	.585	.730	.834	.802
Dhulia	.562	.714	.697	.787	1.025
Jalgaon	.575	.710	.767	.809	.926
Nasik	.642	.782	.689	.821	1.135
Ahmednagar	.488	.761	.572	.641	1.331
Belgaum	.284	.412	.684	.688	.603

Bijapur	.351	.373	.695	.940	.536
Dharwar	.296	.412	.796	.718	.518
Bajra					
Ahmedabad	.252	.512	.617	.531	.830
Kaira	.422	.543	.568	.778	.956
Dhulia	.577	.583	.641	.988	.906
Jalgaon	.515	.624	.837	.825	.746
Nasik	.622	.637	.656	.977	.971
Ahmednagar	.549	.536	.615	1.024	.873
Poona	.731	.533	.638	1.371	.835
Sholapur	.255	.386	.428	.662	.901
N. Satara	.674	.597	.633	1.129	.943
Belgaum	.529	.501	.622	1.055	.805
Bijapur	.446	.450	.575	.990	.783
Cotton					
Ahmedabad	.541	.497	.672	1.088	.740
Broach	.691	.601	.769	1.149	.782
Surat	.694	.608	.750	1.142	.811
Dhulia	.584	.553	.759	1.056	.733
Jalgaon	.720	.647	.700	1.113	.924
Belgaum	.523	.450	.690	1.163	.652
Bijapur	.514	.467	.644	1.100	.725
Dharwar	.669	.558	.742	1.199	.752
Ragi					
Ratnagiri	.673	.556	.725	1.210	.759
Maize					
Panchmahals	.753	.621	.716	1.214	.867
Gram					
Nasik	.671	.967	.671	.693	1.441
Groundnut					
Jalgaon	.578	.620	1.053	.932	.589

SOURCES: The basic data on the condition factor, and the revenue yields are from the *Season and Crop Reports* of the Bombay Presidency from 1886 to 1947, the *Season and Crop Reports* of Bombay State from 1947 to 1960, of Mysore from 1950–6, of Maharashtra and Gujarat after 1960. For the crops discussed in this paper, crop cutting estimates were introduced officially in 1950 in the *Season and Crop Reports*. For the period 1946–50, the crop cutting yields were presented by Khosal (1950). The revenue yields for the period 1906–20 are from P. C. Patil (1922). During the period 1885–6 to 1896–7, the condition factor was reported in annas, and converted on the basis of 16 annas = 100. From 1897–8 to 1904–5, the annas were converted on the basis of 12 annas = 100, after which date the condition factor was reported on an index basis. The standard yields were published in *Agricultural Statistics of India*, and have been presented in the *Annewari Report*, and after 1950, were published in the *Season and Crop Reports*.

substantial reduction in standard yields about 1897, tended to offset the change in annas of this actual yield. By our estimates, the decline in standard yields between 1884 and 1897 for the four major food grains and cotton when weighted by acreage in each district was 38 per cent. This was larger than the decline in the norm of the condition factor of 25 per cent (4 out of 16 annas). This means that if on average for the same type of season, in say, 1895, an 8 anna crop would actually generate a larger estimate of yield than an 8 anna crop after 1898 because the rise in the condition factor (from 8/16 to 8/12) would be less than the decline in standard yield. In addition, enough extraneous factors, particularly the famine years from 1899–1901, enter into the Bombay picture to make the effects of this change in annas for a normal crop and the standard yields hard to decipher.

Another change in the revenue system in Bombay occurred in 1906, forming another breaking point in our analysis. According to its architects in Bombay the revenue system was designed to cover good and bad years alike on the average. From about 1890 to 1910 the Bombay government with guidance from Calcutta developed the practice of adjusting the assessment for good and bad years on the basis of the annewari of the crops in particular years. (*Report of the Annewari Committee*: 1966, pp. 136–202).[16]

---

yield, a point with which I would disagree at least for Bombay given the evidence of Table 1). Stuart's suggestion was adopted for Madras and several other areas, so the condition factor considered normal in Madras and several other areas, was 13.3 annas. This accounts for the discontinuity observed by Blyn (1966, p. 50) in Madras yields that went up in 1916–17 after the introduction of this change in normal annas from 16 to 13.3.

[16] The basic statement here is the Resolution of 25 March 1905 of the Department of Revenue and Agriculture Land Revenue, Calcutta, GOI. In this resolution it is stated that local government may wish to suspend revenue when crops are below a certain standard. (On a 16 anna normal crop, 25 per cent suspension for crops of 6 and 7 annas, 50 per cent for crops of 4 and 5 annas and 100 per cent suspension for crops less than 4 annas was a guideline.) Two further points were that local governments may not wish to ask for repayment of the suspended revenue until at least one normal crop had been harvested and that suspended revenue should be remitted if not collected in three years. And the Resolution is very explicit that any remission of revenue to the payee should be passed on to the sub-tenants. This, to my knowledge, is the first explicit acknowledgement that the revenue payer might be in much less need of revenue suspensions than sub-tenants. This resolution is reproduced in *Report of the Annewari Committee* (1966, pp. 162–180).

According to the 1906 regulations in Bombay, in any year when a crop was valued at above 8 annas in a taluka, the land had to pay full revenue plus some portion of suspensions due from previous years. If the crop was valued from 6 to 8 annas, only current land revenue was due; if 4–6 annas, one-half revenue was due; and if under 4 annas no revenue was due. Now pressures on revenue administrators might arise not simply to declare a year bad so that half or no revenue need be paid: since in order for the benefit to be permanent, subsequent years had to be below 8 annas in order not to pay arrears. Under the regulations, arrears would lapse (i.e. be remitted) after 2 or 3 years depending on the area. So if this year is a 4 anna year, the benefit will become permanent so long as the next two or three years are under 8 annas.

On the possible consequences of this regulation let me quote G. F. Keatinge, a former Director of Agriculture in Bombay. Keatinge says,

> In this connection I would point out that in recent years, since the new rules governing the remission and suspension of land revenue have come into force, the importance of the anna estimate is far greater than it formerly was. Formerly the anna estimate was of little importance except for statistical purposes, and received but little attention on the part of district officers. Now-a-days it may make all the difference to the question of remitting or suspending lakhs of rupees whether anna valuation is fixed at 7 or 8 annas. Accordingly in some districts the Collectors are devoting much attention to this matter and are issuing detailed instructions on this subject, which I imagine, must have the effect of altering the general pitch of these anna valuations, which have to serve not only for their own revenue purpose, but also for the statistical purposes of the office. This is bound to have a very disturbing influence on the outturn statistics.

The remaining periods are 10 years each. There is some reason for a change in 1917, since this is the first year that the *Season and Crop Reports* in Bombay actually give estimates of outputs for all areas of the Presidency, including reporting and non-reporting areas.[17] The remaining decades were chosen mainly to approxi-

[17] Prior to 1917, the *Season and Crop Reports* only gave the acreage and condition factor for crops, though an estimate was made for the purposes of Agricultural Statistics in India.

mate the previous ones in length. The results of our analysis of condition factor for the major food crops and cotton are given in Table 3.[18].

The average was computed by using the acreage planted in each district as the weight. The total acreage of the important districts for each of the crops is given in column 7 of Table 3. The fifth row of Table 3 gives for each period the weighted average (by acreage) of the four foodgrains, and the seventh row foodgrains plus cotton. An analysis has also been carried out for maize for Panch Mahals district, and for ragi in Thana, Kolaba, Ratnagiri, and Kanara, with apparently the same results.

There are several patterns in Table 3. First the highest level of

One problem in estimating output in British areas was that some alienated areas, like khoti tenure in Ratnagiri, or talukdari areas in Ahmedabad, did not report on areas planted to crops or the condition of crops. Beginning in 1917, in the *Season and Crop Reports*, an assumption was made about these non-reporting areas, namely the Bayesian assumption that they were the same as reporting areas, and estimates for all of the Presidency were published.

[18] There was one difficulty in constructing Table 3 that should be mentioned, namely that until 1917, only the condition factor was published in the *Season and Crop Reports*, but after that time the actual production was published. For the foodgrains I have only had available the output and acreage figures after 1917, except for 1928–29, and 1933–34, when I have available both the output and the actual condition factors. In other words for the three decades from 1917 to 1946, I have derived average condition factors by estimating the condition factor in each year as the ratio of the reported yield to the standard yield. This is a straightforward calculation, except for the following problems. In what follows, there are large differences in the standard yield of irrigated and non-irrigated wheat, and we have had to estimate for each district a weighted average of the standard yield of irrigated and dry wheat on the basis of acreage. Further, for jowar, there are some districts in which yields of rabi and kharif crops differ, and in these districts we have computed a weighted average condition factor. The average condition factor for the 19 districts of the Bombay Presidency are given for rice, wheat, jowar, bajra and cotton in Table 3.

The reader might ask if this is not also a problem in Tables 1 and 2. In comparing the crop cutting yields to the standard yield, we have used for wheat the standard yield for dry acreage. Thus if irrigated wheat is included in the crop cutting samples then the crop cutting yield would have an upward bias relative to the standard yield. Since the standard yield is still always above the crop cutting yield, we can conclude that if anything we have underestimated the upward bias in the standard yield of wheat. In the case of jowar, the standard yield in Table 1 for each district is that of the type most frequently grown, and since in most of the districts growing substantial amounts of both rabi and kharif jowar, there is little difference in the standard yields, the results in Tables 1 and 2 are not affected.

Table 3. Average Condition and Rainfall Factor for Major Crops in Bombay and Index of Average Total Rainfall for Each District, 1886–1947

Crop/District	1886–97	1898–1906	1907–16	1917–26	1927–36	1937–46	Total or Average
	(1)	(2)	(3)	(4)	(5)	(6)	(7)
			A. CONDITION FACTOR				Area (acres)
Crop							
Rice	72	72	82	79	86	74	1989
Wheat	67	55	68	74	70	63	1404
Jowar	63	56	66	63	71	58	8005
Bajra	64	59	65	63	71	62	3925
Cereals	65	59	68	66	73	62	15325
Cotton	61	62	73	70	65	62	4117
Total	64	59	69	67	71	62	19440
			B. INDEX RAINFALL (1886–97 = 100)				Base Rainfall (in inches)
District							
Ahmedabad	100	76	94	86	127	102	31.6
Kaira	100	74	77	71	93	80	38.9
Panch Mahals	100	78	96	87	129	97	41.1
Broach	100	74	85	74	75	84	42.8
Surat	100	64	87	82	100	104	47.0
Dhulia	100	77	77	93	96	93	26.0
Jalgaon	100	83	106	89	123	110	28.8
Nasik	100	76	97	78	103	83	31.7
Ahmednagar	100	75	91	91	108	93	25.5
Poona	100	78	103	82	98	99	27.0
Sholapur	100	82	83	86	92	82	30.1
Satara	100	76	94	75	101	96	44.2
Belgaum	100	93	105	94	101	104	50.8
Bijapur	100	80	76	74	90	83	26.2
Dharwar	100	105	132	135	144	112	24.2
Thana	100	86	89	85	97	102	105.7
Kolaba	100	84	86	83	94	83	94.6
Ratnagiri	100	92	95	113	97	99	100.5
Kanara	100	98	90	93	103	97	123.9
Average	100	82	93	88	104	95	

the condition factor for all crops is for the period 1927 to 1936, and the lowest for the period 1897–1906. Also, the very clear result from Table 2, that the condition factor circa 1947 was lower than during the period 1906–20, is also evident in Table 3. Since one of the principal, if not the only reason save pests and disease, for fluctuation in the condition factor is the weather, we have included in Table 3 a very simple analysis of total rainfall. Total rainfall, of course, is only one element of the season—timing of rains, wind and hail storms, temperatures, and intervals between rains may all affect the season, as has been discussed by Harold Mann and others. But total rainfall is the most easily measured seasonal influence, sufficient for this analysis.

An index of the total amount of average rainfall in each district, for each of the six periods is given in Table 3. Average rainfall is not as simple a concept as it appears; it usually is only measured for one center (or taluka) in each district; some of the centers underlying the district averages in Table 3 changed during the period; and there is a belief that the accuracy of the measurement of total rainfall was subject to larger error in the earlier periods. The average of the index of rainfall for the nineteen districts has also been calculated in the last row of Table 3. There was no general trend in rainfall over the period. Further, comparing the period 1907–16 with the terminal period (column 6), shows that for all of the districts rainfall was greater in the terminal period, and that this pattern existed for 12 of the nineteen districts. Since Table 2 and Table 3 showed that the condition factor was higher in 1907–16 than in 1937–46, we can conclude that on the basis of the most influential ingredient, there is no reason for this decline in the average condition factor.

The decline in rainfall in all but one district from the period 1886–97 to 1898–1906 is another general pattern. The average condition factor also declined, as one would suspect based solely on the weather, including some failures of rain and major famine in the years 1899 to 1901. However, this also marked the time when the normal condition was changed from a 16 to 12 anna rupee, and our contention that the effect of this change should raise the average condition factor, really is evident in comparing the period 1898–1906 with the period 1907–16, when rainfall went up slightly, but the condition factor increased considerably. While rainfall in the third period was lower than the first period the condition factor was higher, reflecting the delayed impact of the change in the normal condition factor from 16 to 12 annas.

The final point I wish to make about Table 3 is that I believe in periods two through five, the revenue yields and the rainfall are related in the expected manner, but that in the last decade before Independence the condition factor declined more than was warranted by changes in the rainfall. I have also examined 74 correlations of rainfall and the condition factor generated from data of the 5 crops and 19 districts underlying Table 3. The evidence is mixed, as might be expected, but on balance these correlations suggest that the relation of rainfall and the condition factor was weak overall and holds mainly in the middle four of the six periods.[19]

There is another point about Table 3 to be made clear. Because the standard yields are substantially the same between 1897 and

[19] These statements refer to simple correlations of 6 observations (for the six time periods of Table 3) of the index of average annual rainfall and the average condition factor. If a district had all five crops, then five correlations would be available for that district—in fact of the potential 95 correlations (5 crops and 19 districts), only 74 were available. Summarizing these results, there was a positive simple correlation of the condition factor and rainfall in 52 of the 74 cases. Because there were few observations underlying each estimate, very few of the relations were statistically significant; in addition most of the relationships were weak. This, we suggest, is because the condition factor was subject to administrative influences that outweighed influences of the season, thus producing weak correlations between the condition factor and rainfall. To test this explanation we examined the residuals of the equations relating rainfall and the condition factor with the following results. If the predicted value of the condition factor based on rainfall, is greater than the actual value, the residual will be negative. It is our argument that the residuals in period 1 and period 6, when we believe the condition factor is low, are negative. The reason for period 1 is the change in the number of annas considered normal, and for period 6 is given in the text below. For each of the 74 equations we analyzed the sign of the residuals in the two periods which were similar in pattern a total of 148 residuals. They were converted to a percentage of the actual value and then grouped as below:

Number of cases where residual as per cent of actual condition factor is	more than 10%	5 to 10%	5 to −5 %	−5 to −10%	less than −10%
	9	12	55	24	48

Since the strongly negative residuals (72) are over three times the number of strongly positive residuals, the results of this analysis certainly suggest that the condition factor in both the periods 1887–97 and 1937–46 was unusually low.

1946, the condition factors in periods 2 through 6 substantially reflect estimated revenue yields per acre in the five periods — i.e., revenue yields are condition factors times standard yields (which are virtually constant between 1897–1946). However, for the first period, the standard yields were 38 per cent above the 1897 standard yields. This means that condition factor of 64 in the period 1886–97, implies an estimated revenue yield per acre in period 6 when the average condition factor is 62, that is 60 per cent of that of the former period (62   62/64   100). This decline in estimated yields is in excess of that given by Blyn, in part because there are a number of non-comparabilities.[20]

Conclusions

One crucial element in yield estimation by the revenue method, as used in India from 1886 to 1946 (and beyond for certain crops and regions) is the standard yield per acre. In Bombay the research underlying the standard yield was inadequate, and the method for introducing changes after 1897, except perhaps in cash crops, was ineffective. As a consequence standard yields were substantially unchanged in the fifty years from 1897 to Independence. Further the standard yields were (relative to crop cutting experiments in Bombay) always high — they were not an average yield. Except in Punjab, there is every reason to believe that these same conditions prevailed in other areas using the revenue method (Assam, Ajmer-Merwara, Madras, Central Provinces, Sind, Mysore, Berar, and the United Provinces and some other princely areas).

One consequence of this stability in standard yields was that after 1897 any trend in estimated yield by the revenue method had to result wholly from a trend in the condition factor. Since the condition factor should reflect principally rainfall and its distribution, and disease, and there has been no trend in these variables there should have been no trend in the condition factor. However, a downward trend in the condition factor, and yields was found for the major foodgrains, which we traced to administrative changes in earlier periods, and linked to political pressures toward the end of

[20] In particular, in the data used by Blyn, wheat and cotton were available in 1891 for Bombay, but not rice, bajra and jowar, the most important crop in terms of acreage until 1912. Further Blyn's figures include allowances for pulses and other cereals, and for Bombay include estimates for princely areas.

the period.[21] The change introduced in the revenue system in 1907 had built into it an inducement for the continual reporting of lower condition factors. That is, if this year is poor, current revenue payments and arrears are suspended, *and if* subsequent years are also poor, the suspensions are remitted. I am suggesting that from the inception of this regulation until 1947, and even thereafter, there were increasing pressures on local revenue officers to accept lower condition factors.

The nationalist agitation which took the form of no-rent campaigns, such as the agitation in Bardoli taluk in Surat district in 1928 was one source of pressure. In earlier periods, land revenue was not only an important source of revenue for the British, but also of income to local administrators who received a proportion of increased land revenue, thus ensuring their personal interest in its collection. However, land revenue declined as a source of total revenue relative to tariffs and indirect taxes, and political stability replaced revenue as an interest of a local administrator. One way to keep an area free of no-rent campaigns, i.e. not to raise taxes, and perhaps even to lower them, became possible administratively under the 1907 regulations. In other words a decline in the average condition factor such as occurred in the periods 1907–16 to 1937–46, and particularly 1927–36 to 1937–46, is likely to be simply a reduction in taxes of the rural population. The fact that this also produced a decline in the estimated yield of crops was of no consequence.[22] It did not affect the revenue officers; it probably

[21] Also, we have shown that any apparent increases in the level of the condition factor from its initial publication in 1886 until 1916 can be traced to changes in the number of annas of a crop considered normal in 1897. My interpretation of this early period is that any increase in revenue yields between 1886 and 1897 is well within the range of error due to changes in the reporting system.

[22] The argument above suggests that there would be a decline in land revenue in Bombay during the period, and indeed there was. Two other factors also reduced revenue demand but they are also consistent with the view that political influences were important; namely special remissions of revenue during the 1930s, and revisions of land settlements (the usual period of settlement was 30 years in Bombay), that undoubtedly reduced revenue demand during the period 1937–46. Some figures of land revenue in Bombay are a high of Rs 44.87 million (39.6 per cent) in 1922–3, a low of Rs 31.96 million (25.7 per cent) in 1937–38, reaching a smaller peak during W. W. II in 1942–3 of Rs 40 million (20.6 per cent). The land revenue figures are from Joshi (1959: 182–89 and 1947: Appendix A), and the figures in brackets are the per cent of

perturbed the agricultural department but with the retrenchment in staff in the 1920s and 1930s, they were likely to have been fully occupied with their reports. The only persons affected I suggest are those trying to understand the trends in yield in India under the British, and the consequences are clear.

There is no evidence for Bombay that suggests that the reported declines in yields per acre during the period 1886–1947, correspond to the agricultural history of the period—to administrative and political history yes, but to reality, no. It should be clear that I am offering no evidence that yields per acre did not decline, but rather I am saying that from the way yield estimates were formed in Bombay during the period, there is no reason to conclude that there was any trend in yields upward or downward.

Blyn (1966:150–64) and others, e.g. Dantwala and Shah (1961), who have accepted the reported decline in yield as valid, have discussed a number of reasons why it might have occurred. I would accept a number of these reasons, like (1) decline in dung availability due to its use as fuel when wood becomes expensive due to deforestation, (2) movement on to less productive lands, and (3) shift of better grain lands to cash crops, as reasonable explanations. However, in addition to improved seeds and techniques, there is another basic trend that should have operated to increase yields per acre, namely the growth in workers per acre. Since most studies show that more workers per acre produce more output per acre in Indian farm studies, one might also suspect that as Indian agriculture became more intensive over the period, yields per acre would rise. In any event, on *a priori* grounds, the case for secular decline in yields per acre is not convincing to me. The two components of the estimated yield are independently suspect. The 1897 standard yields are always greater (frequently by 30 per cent or more) than yields found by crop cutting at Independence and there is nothing in the generation of the 1897 standard yields that suggest they should be treated as sacrosanct. The condition factor was a tool of the revenue system, that was inherently subjective,

---

land revenue to total tax and other receipts in each year. The fact that land revenue did absolutely rise by about 30 per cent during the war (while still absolutely below the level of the 1920s), should be viewed against the rise in wholesale prices from 100 in 1939 to 241 to 1943. This small war time rise in land revenue is probably due to the end of the special remissions that had been granted because of declining prices in the 1930s.

and was used in estimating production only as a by-product. The fact that the condition factor was never near 100 during any period, again suggests its rather peculiar nature. It is probably true that the condition factor accurately reflected the change in direction of the seasons, up and down, from year to year, but that the level and magnitude of the fluctuation over the period are considerably less reliable. However, this is a subject that deserves more study for Bombay and other parts of India.[23]

One possible objection to this analysis is that in many cases in Bombay and other areas of India and Pakistan the yields estimated by the revenue methods at Independence were higher than crop cutting yields. In Table 1, for example, in about half the cases the revenue yields (column 4) are greater than crop cutting yields (column 5) though for most of subcontinent the general case was that crop cutting yields exceeded revenue yields.[24] My answer is that there could be a secular decline in the condition factor, but that the end result could either produce an estimated revenue yield above or below crop cutting yields. This is so because the standard yields are almost always above average yields, so whether revenue yields circa 1947 are above or below crop cutting yields depends on whether the upward bias in the standard yield (relative to average crop cutting yield) exceeds the downward bias in the condition factor. Until more is learned about these relative biases for all parts of India, there is little one can infer about the trends of yield from the relation of the revenue yields and crop cutting yields in the period about 1946–50 and later when they overlapped.

How generally does the argument of this paper apply to the rest of India? Until more research is done, we can only say that all of the factors that we have suggested operated in Bombay, were operative in other parts of British India as well, i.e. an initially

[23] We earlier mentioned the work of Mann (1955). Also, N. G. Bapat (1972) has been doing an intensive analysis of the agricultural development in Ahmednagar district, including the crop weather relation.

[24] See Panse and Sukhatme (1951, pp. 104–20). Also, there was an interesting exchange between C. H. Shah (1962) and Panse (1963), on this issue of the pitch of revenue and crop cutting yields. In Pakistan, where a Committee was asked to examine crop cutting and revenue yields, the crop cutting yields for wheat were greater than revenue yields. It has been suggested that because acceptance of crop cutting yields would have implied less need for food imports (even though population was also probably underestimated), that revenue yields be retained for official estimates.

experimental period, stable and high standard yields after 1897, an initially low condition factor based on a 16 anna normal crop, the introduction of regulations allowing suspension and remission of revenue based on the condition factor, and agitation against revenue demands that could be met in part by a decline in the reported condition factor. While work needs to be done on these questions, as well as on areas where revenue was indirectly collected like Bengal and the Princely states, the only real exception to my argument is apparently Punjab, where crop cutting experiments were more frequent and bore more relation to standard yields.

If we have no reason to believe that there were declines in the yields of foodgrains and cotton in Bombay from 1886–1947, and if this pattern is true for other parts of India, there are a number of implications. For example, estimates of the trends in output per acre, in output per man (which are also used as a basis for estimates of output per man in other sectors, like services, in generating estimates of value added), and in food availability would have to be revised. I do not want to further explore these implications of my argument, but only to make clear that these are some of the issues involved.[25] Rather, I hope that this paper will be a part of a discussion with others that can contribute toward a consensus on how the official figures on agricultural output in India during the past century should be treated in historical studies, and in time series for agricultural planning.

[25] I would also like to make clear that some of the scepticism about the official statistics in this paper is built on the work of others. M. Mukherjee, who was closely associated with the first National Income statistics for independent India is one such sceptic. He would agree that if one accepted the official agricultural statistics one would have to conclude that per capita income declined over the 1890–1947 period. However, he believes that this was not the case and produces a synthetic set of national income figures that are not consistent with a declining per capita availability of foodgrains (1965: p. 703). In doing so, however, he does not explicitly state in what ways the trend given by the agricultural figures are incorrect – this is more of an assumption than conclusion. Another sceptic is M. D. Morris, who reasons this way. If there were a decline in per capita availability of food grains, would you expect the increase in population that India experiences especially during the period after 1921, which was also the period when population growth increased and yields per acre most decreased, Morris (1963, p. 17). Angus Maddison (1971, pp 51–2 and Appendix B) has made a similar analysis. He makes revised estimates of output using the average figure of Sivasubramoniam and the yield figures of Blyn.

References

Anderson, Hartnell F. G., (1929). *Facts and Fallacies about the Bombay Land Revenue System*, Printed by Author, Poona.

Anderson, Hartnell F. G., (1948). *Manual of Revenue Accounts of Villages, Talukas and Districts of the Bombay State*. 5th edn, Revenue Department, Government Press, Bombay.

Annewari Committee for the Determination of Standard Yields (1966). Revenue and Forests Department, Government of Maharashtra, Government Press and Printing, Nagpur.

Bapat, N. G. (1972). 'Trends in Agricultural Production, 1881–1960, in Ahmednagar District', (mimeographed, Marathwada University, Aurangabad).

Blyn, George, (1966), *Agricultural Trends in India, 1891–1947; Output, Availability, and Productivity,* Univ. of Pennsylvania Press, Philadelphia.

Dantwala, M. L. and Shah, C. H., (1961). 'Trends in Yields per Acre'. *Changing India, Essays in Honour of D. R. Gadgil*, Asia, Bombay.

Digby, William, (1901). *Prosperous British India: A Revelation from the Official Records*, London.

Government of Pakistan (1965). Final Report of the National Income Commission.

Joshi, T. M., (1947). Bombay Finance (1921–46), Gokhale Institute of Politics and Economics, Publication no. 16, Poona.

Joshi, T. M., (1959). Agricultural Land Revenue in the Bombay State. Doctoral Dissertation, University of Pennsylvania, Philadelphia.

Khosal, R. S., (1950). *A Review of Crop Cutting Experiments in the Bombay State during the Period 1945–6 to 1948–9*, Bulletin no. 1 of 1950, Department of Agriculture, Bombay State, Poona.

Mann, Harold (1955). *Rainfall and Famine in the Bombay Deccan*, Indian Society of Agriculture Economics, Bombay.

Mollison, W. (1910). *Textbook on Indian Agriculture*, Department of Agriculture, Poona.

Moray, P. E., (no date). 'Crop Yield-Weather Relationships Studies in India by using Multiple Regression Technique', (Mimeo) Meteorological Office, Poona.

Maddison, Angus, (1971). *Class Structure and Economic Growth: India and Pakistan since the Moghuls*, W. W. Norton Company, Inc. New York.

Morris, D. Morris (1963). 'Towards a Reinterpretation of Nineteenth Century Indian Economic History', *Journal of Economic History*, vol. XXIII.

Mukherji, K., (1965). *Levels of Economic Activity and Public Expenditures in India*, Asia, Bombay, chp. 2.

Mukherji, M., (1965). 'National Income' in V. B. Singh (ed.), *Economic History of India 1857–1956*, Asia, Bombay.

Naoroji, Dadabhai, (1901). *Poverty and Un-British Rule in India*, Swan Sonneschein and Co., London.

Noyce, F., (1919). Proceedings of the Board of Agriculture in India, Superintendent of Government Printing, Calcutta, p. 23.

Panse, V. G., (1961). 'The National Sample Survey, Agricultural Statistics and Planning in India', in N. V. Sovani and V. M. Dandekar (Eds.), *Changing India, Essays in honour of D. R. Gadgil*, Asia, Bombay.

Panse, V. G. (1963). 'Why Crop-Cutting Surveys?', *Indian Journal of Agricultural Economics*, vol. XVIII, no. 2.

Panse, V. G., and Sukhatme, (1951). 'Crop Surveys in India—II,' *Journal of Indian Society of Agricultural Statistics*.

Patil, P. C., (1922). *The Crops of the Bombay Presidency, Their Geography and Statistics*, Bulletin no. 109 of 1921, Department of Agriculture, Bombay.

Report of the Indian Famine Commission of 1880, vol. III, London, no date. Evidence in Reply to Inquiries of the Commission. 'Note on Crop Experiments', James S. Peile, pp. 64–8.

Shah, C. H., (1962). 'Comparison of Yield Estimates Prepared on the Basis of Traditional and Crop-Cutting Methods', *Indian Journal of Agricultural Economics*, vol. XVII, no. 4.

Sinha, H., (1934). 'Indian Agricultural Statistics', *Journal of the Royal Statistical Society*, vol. XCVII.

Sivasubramoniam, S., 'Estimates of Gross Value of Output of Agriculture for Undivided India (1900–1 to 1942–3)', Paper presented to the Preliminary Conference on Research in National Income, January 1957.

Stuart, G. A. D., (1919). 'The Season Factor in Crop Statistics: A Method of Correction for the Inherent Pessimism of the Farmer', *Agricultural Journal of India*, vol. XIV.

Chapter 3

Revenue Administration and Agricultural Statistics in Bombay Presidency

[1978]

ASHOK V. DESAI

George Blyn (1966) showed, on the basis of a careful analysis of official statistics, that average crop yields as well as per capita supply of foodgrains declined between 1890 and 1947. Heston (1973) confirmed the fall in yields for the Bombay Presidency; but he argued that the fall was due to biases in official statistics and not genuine. He further felt that his arguments applied to all of India except Punjab and hence cast doubt on Blyn's overall conclusions.

On looking more closely at Heston's argument, I found some strange features, of which I shall touch on only major ones.

(*a*) Good and bad crops, being dependent on climatic variables, are not purely randomly distributed but tend to cluster; averaging over a few years does not therefore eliminate non-systematic fluctuations. To get over this difficulty Blyn (1966:82) calculated exponential rates of change over overlapping decades and then averaged them. Heston chose instead to compare two arbitrary periods. His initial period was neither the earliest permitted by available data—presumably 1886–95—nor the period in which official yields should have approximated closely the actual yields—1897–1909. It happened to be 1906–20, when a series of good harvests produced the peak foodgrain outputs reached before 1947 (Blyn 1966: 95). Heston compared the *revenue* yields of 1906–20 with the *crop-cutting* yields of 1946–54 (a period which went beyond the end of Blyn's study) which were far below revenue yields of 1945–54. In both ways he exaggerated the decline in yields—just how serious the exaggeration was can be seen from Table 1.

Blyn's figures for Bombay Presidency show a sizeable fall—13

Table 1. Changes in Yields between Different Periods

	Yields (lb/acre)				Changes in Yields (per cent)		
	I 1897– 1909	II 1906 1920	III 1937- 1946	IV 1950– 1958*	I–III	II–IV	I–IV
Rice	898	926	886	761	−1.3	−17.8	−15.3
Wheat	510	584	482	388	−5.5	−33.6	−23.9
Jowar	410	456	358	336	−12.7	−26.3	−18.0
Bajra	259	283	274	225	+ 5.8	−20.5	−13.9
Ragi	641	648	668	642	+ 4.2	−0.9	+ 0.1
Sugarcane	5,259	5,821	6,098	6,084	+ 16.0	+ 4.5	+ 15.7
Cotton	74	81	104	81	+ 40.5	0	+ 9.5
Groundnut	934	1,267	970	531	+ 3.9	−58.1	−43.1

* 1950–8 is taken instead of 1946–54 preferred by Heston because the status of published official statistics before 1950–1 — whether they are based on crop-cutting yields or not — is uncertain. Years beyond 1957–8 are excluded because Bombay was then divided into Gujarat and Maharashtra; concomitant border changes make subsequent figures non-comparable.

SOURCES: Blyn (1966), India (1956, 1957)

per cent — in the yield of one crop, small decreases in the yield of two, and *increases in the yield of five*. Heston gives no figure that can be compared with Blyn's; but figures calculated in his fashion show a slight increase in the yield of one crop, no change in the yield of one, and *falls in the yield of six crops*.

More explicitly, Blyn's conclusion that average yields in India declined depended largely on the fall in yields in Bengal, Bihar, Orissa and UP, and not at all on yields in Bombay-Sind, which in his reckoning went up slightly. Heston tried to throw doubt on Blyn's conclusion by choosing periods and sources so as to obtain large declines in Bombay yields.

(*b*) In building up his case against the quality of official statistics, Heston somehow omitted all official references — even references to mere descriptions of how the statistics were compiled. This omission could well be due to ignorance. But more interestingly, he omitted references *within the works he cited* to their authors' comments that went against his case. For instance, he quoted Patil's (Bombay 1922: 51) unfavourable comment on standard yields. But in the very next paragraph Patil approved of revenue yield estimates, against which Heston's paper is essentially directed; further, Patil *used* the revenue yield statistics to work out fodder supplies in the same study. Harold Mann (not T. E. Main, *pace* Heston), the then Director of Agriculture, did not accept responsibility for the conclusions of another study of Patil (1932). Heston interpreted this 'to reflect a heightened sensitivity of British administrators' (1973:313–17). He forgot, however, to give Mann's own reason for reserving judgement on Patil's study, namely that it was based on statistics for a single, long-past year, 1914–5; in fact, Mann further expressed the hope that more studies like Patil's would follow his preliminary effort.

(*c*) Heston gave data for districts only, and not for the Presidency or its parts. He did not give crop acreages in various districts or indicate in any other way that many of the districts he listed were relatively minor producers of the crops he included. He omitted districts from the sources available to him on the basis of no stated principle.

(*d*) Any attempt to trace Heston's references to sources or his column references to his tables is apt to drive one to despair.

In the circumstances, it would be tempting to regard Heston's paper as rather resolutely one-sided and to assume that the truth lay the way: that the output statistics are reliable enough to support Blyn's limited conclusions. That is the truth but not the whole truth, which in this case happens to be stranger than fiction.

Revenue Assessment

The truth is that contrary to Heston's impression—and my own—*the revenue assessment did not depend in the least on annual output statistics.* Harold Mann, writing as Director of Agriculture in 1925, could not have been clearer on this.

> The land is subject to a charge, assessed according to its productive capabilities and liable to revision at intervals of thirty years. The first assessment was strictly by the condition of each field as found, but after this first survey . . . the relative valuation of the survey fields cannot be altered except by reason of improvements effected at the cost of Government. The revised assessments are based on general considerations of the rise and fall of the prices of agricultural produce and not on a re-examination of the conditions of each field. It must be carefully noticed further that the rent-charge on the land is scrupulously graduated by the regularity and certainty of rainfall in each group of villages. Thus in tracts chronically liable to failure of crops a due discount is allowed . . . (Bombay 1925:6).

Thus, the revenue rates per acre in areas of uncertain rainfall were kept below those in areas with more stable rainfall. But they had nothing to do with the variation in output from year to year.

But surely, the 30-year revenue settlements must have had some relation to output? The answer, I think, is, sometimes and in some places. When the British took over revenue administration in Maratha territories in 1819—not in 'the early 1800s' (Heston 1966:306)—they tried to collect the *kamal* (standard) rates fixed by the Maratha administration, but managed to collect only a fraction. Hence, an official—Pringle—was sent around in 1830 to fix the rates anew. He was supposed to have estimated actual production and to have fixed rates in proportion to it, but the rates he fixed proved even less capable of collection, and another three officials—Goldsmid, Nash and Wingate—were sent out in 1836–7 to make a new settlement. The principles of this settlement are not clear, but it must have been based on negotiations with village worthies—on what the traffic would bear—for the settlement worked well for 30 years (India 1883). Further 30-year settlements followed in 1866–7 and 1896–7.

Mann says that revised assessments were not based on 'a re-examination of the conditions of each field'. Actually, the Bombay settlements took account of almost everything but yields. According to W. G. Pedder, Revenue Secretary of the Government of India.

The Bombay method is avowedly an empirical one. When a tract [usually the *taluk* or subdivision of district] comes under settlement, original or revised, its revenue history for the preceding 50 or more years is carefully ascertained and tabulated in figured statements and diagrams. These show in juxtaposition, for each year of the series, the amount and incidence of the assessment, the remissions or arrears, the ease or difficulty with which the revenue was realised, the rainfall and nature of the season, the harvest prices, the extension or decrease of cultivation, and how these particulars are influenced by each other. The effect of any public improvements, such as roads, railways, canals, markets, on the tract, or on parts of it, is estimated. The prices for which land sold, or the rents for which it is let, are ascertained; and the tract is compared as regards the above particulars with other tracts similar to it in soil, climate, and situation. Upon the consideration of all these data the total assessment is determined. That amount is then apportioned pretty much in the same manner upon the different villages; and the total assessment of each village is then distributed over its assessable fields in accordance with their classification, which determines their relative values in point of soil, water supply and situation (India 1886:24).

Elsewhere revenue assessment had even less to do with output. In the lower Gangetic plain, whose revenue administration came earliest into British hands, the government aimed to get a certain proportion of what the landlords got from peasants; it was not even faintly interested in what the peasants got from the land. And since those tracts came under Permanent Settlement there was no question of reassessing their revenue.

In Madras, the Board of Revenue did initially (between 1800 and 1810) try to estimate yields as a basis for revenue assessment and obtain a few records of physical output, some of which were for areas where revenue was still determined by crop-sharing in the field; I hope to publish a further account of them later. The principle of crop-sharing underlay all Madras settlements. But in practice, all settlements after the first ones at the turn of the century started from past revenue records, and adjusted revenue where developments after the previous settlement justified it; the system functioned much as in Bombay.

Under the Madras system the average yield of certain staple crops per acre is ascertained by a great number of actual experiments extending over a series of years. The average gross produce is converted into cash at 'the commutation rate,' or average harvest price of 20 or more years preceding the settlement. The average cost of cultivation and profits of stock are then ascertained by careful and extensive investigation, and the amount arrived at being deducted from the value of the gross produce is net produce. Half the net produce is the 'revenue rate' per acre. . . .

Such is the theory of the Madras settlement . . . the first step in the Madras settlement practically is to determine, on general considerations, whether a tract . . . requires a decrease or will bear an enhancement of its revenue and to what extent. The total amount of assessment having been decided on, the results of the process described above are adjusted so as to yield it. The estimates of average yield are reduced to allow for error or for exceptionally bad seasons, and the commutation rate is lowered to cover possible fluctuations of prices in the future . . . (India 1886:24).

Punjab and western UP, which were first settled in the 1840s, fell into the pattern of Bombay and Madras. Thus, I would assert that at the time when agricultural output statistics began in India—the 1880s and 1890s—revenue assessment neither required nor generated them anywhere. It did generate statistics of area under cultivation, but not of yields.

Famines and Production

Yield statistics owed their origin to the famines of 1870s. There were the Bengal famine in 1874, the Great Famine and riots in Bombay in 1876–7 and an equally severe famine in Madras in 1878–9 which spread eventually to most of India. Reports of the last one partly agitated public opinion in Britain, and led to the appointment of the Famine Commission which reported in 1880 (Great Britain 1880–5).

After the famines of the 1870s it was clear that British opinion would require the Government of India to assume responsibility for preventing mass starvation; the Famine Commission spelled out the implications of this responsibility, of which two are relevant here. One was that the interest of the government in agriculture should not be confined to revenue collection but should extend to the improvement of agriculture and its fortification against vagaries of weather. The other was that when famine threatened, the government must procure, store and transport grain so as to avert mass starvation: for this purpose it needed *early* information on agricultural output. To undertake these new tasks, the provincial governments (for then as now, agriculture was a provincial responsibility) set up Departments of Agriculture. The old Revenue Departments were, however, too strong to tolerate equal competitors; everywhere the new departments were placed squarely within Revenue Departments, and Directors of Agriculture were made subordinate to Revenue Secretaries. Nor could Agriculture Departments have their own field organization; for contact with the field they had to rely on the vast revenue hierarchy. They had at least the bureaucracy for field organization; of specialist research staff they had virtually none. The result was that for the first decade after their creation they were largely concerned with statistical work, including the compilation of the first output statistics (India 1915:2–8).

Why was the annawari system adapted for estimating output? It was initially used to classify land for revenue assessment in the 1830s (Dodwell 1932:256). As applied to yield estimation, it no doubt imposed a low administrative work load. But the basic cause was that *only the annawari system could furnish statistics of total output fast enough for timely action against famines.* It was not as if the civil service had not heard of crop-cutting experiments or was innocent of statistical methods. But crop-cutting experiments had to await the harvest; and compilation of reliable estimates would have required averaging and aggregation of figures collected over a vast area, and would have stretched over months. Famine spread much faster than statistics could be gathered: as soon as the traders learnt that a crop was likely to be poor, prices started rising. What the government needed was quick forecasts of crops rather than accurate estimates; this is why the major crops are still officially described as forecast crops.

Standard Yield

Heston makes much play with the unclarity in the concept of the standard yield, and cites the doubts of two civil servants, one from Bombay and another from Madras. The ignorance of two twentieth century civil servants may prove something about them and how they must have worked the annawari system. But the meaning of the standard yield is clear from the origin of the system and the statistics it generated.

As mentioned earlier, annawari was initially used to classify land for revenue assessment in the Bombay settlement of 1830, although it might have been a part of vernacular usage before that date. Under it, 16-anna land was the best land, and bore the highest revenue rates.

When crop forecasts were adopted in the 1870s, annawari came to be used to describe the condition of the crop. By analogy with land classification, a 16-anna crop was taken to be a good crop—a crop which would be harvested in a year of well-distributed, normal rainfall. This is how annawari is interpreted even now in vernacular usage—no one ever heard of an 18-anna or 20-anna crop. And that is how it was interpreted officially; a clear proof is that the average of condition factors everywhere is much below 100 per cent.

Stuart (1919:276), who did not work in Bombay anyway, was

plainly wrong even about Madras. It was nonsense to say that 'the village accountant . . . thought poorly of most crops': he had an adequate idea of a 16-anna crop as an excellent crop, and could judge the annawari perfectly well. It was no use telling him that '12 as represents a normal crop'; a Director of Agriculture, who was there one day and would be gone the next, could hardly aspire to change the common usage overnight. Since the method of yield estimation underwent no change at all, Stuart's rationalization of the increase in yields was pure statistical idiosyncracy.

Heston can only cite Stuart in support of his contention that the 'normal' crop was changed from a 16-anna to a 12-anna crop in 1897–8 in Bombay; there is considerable doubt that any such change took place. If it did, the standard yields in Bombay should have *risen*, as they did in Madras in 1916–17; in fact, they *fell* by 38 per cent according to Heston's calculations. And if the annawari came to be based on 12 instead of 16 annas, it should have *risen* by a third on the average; in fact, according to Heston's Table 3 (1973:322) the condition factor *fell* marginally between 1886–97 and 1898–1906.

Heston (1973:324) argues that it rose belatedly in 1907–16, 'when rainfall went up slightly but the condition factor increased considerably.' By Heston's own reckoning it rose a mere five points over 1886–97, whereas it should have risen 21 points. Besides, it is odd that the change should have taken twenty years in Bombay. It was not an administrative measure, but merely involved a change in the way annawari was converted to percentage. It could not have involved the village accountant, for according to Heston's paraphrase of Stuart, 'you do not want to inform him that standards in annas of yield are different, or he would adjust his evaluations downward'. In fact, the change could have been made in the Director of Agriculture's office, and would not have involved more than a day's work. Madras introduced it in a single crop year; why did it take Bombay twenty years?

The fact is, it did not, for Bombay never introduced it. What Bombay did was to revise standard yields in 1897 on the basis of accumulated statistics. What happened becomes clear with the help of the following description of Bombay standard yields in 1892:

> The statement for Bombay Presidency has been compiled on the basis of certain standard outturns prepared in 1884 for the purpose of estimating the produce of harvest. These standards were formulated by a

committee appointed by the Government of Bombay upon a full consideration of all the available sources of information existing at the time, including the results of ten years' crop cuttings. Systematic crop cutting . . . experiments, the records of which are scrutinized with great care by the Land Records and Agricultural Department, have since been regularly carried out and ledgered year by year and in some respects they confirm the standards of 1884; but in others they indicate that those estimates must be accepted with caution. But the experiments are not yet sufficiently numerous or complete to supply information for the principal crops of each district which would justify a general revision of the standards of 1884, and these are still accepted as the best index of outturns at present forthcoming (India 1892: 1).

Evidently, the Government of Bombay was convinced by 1892 that the standard yields laid down in 1884 were inaccurate, but was not sure how far to correct them. By 1897 it had collected enough data to make a general revision, mainly downwards.

In 1897 the Government of Bombay was satisfied with its standard yields in the sense that the revenue yields they were used to derive gave a reasonable approximation to actual yields as established by crop-cutting experiments, Crop-cutting experiments continued till 1909. The revenue yields in 1897–1909 came closest to reality, and were therefore taken as the initial basis of comparison in Table 1.

A comparison of 1897–1909 revenue yields with 1950–58 crop-cutting yields shows falls of 14 to 24 per cent in the yield of the four major foodgrains—rice, wheat, jowar and bajra—a fall of 43 per cent in the yield of groundnuts, and rises in the yield of sugarcane and cotton. This is the best conclusion that can be reached on the basis of available statistics. It differs substantially from the picture emerging from Blyn's revenue yield figures, and we owe it to Heston's—albeit incomplete—researches into Bombay revenue history.

Heston claims that standard yields were remarkably stable and takes the stability to be an indication of neglect. He is probably right, and the great excess of revenue yields over crop-cutting yields shown by him in 1946–54 support his claim. Unfortunately, it goes against his supposition that revenue yields in the inter-war period were marked down for political reasons; in any case the yearly revenue collections were quite unrelated to annawari—except in very poor years to which we shall turn now.

Revenue Remissions and Suspensions

Heston (1973:320) says:

> According to 1906 regulations in Bombay, in any year when a crop was valued at above 8 annas in a taluka, land had to pay full revenue plus portion of suspensions due from previous years. If the crop was valued from 6 to 8 annas, only current land revenue was due; if 4–6 annas, one-half revenue was due; and if under 4 annas no revenue was due. Now pressures on revenue administrators might arise not simply to declare a year bad so that half or no revenue need be paid: since for the benefit to become permanent, subsequent years had to be below 8 annas in order to pay arrears. Under the regulations, arrears would lapse, (i.e., be remitted) after 2 or 3 years depending on the area.

This happens to be a complete misstatement. The fact is that from the beginning of British rule in Bombay and Madras, the two Presidencies whose early records I have checked, District Collectors had the power to remit or suspend revenue payments. Collectors never asked for permission to remit and suspend; they *reported* remissions and suspensions. In the early years of British rule remissions sometimes exceeded half the year's revenue. While collectors explained their reasons for remissions in every case, persistent remissions were taken to be a reflection on the settlement rather than on collectors. Gradually settlements were revised; as they approached the practical taxation capacity, remissions grew rarer and collectors got out of practice in the use of their powers. By the 1870s they would not use the powers even when the interests of the government required it: for instance, when peasants were getting into debt to pay land revenue and being forced off their land in the early 1870s in the Deccan.

Once remissions became infrequent, collectors were loath to remit or suspend revenue for an obvious reason: namely, full and prompt collection of revenue was rewarded by good marks from the Revenue Department and improvement of career prospects, while remissions and suspensions were a failure that called for explanations.

The legislation from the 1870s onwards was designed to *encourage* collectors to use their powers by giving them the protection of the law. Following the recommendations of the Deccan Riots Commission in 1875, the resumption of land by moneylenders was controlled: mortgages on agricultural land had to be registered.

The idea was to give collectors advance information on the indebtedness of peasants, so that they would relax the revenue regime when peasants were in difficulty.

The Debt Relief Act proved inadequate in preventing resumption of land; so the Land Revenue Code was amended in 1901. Where a peasant was falling behind revenue payments and at the risk of losing his land, a collector was authorized to change his tenure from the Mirasi tenure, with its unlimited right of ownership and transfer, to a restricted tenure in which the right of transfer by private contract or sale under attachment by Court was taken away. If a peasant's tenure was restricted, he could no longer borrow on its security; neither, however, could the government force him to sell it in order to pay revenue.

Even with the amendment, peasants whose tenure was restricted could become hopelessly indebted to the government for revenue. To prevent such impossible accumulations of dues, collectors had to be pursuaded to use suspensions and remissions more frequently. The Regulations of 1906 tried to do so by authorizing collectors to give blanket remissions or suspensions to all peasants in a tract on the basis of crop conditions instead of on enquiry into individual peasants' economic conditions. They thereby eliminated a great deal of paperwork and explanations; but they did *not* make either remissions or suspensions automatically follow from reported crop conditions. Let me quote Harold Mann in substantiation:

> *Suspensions and remissions of land revenue.* Another measure in the same direction is the introduction of a regular system of suspensions and remissions of land revenue when the crops fall below a certain standard or when the water supply on the irrigated lands fails. The assessment fixed under the survey settlement is a fixed demand and represents the revenue capable of being paid on an average in a series of years, the original idea being that on the average the *rayat* saves in a good year sufficient to enable him to pay the assessment without borrowing in a bad year. Experience, however, showed that among the smaller landholders and in tracts subject to frequent vicissitudes of the season, this idea was fallacious, and in 1906–7 a regular system of suspensions was introduced.
>
> The system authorises the Collector, when he has ascertained by local enquiries that owing to partial or total failure or destruction of crops throughout any tract, suspension of collection of land revenue is

necessary, to grant suspensions according to a scale to all occupants, agriculturists and non-agriculturists alike, without enquiry into the circumstances of individuals. As regards remissions, the grant of them depends on the character of three seasons following that in which the assessment is suspended (Bombay 1925:7).

The possibility raised by Keatinge (Heston 1973:320–1), whose source reference Heston has characteristically omitted, certainly existed: if a village revenue official wanted to get remissions for his village, he could after 1906 make a case to the collector on the basis of crop conditions, and to this extent he would have had an incentive, if he had the interest, to adjust annawari downwards. But he would have exposed himself if he had not obtained the collusion of large numbers of his counterparts in contiguous villages since climatic conditions could not vary drastically from village to village; and he could not have understated the crop to a substantial degree since it was there for all to see including the collector who had himself to make local enquiries before granting remissions. Heston has failed to carry out the simplest tests of the bias he postulates: for instance, counting whether triennial successions of crops below 8 annas were more common before than after 1906, or finding out the annual remissions from Bombay revenue budgets. A supposition falls considerably short of a demonstration.

Annawari and Rainfall

Heston's conclusions about the relationship between the condition factor and the rainfall (1973:324–5) just do not hold statistical water. He says that the condition factor and rainfall were positively related in 52 out of 74 correlations, but that most of them were statistically non-significant. He blames this on there being only six observations in each correlation. In fact he had an average of 90 observations for each crop for the 15 districts he selected, and by pooling districts he could have got ample degrees of freedom. Heston's results could be non-significant owing to few degrees of freedom, although he has failed to use the degrees of freedom available to him; on the other hand, all their features can be due to misspecification, of which there is no doubt.

A priori, a bivariate relationship between the condition factor and total rainfall, *if there is any*, should fulfil the following conditions:

(*a*) The condition factor should increase with rainfall up to a certain point, that is, the slope of the regression should be positive.

(*b*) The condition factor should fall to zero at some positive level of rainfall: in other words, there must be some level of rainfall—may be three inches, maybe ten inches—which is just too low to raise any crop. The intercept of rainfall must be negative.

(*c*) There must be some level of rainfall above which the condition factor must rise at a slower rate, and a higher level above which it should fall. The slope must decline beyond a certain point and become negative at some point. And at some peak level of rainfall, the crop must be washed away and the condition factor fall to zero.

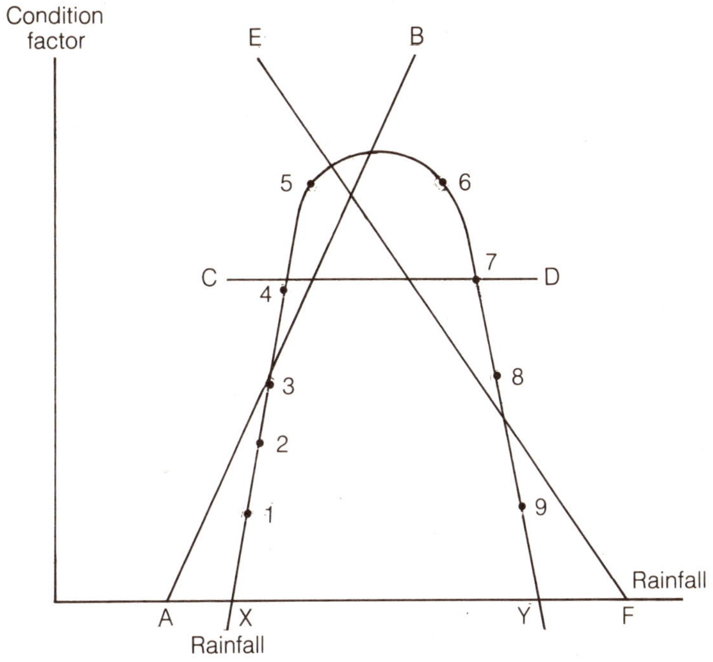

Figure 1. Relationship between rainfall and condition factor.

Fig.1 depicts a relationship XY which satisfies conditions (*a*)–(*c*), and points 1, 2 . . . 9 representing observations confirming to the relationship. Suppose now that we fitted regressions to 6 of the 9 observations as done by Heston. From observations 1–6 we would get a regression AB with a positive slope and a negative intercept; from points 3–8, a regression CD with zero slope and from 4–9, a regression EF with a negative slope. And by mixing observations suitably we could generate regressions of virtually any slope and any degree of non-significance, *although the underlying non-linear fit is perfect.*

Note, further, that a misspecification of this kind could generate all the peculiarities discovered by Heston. For instance, if observations fit a regression AB with a negative intercept, they will show greater than proportional changes in the condition factor than in rainfall. Heston (1973:324) finds that between 1898–1906 and 1907–16 rainfall went up slightly and the condition factor rose considerably. This is precisely what is to be expected; it is no evidence of a change from a '16 to 12 anna Rupee.' Again, for all the linear regressions, whether AB, CD or EF, the extreme observations will always give negative residuals; residuals for 1886–97 and 1937–46, which experienced relatively high levels of rainfall, would therefore be expected to give a predominance of negative residuals. Here again, the conclusions Heston wishes to draw on the shortcomings of condition factors in the two periods crumble.

Conclusions

Heston did well to show that crop-cutting yields around the mid-century in Bombay Presidency were much below the revenue yields of early twentieth century. But he was hasty in concluding that revenue yields were therefore unreliable and biased: they were both, but not uniformly so throughout. They were too high at the outset from the 1870s till 1897; they were also too high by the 1940s. But they were based on crop-cutting experiments and came reasonably close to actual yields in 1897–1909. Revenue yields in that period for four major foodgrains were appreciably above crop-cutting yields in 1950–8; for those crops yields declined much more over the half century than revenue yields would have suggested. To that extent Blyn's conclusions, based as they were on revenue yields only, need correction: the fall in yields he showed for the lower Gangetic plain extended to western India as well.

References

Blyn, George (1966): *Agricultural Trends in India, 1891–1947: Output, Availability, and Productivity*, Philadelphia, University of Pennsylvania Press.

Bombay (1922): Department of Agriculture. *The Crops of Bombay Presidency: Their Geography and Statistics.* Bulletin no. 109 of 1921 by P. C. Patil, Bombay.

Bombay (1932): Department of Agriculture, *Preliminary Studies of Important Crops in the Bombay Deccan in the Postwar Period.* Bulletin no. 168 by P. C. Patil, Bombay.

Bombay (1925): Director of Agriculture. *Statistical Atlas of the Bombay Presidency*, 3rd ed. Bombay.

Dodwell, H. H. (ed.) (1932): *The Cambridge History of India, vol. VI: The Indian Empire 1858–1918.* Cambridge.

Great Britain (1880–85): Report of the Indian Famine Commission, London.

Heston, Alan W. (1973): 'Official Yields Per Acre in India, 1886–1947: Some Questions of Interpretation', *Indian Economic and Social History Review* X(4), pp. 303–32.

India (1883): Papers connected with the Bombay Revenue and Settlement System, Calcutta.

India (1886): Revenue and Agriculture Department. *Statistical Atlas of India prepared for the Colonial and Indian Exhibition 1886*, Calcutta.

India (1892): *Return of the Yield per Acre of the Principal Crops cultivated in India*, Simla.

India (1915): Agriculture Department, *Agriculture in India* by J. MacKenna, Calcutta.

India (1956): Directorate of Economics and Statistics. *Estimates of Area and Production of Principal Crops in India: Summary Tables 1954–5*, Delhi.

India (1957): Directorate of Economics and Statistics. *Abstract of Agricultural Statistics*, India 1957, Delhi.

Chapter 4

A Further Critique of Historical Yields per Acre in India*

[1978]

ALAN W. HESTON

I welcome Ashok Desai's interest in my article (Heston, 1973) on yields per acre in Bombay during the 1880–1947 period. In Part I of this paper I will reply to what I believe is Desai's principal criticism of my paper, namely his claim that, contrary to my paper, actual declines in yield per acre in Bombay were greater than those given by Blyn (1966). In Part I, I reject Desai's claim and extend my argument to other parts of India. In Part II, I take up other issues raised by Desai and present some additional analysis of Bombay data that further throws into question the quality of historical yields. The concluding section restates my position and suggests alternative ways of using official data on historical yields.

I

Prior to the systematic use of scientific crop-cutting estimates in the period 1944–52 (and for some crops even later), estimated crop yields were in most areas based on the formula:

Estimated yield per acre = (standard yield per acre) times (a condition factor), reflecting whether the season was good or bad.

Combined with acreage this yield allows estimates of output. This yield, which is termed 'revenue yield', was usually estimated for principal crops in districts, although standard yields were also given for the provinces. The condition factor for a district was built up from village and taluka reports on the season. This method of yield estimation covered some native states, and British India, though areas of less direct administration, like zamindari areas, had

* For their helpful comments, I would like to thank but not implicate Carl Pray and Raj Saah.

less local reporting. After 1920, the yield per acre was estimated directly in Punjab and the Central Provinces, and their story is different.

The point of my article was to explore Blyn's finding that yields per acre of foodgrains declined in India between 1892 and 1947. Arguing from data for the Bombay Presidency, I showed: (1) That standard yields per acre tended to be unchanged from 1897 to 1947. (2) Therefore, the decline in estimated revenue yields per acre of individual foodgrains must be due to an overall decline in the condition factor which, I argued, was implausible.

Let me turn to Desai's main criticism of my paper.

> Heston did well to show that crop-cutting yields around the mid-century in Bombay Presidency were much below the revenue yields of early twentieth century. But he was hasty in concluding that revenue yields were therefore unreliable and biased: they were both, but not uniformly throughout. They were too high at the outset from the 1870s till 1897; they were also too high by the 1940s. But they were based on crop-cutting experiments and came reasonably close to actual yields in 1897–1909. Revenue yields in that period for four major foodgrains were appreciably above crop-cutting yields in 1950–58; for those crops yields declined much more over the half century than revenue yields would have suggested. To that extent Blyn's conclusions, based as they were on revenue yields only, need correction; the fall in yields he showed for the lower Gangetic Plain extended to western India as well.

His first sentence does not reflect my emphasis; I did show that standard yields in 1897 were above crop-cutting yields of the 1950s in all 59 cases; as to revenue yields, sometimes they were above (28 of the 59 cases) and sometimes below crop-cutting yields [Heston, 1973, Table 2, Columns (1) and (4)], but this was not an important part of my discussion. Desai's second sentence is erroneous; I did not conclude that revenue yields were incorrect because they differed from crop-cutting yields (nor for that matter do I think my conclusions were hasty). Rather I concluded that revenue yields were incorrect because they declined due to a secular decline in the condition factor, for which there seems no justification in reality.

It is difficult to know what Desai means in the next two sentences. First, revenue yields were not based on crop-cutting experiments in Bombay or most other areas of India before 1920, and then mainly in Punjab till after 1944. Standard yields were based on casual non-random crop-cutting experiments, while revenue yields were derived from standard yields. But my main problem with Desai is sentence four above. How does Desai know about actual yields in the period 1897–1909, so that he can say anything about whether they were close to revenue yields? The answer is, he does not. The only conceivable data to be brought to bear on actual yields in the 1897–1909 period would be the non-random crop-cutting experiments from 1872–1909.

Bombay put together standard yields in 1884 which were revised in 1891 and 1897, and very little thereafter. The 1884 standard yields were based on crop tests or experiments between 1872–3 and 1882–3 (*Annewari Report*, p. 39), and were more ambitious, but not therefore more accurate than later estimates.

The standard yield estimates of 1897 in Bombay were an improvement over 1891; Mollison took account of some additional tests between 1890 and 1896, and produced some important downward modifications of the 1884 and 1891 yields which were extraordinarily high.

In my article I had commented negatively on these 1897 yields quoting P. C. Patil (1922, p. 51) who said, 'These yields have been fixed without elaborate and careful tests and the same handed down with slight modification made at revisions conducted every 5 years.' Desai (p. 2) passed off this criticism saying that Patil goes on to use the revenue yields derived from these estimates, which comment to me seems irrelevant. The national income statistician does not criticize the basis of his estimates, but goes on to use his estimates as the best he has at that time; pushing this point further, national income statisticians revise their estimates if they get new information on their subject. The analogy with yields is that the coexistence of crop-cutting yields and revenue yields *circa* 1947 provides a basis for comparison, and I would say the principal basis we now have, for evaluating historical yield figures; and such comparisons suggest revisions are called for in our use of revenue yields.

Then Desai (p. 8) says, 'In 1897 the Government of Bombay was satisfied with its standard yields in the sense that the revenue yields they were used to derive gave a reasonable approximation to actual yields as established by crop-cutting experiments.' Desai offers no evidence of this satisfaction and it is also quite unclear what he means. The crop-cutting experiments were used to estimate standard yields, and it was not true that estimated revenue yields (standard yields times the condition factor) in Bombay were checked against crop-cutting experiments. The *Season and Crop Reports* of Bombay did not see fit to publish their production estimates until 1916, and provincial estimates were forced upon the provinces and framed in part by the compilers of *Agricultural Statistics*. There is no evidence in the Bombay records of this period that experimental yields were ever compared to estimated revenue yields, so it is not clear what Desai means. If he means to imply that standard yields were close to actual yields in the 1897–1909 period, then this is clearly inconsistent with other points in his paper.[1]

The quotation which Desai uses to discuss the 1897 yields is *Agricultural Statistics*, which is quite an inappropriate source for an accurate appraisal of Bombay procedures. A summary of the history of these tests including quotes from Keatinge, who was Director of Agriculture in Bombay during the period when crop cutting was abandoned, is given in a note of F. G. H. Anderson, ICS Settlement Commissioner and Director of Land Records in Bombay in the 1920s (Note to Resolution of Revenue Department, no. 7773–B, 23 June, 1927, reproduced in *Annewari Report*, pp. 219–28) which summarizes the history of Bombay crop experiments.

The next stage was in 1872. The Government of India then sanctioned Rs 2,000 for crop experiments pointing out that their value depended altogether on the selection of the land. They must be carefully conducted; must be numerous; must extend over every description of soil and season, and include every mode of culture (R 3859-72). The Bombay Government orders then followed that fields should be selected of good and middling quality, (i.e., excluding the lower grades) with reference to the classification, thus at once negativing the directions of the Government of India which applied to every descrip-

[1] If, as Desai seems to say, crop-cutting experiments gave correct standard yields in 1897, then for revenue yields to equal actual yields it would require that the average condition factor be 100 in this period. But (p. 6) Desai has previously said that he has given a clear proof of why 'the average of the condition factors everywhere is much below 100 per cent'. But Desai must understand that you cannot have condition factors averaging 80 per cent, and standard yields equal to actual yields, and get a revenue yield estimated as equal to the actual yield, so I am unsure of what he believes is the relation of revenue yields and standard yield.

tion of soil. . . . After 37 years, it was finally decided in R 8719–09 to discontinue these experiments. It was reported that 'the experimenters were inexpert. Everything depended on the anna valuation of the soil, which they had not paid attention to. Their results could not be used to test the expert formula of the Agricultural Department. . . .' Mr Keatinge reported that the tables of standard outturn which his Department had been using were based not upon experiments or upon records of the farms, but were mere guesses, 'revised upon suggestions' of Mr Mollison, the Deputy Director. He then very rightly observed 'it is probable that a careful series of experiments conducted by this department and checked against the figures of the control plots which we have in our farms would give trustworthy data for the revision of the outturn figures' (3rd July 1909). Thereupon Government ordered the crop experiments to stop . . . (pp. 226–8).

In fact, Anderson goes on to complain that Keatinge's suggestion was not followed, and that Bombay still needs to find out what are correct yields.

So during the period 1897–1909 when Desai equates revenue yields with true yields on the basis of crop experiments, the Agricultural Department in Bombay was giving up these experiments as inadequate. And with very good reason as it is instructive to examine just how inadequate these crop experiments were. My illustration below is from crop-cutting tests during the period 1883–4 to 1891–2, when materials were available to me, but there is every reason to believe the experiments were no better or more frequent before or after this series.

For jowar, the most important cereal, 47 tests in 13 districts were reported, during 1883–4 to 1889–90 in Bombay, an average per district of about one-half a test per year, with important districts like Ahmednagar and Bijapur reporting only one test over these years. There were 16 tests in 11 districts for bajra, 63 tests in 11 districts for rice, 101 tests in 14 districts for wheat, and 30 tests in 11 districts for gram.[2] Even within one year, let alone seven years, so few tests would produce very large sampling errors, even if the fields were randomly chosen. To illustrate, Panse reports that to obtain a standard error of estimate of 3 per cent for the yield of wheat in Lyallpur district, which has less variable yields than Bombay, it would be necessary to sample two fields per village in 78 villages, or 156 tests in a single season (Panse, 1946, Table XII,

[2] Letter from D. L. Cappel (no. 1237 of 1892), Director, Land Records and Agriculture, Bombay, reproduced in *Annewari Report*, pp. 268–81.

p. 37). In Hoshangabad district, a more precarious climate like the Deccan and Gujarat, the required number of tests or cuttings would be 304 to achieve the same level of reliability for a single crop in a single year. Clearly the Bombay Presidency methods for estimating standard yields in the 1880s and 1890s were completely inadequate compared to scientific requirements. Yet these are the kind of tests which were used to frame the standard yields which were used in output estimation for almost 60 years.

But one might ask, can't a knowledgeable observer come close to estimating true yields? In his 1943–4 survey cited above. Panse asked owners of fields, their neighbours, agricultural officers, and his own crop-cutting teams to sight estimate yields on chosen fields before harvest; their estimates were then compared with the actual harvest from the fields. When the field estimates were averaged over tehsils it was found in Lyllapur that the owner generally underestimated yields by 5 to 21 per cent across tehsils, while other cultivators underestimated by 15 to 39 per cent. In Hosangabad the errors were smaller and were both plus and minus but correlations of sight estimates with actual estimates were only about 0.5. The agricultural staff erred from 3 to 14 per cent between tehsils in Lyllapur, while the range was 4 to 86 per cent within Hosangabad (Panse, 1946, Tables XIII and XIV, p. 38). Thus trained staff, who knew the rough magnitude of true yields, made large errors in eye or sight estimates, the bastis of most estimates in India before 1947. If, in addition, such trained agricultural officers did not have a random sample of fields and too few fields, their errors would be compounded. Choice of fields is probably the largest source of error and one of the indicators of the lack of precision of investigators in the 1880s is that despite the fact that Bombay settlements were famous for allowing for the quality characteristics of the soil, reports of crop tests in Bombay never took note of the soil classification of the fields on which the crop tests were made. In short, if there were well-trained staff in Bombay in the 1880s and 1890s, their estimates were too few and subject to large errors, invalidating their efforts; and in fact the staff was not well trained until the twentieth century when crop cutting had been discontinued in Bombay.

This account of experiments in Bombay in comparison with modern crop-cutting experiments indicates why I have little faith that revenue yields around the turn of the century were close to actual yields as Desai contends. My conclusion was that we have no real historical basis to ascertain for most crops what actual yields were in Bombay (or in many other provinces) before 1944, and Desai has provided no evidence to dissuade me from this view. The remainder of Desai's conclusion rests on his *unsupported* assumption that revenue yields represented true yields in Bombay at the turn of the century; therefore I must reject his principal criticism of my discussion of yield changes in Bombay.

This discussion of Bombay is relevant to the rest of India, and I want to take this opportunity to extend my argument. First, let me deal with aggregate data. Table 1 presents in columns (1), (2) and (3) the standard yield in 1946–7, the average revenue yield for the period 1936–7 to 1946–7, and the average crop-cutting yield during 1949–50 to 1955–6 of principal crops in India where a quarter or more of the area was subject to random crop-cutting experiments in 1951–2. (The crop-cutting area is given in columns 7 and 8.) For ragi, gram and jute, where crop cutting only became important by 1955–6, the averages were computed from 1944–5 to 1952–3 for revenue yields, and from 1952–3 to 1957–8 for the crop-cutting yields.[3] Since there is necessarily some years of overlap between revenue yields and crop-cutting yields (columns 2 and 3) because crop cutting was introduced gradually, the ratios of revenue yields to crop-cutting yields (column 6) probably understate differences between the two. For all of India from Table 1, the crop-cutting yields range from 7 per cent under revenue yields (jute) to 25 per cent above revenue yields (maize) with crop-cutting yields most frequently below revenue yields. A mixed pattern was observable in the data for districts of Bombay during the period when both revenue yields and crop-cutting yields were simultaneously available, namely 1946–61, though in fact crop-cutting yields were more often above revenue yields than below. A further analysis of these Bombay data is given in Part II. R. C. Desai in his comparison of crop-cutting and revenue estimates for rice, wheat, and jute in Bengal, Bihar, Orissa, Punjab, U.P., Bombay, Madras, C. P., Sind and N.W.F.P., finds

[3] Several important crops are excluded from Table 1 because crop-cutting began in the late 1950s. This includes sugarcane, sesamum, linseed and tobacco, for which column (4) is respectively 0.86, 0.71, 0.83 and 0.79. Few standard yields or revenue estimates were available for groundnuts and other oilseeds, potatoes, bananas, and many other crops for which scientific estimates have been developed in the late 1950s and in the 1960s.

Table 1. All India Yields for Selected Crops about 1947

Crop	Yield per Acre			Ratio to Standard Yield of		Ratio of RY to CCY	Per cent of Area for which yield estimated by Random Crop-cutting	
	Standard Yield 1946–7	Revenue 1936–7 to 1946–7	Revenue 1949–50 to 1955–6	Revenue Yield (2)/(1)	Crop-Cutting Yield (3)/(1)	(2)/(3)	1951–2	1955–6
	(1)	(2)	(3)	(4)	(5)	(6)	(7)	(8)
Rice	902	740	703	.82	.78	1.05	64	83
Wheat	828	595	630	.72	.76	.94	68	96
Jowar	580	392	369	.68	.64	1.06	47	100
Bajra	437	324	270	.74	.62	1.20	37	100
Maize	946	665	531	.70	.56	1.25	30	57
Barley	877	733	721	.84	.82	1.03	82	92
Ragi[1]	937	538	660	.57	.70	.82	0	78
Gram[1]	722	474	481	.66	.73	.90	0	96
Jute[1]	1,295	976	960	.75	.74	1.02	0	56

SOURCES: Column (1) from *Abstract of Agricultural Statistics, India, 1950*, Ministry of Food and Agriculture (Delhi, 1952); Column (2) from Blyn (1966); Column (3) from *Area, Production and Yield per Acre of Forecast Crops, 1949–50 to 1959–60*, Directorate of Economics and Statistics, Ministry of Food and Agriculture (Delhi, 1961); Columns (7) and (8) from *National Income Statistics, Proposals for a Revised Series*, (Delhi, 1961), p. 18.

[1] For these crops for which random crop-cutting was not used until after 1951, the yield in Column (2) was calculated from 1944–5 to 1952–3, and Column (3) from 1952–3 to 1957–8.

that between 1943 and 1946–7, provincial estimates range from 25 per cent under-estimation of rice in Orissa by revenue methods to a 29 per cent overestimation of wheat in U.P. R. C. Desai concludes there is no overall direction of difference between crop cutting and revenue yields.[4] This is also the conclusion of Sukhatme and Panse as well as K. Mukerji.[5]

This discussion has concentrated on the differences between crop-cutting and revenue yields around 1947. What can be inferred about historical trends in yields from the evidence at Independence? First, there is no general relation that can be expected between random crop-cutting yields (CCY) and what we observe historically, namely the standard yield (SY) and the revenue yield (RY), or the condition factor (CF = RY/SY). Can we infer that the relation for a particular crop in a province will hold historically? For example, the average CCY for wheat in U.P. was 628 pounds per acre during the three years 1943–4 to 1945–6, when the SY was 950 pounds, or CCY/SY = .66.[6] Can we assume that the CCY was always .66 of the SY for wheat in U.P. in earlier periods? I would argue that this is not a fruitful assumption, because the standard yield often changed in large discrete jumps related not to changes in underlying factors influencing trends in CCYs, but adjusting to earlier errors in the initial estimates of SYs. A further problem is that for annual data one would need to take account of seasonal fluctuations and these are not allowed for by a simple assumption linking CCYs to SYs.

The next question is whether we can assume that the ratio of CCY/RY was constant historically for different crops in the different regions. For example, the CCY for winter rice in Orissa in the two seasons 1944–5 and 1945–6 was 765 pounds per acre while the RY was 560 pounds, the ratio CCY/RY being 1.37. If the RY for winter rice in Orissa were 650 pounds per acre in 1900, could we

[4] R. C. Desai, *Standard of Living in India and Pakistan 1931–2 to 1940–1*, Popular, Bombay, 1953, pp. 14–18.

[5] P. V. Sukhatme and V. G. Panse, 'Crop Surveys in India', *Indian Journal of Agricultural Statistics,* vol. III, no. 2, 1951, pp. 98–168. K. Mukerji, *Levels of Economic Activity and Public Expenditure in India*, Asia, Bombay, 1965, p. 18. Mukerji notes that of 36 cases permitting comparisons of crop-cutting and revenue yields, in 19 crop-cutting exceeds revenue yields and the opposite is true in 17 of the cases.

[6] The crop-cutting yields in these illustrations are from R. C. Desai, p. 15, while the SYs are from *Average Yields of the Principal Crops of India, 1951–2.*

safely estimate the CCY in 1900 as 890 pounds (1.37 × 650)? Since in most cases RYs declined, can we therefore infer that CCYs declined, even if we discard the absolute levels of RYs?

It was the contention of my original article that on the evidence for Bombay, neither trends nor levels in RYs could be accepted for major food crops, and I am now convinced that this is true for much of the rest of India. For Bombay, most of SYs were constant between 1897 and 1947, so declines in RYs came about due to a decline in the average CF; since there was no natural justification for this decline in the CF, it was my contention that it should not be accepted. Fluctuations in the CF from year to year might be useful, but the notion that there would be a trend in the CF is not plausible, on the basis of what we know about climatic trends in Bombay.

What of other provinces? In other provinces the decline in RY, where it occurred, was due to changes in the SY as well as the CF. Blyn was most concerned with this problem, especially for rice in Bengal, which crop we may take as an illustration. Using two ten-year periods, one the 1896–7 to 1905–6 period, which Desai chose, and the last ten years available from Blyn, 1937–8 to 1946–7, the RY for rice for all of British India goes from 890 pounds per acre to 764 pounds, a decline of 16 per cent on the latter base. For Bengal, the SY of the most important rice crop, Aman or winter rice declined from 1234 pounds per acre in 1937–8 to 1024 in 1946–7, while for the Aus rice crop the SY increases from 800 to 865 pounds per acre over the period (CCYs were about 720 pounds for winter rice during 1943–4 to 1944–5, and 655 pounds during 1944–5 to 1946–7, from R. C. Desai, p. 15). The decline in the RY in Bengal was much larger than for British India during 1916–47, declining from 969 to 751 pounds per acre, or 29 per cent, of which 17 per cent can be allocated to the decline in the SY and 12 per cent to the decline in CF. Blyn (p. 185) compared rainfall and yield changes by decade and found their sign matched barely half the time in comparisons for Bengal and U.P., so the decline in the CF is not supported by Blyn's analysis of rainfall.[7]

[7] This is what led Blyn to produce a modified series for Bengal (p. 346) which assumed a constant level of rice yield at the 1912–13 level, which is approximately the crop-cutting level in 1947. Also for all the provinces discussed, except Madras, Blyn (p. 42) has estimated yields of rice from trends in other crops, so these comparisons are limited. See also M. M. Islam (1973).

As for the decline in the SY, I would argue that this was a continuing downward adjustment from the unusually high levels initially chosen. Consider first that the ratio of the CCY to SY for Bengal was about 70 per cent at Independence; even after there had been a decline in the SY from 1234 to 1024 pounds per acre during the decades preceding 1947. What this means is that there was lots of room for downward adjustment of standard yields, while they still remain above average CCYs, without these changes in the SY necessarily reflecting anything about the trend in actual historical yields.[8]

For Madras, trends in revenue yields are constant, 949 versus 964 pounds per acre in 1897–1906 and 1938–47, as was the SY, 1072 in 1906 and 1133 in 1944. If Stuart's method was in force in Madras, there could be no trend in the CF, which is consistent with the fact that no change in the RY occurred. The only other province with a decline in the yield of rice was U.P., where revenue yields declined from 695 to 581 pounds per acre or 20 per cent, the CCY being about 530 pounds in 1944–5. The SY of rice in U.P. declined from 850 to 800 pounds between 1906 and 1947, a decline of 6 per cent, so 60 per cent of the decline in yield of rice in U.P. would be due to a decline in the CF, for which there is no support in the rainfall statistics.

Without going into the details of each province, the pattern for wheat is similar, except in Punjab, where there were yield increases reported of 15 per cent from 686 to 790 pounds per acre. After 1920, Punjab estimated wheat yields directly, which since new seeds were introduced accounts for the rise in yields.[9] It is interest-

[8] The most common usage of SY in India, which Desai accepts, is that SY should be larger than actual yields, since they reflect something like a median yield where the seasonal yield distribution is skewed towards low yields. In the Annewari Committee (1966, pp. 7–8 and 62–3) for Maharashtra, this was the accepted view and the SY for rice, for example, was generally above the CCY by at least 15 per cent, on average for the eight districts where a comparison was possible the ratio of CCY/SY was .76.

[9] Carl Pray has written on the rise in yields due to improved strains of wheat, cotton and sugarcane in various parts of India. For Punjab, he estimates the increase in yields at about 17 per cent for improved wheat over local wheat in the inter-war period. Acreage under improved varieties of wheat rose from 1 per cent in 1913–14 – 1917–18 to 75 per cent in the period 1942–3 to 1943–4, so that one would have expected SY in Punjab to rise by 10 or 12 per cent over this period, which it did not. Carl Pray, 'The Productivity of Agricultural Research in Punjab 1905–47', paper presented to the University of Pennsylvania Economic History Workshop, Fall 1977, mimeographed, pp. 10 and 16.

ing that between 1906 and 1947, the SY of wheat in Punjab rose only 2.5 per cent, from 816 to 837 pounds per acre. (The crop CCY was about 866 pounds at Independence). If Punjab were appropriately adjusting the standard yield to apparent increases in actual yields it would have risen much more than it did, since SYs were supposedly 15 to 50 per cent above actual yields. The experience in Punjab suggests one of two things; first, Punjab was moving to a concept of the standard yield actually being the average of directly estimated yields suggesting that there were substantial differences in the provinces in this respect; and, second, that one cannot really assume that changes in SY in any of the provinces necessarily reflect any underlying trends in average actual yields.

Sugarcane is another illustration of the dubious relation of adjustments in SYs to underlying production conditions. In Bombay the provincial SY was 6,954 pounds of gur per acre from 1900 to 1947. Experimental yields for a local variety, Pundia, which was more than 90 per cent of sugarcane acreage in 1931–2 was 10,261 pounds per acre. Between 1931–2 and 1936–7, about half the sugarcane acreage came under improved varieties in Bombay, mostly P.O.J. 2,878, where the yield was 21 per cent higher, but this change was not reflected in SYs (*Report on the Marketing of Sugar*, 1943, p. 22). In Bengal, the changes in SYs were in the appropriate direction, rising about 80 per cent between 1900 and 1947, which coincided with the introduction of Coimbatore varieties of cane; and in Bengal the revised SY of 4,444 pounds of gur per acre was not too far off yields for 1934–5 to 1936 estimated from a Cost of Cultivation Enquiry which gave 3,540 pounds per acre (Report, p. 22). But Bengal was the exception and the *Report on the Marketing of Sugar* (p. 20) summarizes the situation as follows:

> It will be observed from the above table that in certain provinces such as the Punjab and Madras, although the standard yields are being revised regularly every quinquennium, they have remained practically unchanged during the last 20 to 25 years, a period in which the cane yields are understood to have appreciably improved. In the Punjab, for example, during the last 15 years approximately 60 per cent of the total cane area has been put under improved varieties, which are estimated to yield roughly 20 to 50 per cent more than desi, but the standard yields fixed in 1936–7 in this province are indeed lower than those laid down in 1921–2.
>
> The fact is that even in those tracts where standard yield are being revised every quinquennium the position leaves much to be desired. . . .

The production in most of the tracts is calculated on the basis of a common standard without any regard to the proportion of the acreage under improved or desi varieties or plant and ratoon, or under wet and dry crops.

Sugarcane is an example of a crop where the underlying yield conditions were known to be improving in most provinces of India in the 1930s, but the adjustments, or lack thereof, in the SYs in the majority of the provinces, only raise more questions about the reliability of levels and changes in SYs.

Although I have also casually looked at SYs, CCYs and RYs for other crops in the provinces, time has not permitted the thorough analysis this topic deserves if we are to correctly describe regional agricultural growth in India. Let me conclude this section by repeating my position that long-term trends in the CF which produce declines in RYs occur in a number of provinces in India in the 50 years before Independence. No climatological support for these trends has been offered by anyone so far.[10] Further, another component of the declines in RY in some provinces is a decline in SYs for certain crops, which often seem to be in the correct direction, namely downward. But since initial SYs were very high in most provinces for most crops, downward adjustments were necessary, regardless of whether actual yields per acre were suffering a declining trend. Since the ratio CCY/SY around 1947 varies widely between provinces for the same crop, and between crops within a province, it seems to me doubtful if most SY adjustments reflected any underlying trends in yields. In Punjab where RYs were reported directly in maunds RYs appear to be stable or rising, which is consistent with my scepticism, in part derived from Blyn, about yield trends in other provinces estimated via CFs and SYs.

II

(A) Turning to Desai's other points in order, he says in (*a*) (p. 1) that averaging over a few years does not eliminate seasonal clustering, with which I agree. But 10 or 15 years, which is the period I

[10] Nor can, perhaps, such evidence be offered. As I understand from very recent studies on this question, there appear at the regional level to be no evidence of trends that are significant for agriculture, nor even strong evidence for clustering of good or bad years for longer periods than two years. *Report of the National Commission on Agriculture*, vol. IV, *Climate and Agriculture*, Ministry of Agriculture and Irrigation, Delhi, 1976.

use, is an average used on the subcontinent (in fact 5 years was thought long enough for standard yields), and Desai offers no evidence to suggest that 10 or 15 years is not long enough to average over clusters of good and bad years. He chides me for using the period 1906–20. My reasons were one, Patil published data, already averaged for this period, that are not available in earlier Season and Crop Reports for Bombay which only gave condition factors by district. Second, while those years included one apparently very good year (1915–16) they are quite enough to average out good and bad years. Desai says, and again I repeat with no basis whatsoever, that revenue yields should 'have approximated closely the actual yields — 1897–1909', and so he used an earlier period than 1906–20. I have no objection to an earlier period, but there is nothing particularly accurate about 1897–1907.

Further, for the purposes of Desai's Table, 1897–1907 is a rather poor period to use since for only wheat, cotton, and groundnuts Blyn does have direct yields; for the remaining five crops the yield estimates have been approximated by Blyn from those of other crops (Blyn, p. 42).

(B) In his point (*b*) Desai chides me for not citing references on the compilation of agricultural statistics, which is odd, since his list is extremely scanty, and it is not clear from his comments that he has consulted the references in my article. For example, Desai (p. 7) goes through a tortured discussion about whether the standard crop in Bombay was a 16 annas initially and then became 12 annas in 1897–8. Though Blyn was not my source, Blyn (p. 48) says, 'Provincial normals were 12 annas — Madras, Bombay, Bengal, Assam; 16 annas — United Provinces, Punjab, North West Frontier Province: Bihar and Orissa — 12 districts at 12 annas, 7 at 13 annas, and 2 at 14 annas.'[11] Now how did the various provinces end up

[11] These figures are also given in Thomas and Sastry (1939, p. 22) where they also give Central Provinces and Berar as a normal of 13 annas and 4 pies, as does Panse (1946, p. 7). The figure for Madras given above of 12 annas is not consistent with the 13.3 anna figure I cite in my fn. 15, p. 319, and with the limited materials now available to me, I cannot clear up this difference. However, the comments of V. N. Visvanatha Rao, Statistical Assistant to the Director of Agriculture, Madras (in *Proceedings of the Board of Agriculture in India, 1924*, Appendix V. pp. 120–1) suggests an answer. Rao (p. 120) says, 'Mr Stuart's formula referred to in paragraph 5 of the Committee's report at page 30 of 1919 Proceedings is used only for the calculation of total yields in the season and crop reports and not for forecasts.' Stuart's formula is that the normal number of annas of a crop for an area is the average number of anna

with different annas corresponding to a normal crop, when they all started out with 16 annas as the normal? The answer of course is that those provinces or districts not using 16 annas as normal in the 1930s must have changed them sometime along the way. And all I said was that Bombay changed from 16 to 12 annas, and Desai apparently from the top of his head, (p. 7) says, 'there is considerable doubt that any such change took place', and 'the fact is it did not for Bombay never introduced it' (12 anna normal crop). How can there be any doubt if Desai had even consulted the source he claims to defend, namely Blyn. The exact year of the change for Bombay is 1897–8, and is recorded in the *Season and Crop Report* of that year.

(C) Desai says no one ever heard of an 18 or 20 anna crop, and again he is wrong. In the season 1889–90, crops of 17 and 20 annas are reported for wheat and bajra in Ahmedabad District, and of 19 annas for rice in Poona (*Season and Crop Report*, 1889–90). Related to this question is Desai's statement in the same paragraph (p. 6) where he points out that the average of the condition factor tends to be below 100. There are two cases here. First, when the condition factor is estimated independently, as in the case of Bombay, this tends to be true. However, in Punjab, particularly, the yield came after 1920 to be estimated directly in maunds at the tehsil level and the condition factor was derived as a ratio of that yield to the normal yield, and in this second case the condition factor does not average under 100. For example, in *Season and Crop Report* for Punjab for the agricultural year ending 30 June 1946 (Lahore, 1947, pp. xxi–xxvi), Sialkot reports a condition factor of 125 for 1944–5 for rice, Ferozepore and Lahore 105 for wheat in 1945–6, several districts are above 100 in Bajra, including Karnal at 170 for irrigated Bajra in 1945–6.[12]

reported over a number of previous years (10 or more). Under Stuart's formula, the standard yield per acre should be the average of actual yields. My surmise is that when as in the text above 12 annas is given as the normal crop in Madras this is for the forecasts of a crop mentioned by Rao above; the normal annas for purposes of actually estimating yield and production in Madras at this time would be based on Stuart's formula. However, Stuart's formula would imply that the anna valuation for a normal crop would change over the years, and it is not clear from Rao as to whether this was the case. In any event, Stuart's formula is what accounts for Berar and C.P. ending up with 13 annas 4 pies as the annas corresponding to a normal crop in those areas.

[12] In the Central Provinces the condition factor for sugarcane averaged 105 from 1929–30 to 1938–9 (*Report on the Marketing of Sugar*, 1943, p. 18).

The problem of condition factors, that average under 100, is that they must be correctly calibrated with the standard yield of an area to produce an accurate estimate of yield per acre. Vernacular usage may be able to have a condition factor average 70 per cent of normal; but unless actual yield averages 70 per cent of the standard yield, the revenue method of estimation would not get you a correct estimate of actual yields.

As has been demonstrated for the district data for Bombay and for aggregate data in Table 1, there is no stable relation between standard yields and crop-cutting yields around independence nor presumably earlier. So unless the primary reporting agents give a condition factor related to the standard yield, it does not matter how much wisdom they bring to the task, the product of the two will not be the true yield. This is why the Board of Agriculture in 1919 recommended that crop-cutting experiments be used to directly estimate yields, a recommendation followed in Punjab, though the number of experiments was not adequate. This point is not recognized in Desai's discussion of the wisdom of the patwari's traditional anna valuation of the crop; the point is that the anna valuation may correctly reflect year to year fluctuations in yields, but this is not sufficient to make the revenue estimates of yield equal to true yields.

Desai (p. 9) remonstrates me at some length about suspensions and remissions, for reasons not clear. My quotation refers to the last decades of the nineteenth century, and Desai seems to be saying that is not true for the early part of the nineteenth century, and I agree with this. His discussion is interesting and points up to the problems faced by small farmers in bad years.[13] As Desai correctly concludes (p. 11). I did not demonstrate that the new rules which made suspensions and remissions of revenue depend on the anna valuations of the crop led to downward trends in the condition factor. I offered this as an hypothesis to explain secular declines in the CF in Bombay, and I would welcome alternative hypotheses.

(D) Desai's discussion of rainfall is interesting but not particularly illuminating for present purposes unless he claims to have

[13] The quotation that was printed without citation in my article (pp. 320–1) is by G. F. Keatinge, Director of Agriculture in Bombay, which is a letter to the Revenue Department of the Government of India, no. A-7090, 8 October 1910, reprinted in *Annewari Report*, p. 191.

observed clusters of rainfall for ten-year period. The point of his diagram is that the true relationship between the yield of a crop and total rainfall in a season will be an increasing function of rainfall up to some level of rainfall and then yield will fall off. Thus, extremes of low and high rainfall in a season are associated with lower yields. I have no quarrel with this view of the yield-rainfall relationship. However, my ten-year averages of rainfall will 'wash out' annual extremes of rainfall, so Desai's discussion is hardly relevant to the data I present. A period like 1937–46 has rainfall that averages a bit above the 60-year average, but it is hardly analagous to the high rainfall area of Desai's diagram. The variation in year to year rainfall, which is relevant for Desai's diagram, is much larger than between the six longer periods used in my paper.

Further, even if Desai's discussion were relevant to my data, his point is mainly a negative one, namely that my analysis does not show there is no relation between rainfall and yield. With this I agree. However, this objection to my rainfall analysis does not in any way validate a climatological explanation of the observed declines in revenue yields in Bombay. Nor is Desai's interpretation of my data correct within his own framework. He says (p. 12), 'Again, for all the linear regressions, whether AB, CD, or EF, the extreme observations will always give negative residuals; residuals for 1886–97 and 1937–46 which experienced relatively high levels of rainfall, would therefore be expected to give a predominance of negative residuals. Here again, the conclusions of Heston wishes to draw on the shortcomings of condition factors in the two periods crumble.'

The figures on rainfall for the six periods beginning 1886–97 and ending 1937–46 are given below with the sum of residuals for the 75 observations in each time period, which would be expected to be zero if a linear rainfall relation explained the condition factor. If the Desai diagram was appropriate to my data, then one would expect negative residuals to be associated with extreme observations on rainfall. This is only true for the second period when rainfall is relatively low; when rainfall is at its peak in the period 1927–36, the sum of residuals is positive, contrary to what Desai would expect. The residuals for 1937–46 are negative, but this period is not, as Desai says in the above quotation, anything like an extreme value.

Period	1887–96	1897–1906	1907–16	1917–26	1927–36	1937–46
Sum of Residuals	–25.98	–34.49	21.54	28.80	29.57	–19.44
Rainfall Index	100	82	93	88	104	95

However, this re-examination of the residuals does lead me to modify one of my propositions, namely that the decline in the average condition factor was a steady phenomenon from the inception of the rule regarding changes in suspensions and remissions in 1906. According to my proposition, the period 1927–36 should have been a period when revenue yields as estimated from rainfall data would be greater than actual revenue yields, leading to negative residuals. The opposite is the case and the proposition in my article about the reasons for the long-term decline in the condition factor fails to find support in this test.

(E) Desai says that revenue assessment did not depend on annual output statistics and I did not say that they did. Output statistics were desired for their own sake, particularly for export crops, so in the 1860s (not with the famines of the 1870s as Desai says, p. 5) concern for production of export crops like cotton, coffee, chinchona and wheat led to output estimates. Many of these provincial estimates of production of certain agricultural crops were used by Naoroji to frame his estimates of Indian national income in 1869. However, it is also true for Bombay, and Desai says the same for Madras (p. 4) that estimates of output were framed in order to judge revenue paying capacity of an area. Further, estimates of standard yields in 1884, in response to the 1880 Famine Commission, were a direct consequence of an interest in output. I would agree with Desai that what probably determined assessment was past assessment, and that output estimates, which were part of each Bombay settlement, were there in large part to rationalize the level of assessment.

I also agree with Desai that annewari was initially for forecasting the nature of the season for the forecast crops and it was used this way into the 1960s and probably to the present for a few crops. However, anna valuations of crops came to be used as part of the revenue system and as a basis for the condition factor from which yields were estimated. It is in this sense that revenue and output estimates became intertwined in the 1880s and remained that way in many provinces until 1947, and even thereafter.

(F) I would like to conclude my response to the individual points made by Desai by turning to a body of data used in my article that illustrates this intertwining of revenue and output estimates in detail for one province, Bombay. When Bombay introduced crop cutting, the results were the basis of estimates of agricultural output; however, from 1946 to 1961 for a period of 9 to 15 years there also were simultaneous and independent estimates of revenue yields reported along with crop-cutting yields for districts of the former Bombay Presidency. Production was estimated from crop-cutting experiments, but revenue yields, often quite different, continued to be published for revenue purposes, all in the same publication, *Season and Crop Report* (see, for example, Tables V-A and V-B, 1958–9, pp. 256–335).

Table 2 presents an analysis of these data in two forms. In columns (1) to (3) for each crop for each district are given R^2 and the coefficients from the simple linear regression, CCY = a + bRY + u, where u is the error term. These equations were estimated for 60 cases covering five major crops and a few minor crops in those districts where the crop was usually over 200,000 acres. The mean value of the CCY is given in column (4) and the ratios of RY/CCY in column (5). An examination of these regression equations shows that in 35 of the cases R^2 is less than .25, which is not a significant relation at the 5 per cent level. In many of the remaining cases the intercept term is large indicating that the RY is quite different in magnitude from the CCY.

Another way to examine these relations is by decomposing the difference between the CCY and the RY into that due to difference in mean values, that due to differences in variance of the two variables, and that due to low correlation between the two. For a district and a crop we define the average squared deviation $(AD)^2$ as,

$$(1)\quad (AD)^2 = 1/n \sum_{t=1}^{n} (CCY_t - RY_t)^2$$

which may be written,

$$(2)\quad (AD)^2 = (\overline{CCY} - \overline{RY})^2 + (S_{ccy} - S_{ry})^2 + 2\,(1-r)S_{ccy}S_{ry},$$

where the index t runs from 1 to n, the number of years for which data are available, $\overline{CCY}$ and $\overline{RY}$ are the mean values of CCY and RY over the period, S_{ccy} and S_{ry} are the standard deviations of CCY and RY, and r is the simple correlation coefficient between CCY and RY. Theil (1966, pp. 29–30) has suggested the following measures obtained by dividing both sides of (2) by $(AD)^2$, which give,

$$(3)\ 1 = \frac{(\overline{CCY}-\overline{RY})^2}{(AD)^2} + \frac{(S_{ccy}-S_{ry})^2}{(AD)^2} + \frac{2\,(1-r)\,S_{ccy}S_{ry}}{(AD)^2} = U_m + U_s + U_c$$

Theil has termed U_m the bias proportion because it gives the difference due to average values of CCY and RY being different, U_s the variance proportion, and U_c, the covariance proportion. S_{ccy} $\overline{CCY}$, U_m, U_s and U_c are given in columns (6), (7), (8) and (9) of Table 2. The bias proportion, U_m, is important in accounting for differences between CCY and RY which is another way of pointing out the limitations of the latter. The bias proportion cannot be large if $\overline{CCY}$ and $\overline{RY}$ are close together as for rice in Nasik district. If the bias proportion is very large, it can occur when there is little correlation between RY and CCY, and the variance of CCY and RY are similar as is the case of kharif jowar for Belgaum. Districts with a large bias proportion, over .5, and a low R^2, under .25, make up 47 of the 60 cases in Table 2.

Cotton is the one crop for which some independent checks on output were available through the cotton trade for Bombay, and it is interesting to contrast the U_m of cotton with other crops, since it is generally lower. If cotton were eliminated from the comparison above, we find that 44 of 52, or 85 per cent of possible comparisons in Table 2 have values of U_m over .5, and/or R^2 less than .25. The general conclusion I draw from Table 2 is that revenue yields neither approximated the level or amplitude of fluctuation (the variance of CCYs is usually higher than of RYs, with some notable exceptions), or even the direction of fluctuation of crop-cutting yields for Bombay. More work could be done of this type for other areas of India to see whether this very negative appraisal of RYs for Bombay has the generality that I believe it does.

An examination of either Table 1 or Table 2 reveals large differences that existed between RYs and CCYs when the latter were introduced. Since there appears to be no systematic bias, with CCYs both above and below RYs for the same crop in different regions and provinces, researchers like R. C. Desai and K. Mukherji

Table 2. Results of Regression and Decomposition analysis for Bombay Districts

	Co-re-lation F^2	Regression Parameters Intercept 'a'	Slope 'b'	Mean CCY	Ratio RY to CCY	Cofficient of varia-tion $s/\overline{C}$	Bias, U^m	Variance, Proportions U^s	Covari-ance U^c
	(1)	(2)	(3)	(4)	(5)	(6)	(7)	(8)	(9)
Rice									
Ahmedabad	.3[illegible]	–509	1.22	586	1.53	.28	.64	.13	.13
Kaira	.82	–16	.82	576	1.25	.45	.67	.03	.30
Panch Mahals	.49	48	.56	402	1.58	.63	.66	.05	.29
Surat	.61	–130	.94	839	1.23	.28	.61	.02	.37
Nasik	0	472	.34	721	1.01	.11	.01	.06	.93
Belgaum	0	1,013	–.17	1,006	.70	.08	.84	00	.16
Dharwar	.48	401	.64	960	.83	.20	.64	.02	.33
Thana	0	1394	–.20	1,180	.87	.05	.42	.19	.39
Kolaba	.06	218	.86	1,145	.94	.05	.30	.21	.48
Ratnagiri	0	880	.04	901	.85	.08	.60	0	.40
N. Kanara	0	999	.14	1,142	.71	.04	.81	.08	.11
Kharif Jowar									
Ahmedabad	.05	20	.27	92	2.94	.87	.85	.02	.12
Surat	0	597	–.14	503	.93	.10	.07	.24	.69
Dhulia	.23	50	.72	348	1.20	.27	.32	.03	.65
Jalgaon	.55	–181	1.95	743	.64	.14	.67	.22	.11

Bajra									
Ahmedabad	0	179	.10	223	1.76	.31	.77	0	.23
Kaira	0	322	.16	434	1.29	.16	.36	.16	.48
Dhulia	.16	143	.63	336	.91	.21	.14	.03	.83
Jalgaon	.64	66	.60	226	1.18	.30	.81	.12	.37
Nasik	.22	44	.85	244	.97	.13	.04	.15	.81
Ahmednagar	.08	124	.43	204	.91	.20	.17	0	.83
Poona	0	338	–.39	265	.67	.06	.73	.09	.18
Sholapur	.16	38	.31	76	1.68	.60	.64	.09	.27
N. Satara	0	76	.78	249	.89	.06	.37	.27	.36
Belgaum	.10	1	1.10	230	.90	.12	.17	.30	.53
Bijapur	.62	–33	1.21	149	1.01	.12	.02	.29	.69
Cotton									
Ahmedabad	0	51	.32	80	1.01	.24	0	.21	0.79
Broach	.68	–14	1.28	103	.89	.24	.23	.28	.49
Surat	.55	–58	1.77	95	.94	.15	.07	.58	.35
Dhulia	.04	42	.48	82	.99	.26	0	.02	.98
Jalgaon	.62	–17	1.29	93	.92	.17	.20	.29	.51
Belgaum	.11	–59	2.70	64	.78	.11	.16	.65	.19
Bijapur	0	–15	1.67	50	.79	.11	.20	.54	.26
Dharwar	0	16	.98	65	.78	.08	.18	.58	.76
Ragi									
Ratnagiri	0.2	364	.38	529	.83	.08	.79	0	.21

Table 2. (*Contd.*)

	(1)	(2)	(3)	(4)	(5)	(6)	(7)	(8)	(9)
Maize									
Panch Mahals	.87	−348	1.76	779	.83	.24	.35	.51	.14
Jalgaon Groundnut	0.88	−75	1.10	566	1.08	.21	.13	.15	
Gram	0.08	40	.65	350	1.30	.12	.78	.02	
Tobacco	0	399	.40	750	.99	.21	0	0	
Nasik	0	385	.09	413	.74	.17	.36	.12	.52
N. Satara	0	1	1.30	580	.77	.05	.60	.24	.16
Belgaum	.01	204	.99	562	.66	.09	.81	.07	.12
Bijapar	0	−28	1.32	301	.82	.09	.30	.40	.30
Dharwar	.05	377	.29	532	.97	.27	.02	.25	.73
Rabi Jowar									
Broach	0	167	.49	391	1.19	.21	.32	.04	.64
Jalgaon	.60	−22	1.28	424	.82	.25	.35	.23	.42
Nasik	0	112	.27	196	1.57	.33	.60	.01	.39
Ahmednagar	.72	−178	2.18	278	.75	.15	.50	.39	.11
Poona	.31	−138	1.63	244	.95	.16	.02	.55	.42
Sholapur	.16	.70	.99	272	.75	.20	.35	.20	.45
Bijapur	0	257	−.14	237	1.22	.16	.42	0	.58
Wheat									
Ahmedabad	0	370	−.11	338	1.07	.23	0.5	0	.95
Broach	.81	−103	1.10	271	1.25	.34	.68	.06	.26
Dhulia	.56	−5	.84	394	1.21	.35	.44	.01	.55

Jalgaon	.76	−19	.82	399	1.28	.40	.70	.01	.29
Nasik	.69	−90	.99	288	1.33	.29	.78	.01	.21
Ahmednagar	.37	20	.64	275	1.44	.37	.69	0	.31
Belgaum	.70	−93	1.14	209	1.34	.42	.60	.09	.31
Bijapur	.76	−26	1.14	166	1.02	.35	.01	.22	.77
Dharwar	.77	−1	.74	182	1.35	.62	.63	.06	.31

NOTES: (1) Unless otherwise noted, average crop-cutting yields are calculated for the period 1945–6 to 1960–1 for rice, wheat, and rabi jowar, and from 1946–7 for the remaining crops. The exceptions are rice in Ahmedabad and Nasik which begin in 1950, and rabi jowar which begins in 1947–8 in Nasik and 1948–9 in Jalgaon.

(2) Revenue yields are available until 1955–6 for Mysore districts, till 1959–60 for Gujarat districts, and till 1960–61 for Maharashtra districts. Revenue yields were not published in 1950 and are only available for Ahmedabad, Jalgaon, Nasik, Ahmednagar and N. Kanara districts. Some crops (rice in Ahmedabad and Nasik, kharif jowar in Nasik, and rabi jowar in Jalgaon and Nasik) are only modestly important in these districts, but they are included because the data were readily available from Dr Shah's study.

(3) For the period 1906–20, the revenue yields were available for total jowar only. Therefore in columns (5) and (8), for jowar the ratios are for total jowar to the standard yields or crop-cutting yields of the predominant jowar (kharif or rabi) in the district. An exception is Nasik where both are important and weighted average of the two crop-cutting yields is taken.

(4) Data from 1949–50 onward are from the *Season and Crop Reports* of Bombay State. For the period 1945–6 to 1949–50 the data are from R. S. Khosal (1950). These data include tobacco, which accounts for the 60th case, compared to 59 in my article.

have made no corrections when using revenue yield historically. The justification for this is that on an all-India basis many of these differences between CCYs and RYs would cancel out, which is certainly true.

However, use of revenue yields historically has two major disadvantages. First for any district or province, the differences between CCYs and RYs are unlikely to cancel out. For example, in Table 2, all crops included for Ahmedabad have CCYs below RYs, while the opposite is true for Ratnagiri, and there are many other cases of bias in Table 2. The same is true by province and crop; for example, agricultural production in U.P. would be overstated using revenue yields for two of its principal crops, rice and wheat, which are the only reported examples (R. C. Desai, p. 15). Therefore at any point in time use of RYs will give an incorrect view of regional differences in agricultural output, and this seems to me a very important reason not to use revenue yields for historical work.

The second major problem concerning revenue yields historically is whether their trend is correct. The trend is affected in traditional revenue estimation by changes in standard yields and changes in the condition factor. Standard yields were originally constructed and later adjusted on the basis of small non-random crop-cutting experiments. Initially SYs in most of India were very high, in part because European yields were projected to India, and partly because it made the standard of life seem higher and the pitch of revenue lower if SYs were high. Consequently, a number of downward revisions were in order and many were made in SYs over the subsequent 60 years. However, these declines in SYs often had the effect of producing declines in RYs, whether or not the underlying conditions of production had changed. A counter example to illustrate the point is Punjab, where after 1920 there were underlying changes in yields of wheat as new seeds were adapted. However, during the period 1920 to 1947 when these yield increases were occurring, the SYs were not adjusted upward proportionately.

The second element producing downward trends in RYs was the fact that the average condition factor around 1947 was often lower than in earlier parts of the century, not only in Bombay, but in other provinces as well. Originally I had suggested this might be due to rural agitation associated with the nationalist movement, since land revenue payments would be lowered if the condition factor were low in a number of years. Desai's comments and a second look at my data for Bombay lead me to question that proposition, and at a minimum to suggest better tests than I used should be attempted. However, the reality remains that for reasons that are still to be explained, there was a secular decline in the condition factor in Bombay and other provinces for a number of important crops. This does not seem plausible if the condition factor is to reflect the character of the seasons, which should not in the absence of secular climate changes display any trend.

The figures below illustrate the situation for six of the major food crops in India for the period 1900–47, as taken from S. Sivasubramonian's study (1965) for all of India. For each crop, the average revenue yield is given from 1900 to 1947, the average yield in the years 1949–50 to 1955–6, and the correlation of RYs with time. For these crops a rough accounting of the decline in RYs due to a decline in the SY is presented. For those crops where the earlier SYs were particularly high, namely jowar and bajra, most of the decline in RY is due to declines in SY, and I interpret these declines in SYs to reflect little about trends in actual yields of these crops but rather a belated downward adjustment of these SYs in the appropriate direction. It may be recalled that one of the original errors throughout India in crop experiments in the nineteenth century was that the fields sampled were chosen non-randomly, and generally poorer types of soil were excluded. Since jowar and bajra tend to be grown on poorer soils, their initial SYs were much too high relative to say rice, where most of the crop was and is grown on better grade soils.

Where does this all leave us? My conclusion is that at a minimum the CCYs around 1947 should be used in place of RYs for that period, since there are important differences between CCYs and RYs, especially at the regional level. I think this would improve our historical statistics even if the trends and fluctuations in revenue yields were retained. A further improvement, in my view, would be to assume no historical trend in crop yields in the official agricultural statistics, unless we have independent evidence for improvement, as wheat, cotton, jute, and sugarcane, or independent evidence of decline. My conclusion is based on a belief that the decline in revenue yields is not based on any solid foundation in terms of appropriate crop-cutting experiments. If this view is accepted, one can still retain the reasonable fluctuations

Table 3. Major Food Crops in India

	Crop	Rice	Wheat	Jowar	Bajra	Barley	Gram
1	Average Revenue Yield, 1900–47, lbs/acre	853	661	450	365	840	564
2	Average Yield per acre 1949–50 to 1955–6	703	630	369	207	721	481
3	Correlation of Revenue Yield with time, 1900–4 (linear r)	–.57	–.31	–.58	–.19	–.66	–.68
4	Decline in RY 1900–47 as % of Average RY, Row 1	–25%	–16%	–20%	–16%	–20%	–19%
5	Decline in SY 1906–7 to 1946–7 as % of Row (1)	–12%	–2%	–14%	–12%	–14%	–1%
6	Per cent of decline in RY due to decline in SY (4)/(5)	48%	12%	70%	75%	70%	5%

SOURCES: Row (1) and Row (3) are calculated from S. Sivasubramonian (1965); Row (2) is from Table 1 above. Row (4) is calculated from the standard yields given for 1906–7 in *Indian Agricultural Statistics* weighting yields by acreage in provinces, while the 1946–7 standard yields are given in Table 1.

from year to year, by applying an index of deviations from trend of revenue yields to a basic set of crop-cutting yields around Independence, which is a method (Heston, 1977, App. 2) used in another paper.

References

Annewari Committee for the Determination of Standard Yields (1966), Revenue and Forests Department, Government of Maharashtra, Government Printing Press, Nagpur.

Blyn, George (1966), *Agricultural Trends in India 1891–1947: Output, Availability, and Productivity*, University of Pennsylvania Press, Philadelphia.

Desai, R. C. (1953), *Standard of Living in India and Pakistan 1931–2 to 1940–1*, Popular Book Depot, Bombay.

Heston, Alan (1973), 'Official Yields Per Acre in India, 1886–1947: Some Questions of Interpretation', *Indian Economic and Social History Review*, vol. X, no. 4, 1973.

—— (1977), 'National Income', Chapter IV for the Cambridge *Economic History of India 1857–1957*, forthcoming, Appendix 2.

India (1953), *Average Yield Per Acre of Principal Crops of India, 1931–2 to 1951–2*, Directorate of Economics and Statistics, Ministry of Food and Agriculture, Delhi.

Islam, M. M. (1973), 'The Quality of the Official Crop Statistics of Bengal (1920–47)', *Bulletin of Quantitative and Computer Methods in South Asian Studies*, no. 1, June 1973.

Khosal, R. S. (1950), *A Review of Crop-Cutting Experiments in the Bombay State during the Period 1945–6 to 1948–9*, Bulletin no. 1 of 1950, Department of Agriculture, Bombay State, Poona.

Mukerji, K. (1965). *Levels of Economic Activity and Public Expenditures in India*, Asia, Bombay, Ch. 2.

Panse, V. G. (1946), *Report on the Scheme for the Improvement of Agricultural Statistics*, Indian Council of Agricultural Research, Delhi.

—— (1961) 'The National Sample Survey, Agricultural Statistics and Planning in India' in N. V. Sovani and V. M. Dandekar (Eds.), *Changing India, Essays in Honor of D. R. Gadgil*, Asia, Bombay.

Panse, V. G. and Sukhatme (1951) 'Crop Surveys in India – II', *Journal of the Indian Society of Agricultural Statistics*.

Patil, P. C. (1922) *The Crops of the Bombay Presidency, Their Geography and Statistics,* Bulletin no. 109 of 1921, Department of Agriculture, Bombay.

Pray, Carl (1977), 'The Productivity of Agricultural Research in Punjab 1905–47', Paper presented to the Economic History Workshop, University of Pennsylvania, November 1977, mimeographed.

Proceedings of the Board of Agriculture in India (1924), Calcutta, Superintendent of Government Printing, 1924.

Report on the Marketing of Sugar in India and Burma (1943), Agricultural Marketing in India, Series no. 39, GOI Press, New Delhi.

Sivasubramonian, S. (1965), *National Income of India 1900–1 to 1946–7*, Ph.D. dissertation, Delhi School of Economics.

Theil, Henri (1966), *Applied Economic Forecasting,* Amsterdam North Holland, Third Printing, 1975.

Thomas, P. J. and N. Sundararama Sastry (1939), *Indian Agricultural Statistics*, University of Madras, Madras.

Land resettlement & output stats.

Chapter 5

Accuracy of Official Agricultural Statistics and the Sources of Growth in the Punjab, 1907–47

[1984]

CARL E. PRAY

There has been considerable discussion about the quality of the agricultural data during the first half of the twentieth century, but few attempts at providing alternative estimates on the basis of available data. Desai[1] and Blyn[2] both acknowledge the problems with the yield data and discuss some of the independent estimates of yield per acre. However, they conclude that there is not enough evidence about the direction of the biases to warrant adjusting the yield series. Dewey[3] was very critical of the accuracy of the official output series in Punjab and Bengal, but he does not produce any alternatives to them. More recently, both Dasgupta[4] and Mishra[5] have concluded on the basis of little evidence that the Punjab yield series is accurate.

It is difficult to argue with the conclusion of Desai and Blyn that the errors cancel themselves out for India as a whole and thus the level of yields was unbiased. The topic on which they seem to be on weakest ground is the trends in yields of the major grain crops. There is little reason to believe that the yields of these crops

[1] R. C. Desai, *Standard of Living in India and Pakistan, 1931–2 to 1940–1* (Bombay: Popular Book Depot, 1953).

[2] George Blyn, *Agricultural Trends in India, 1891–1947: Output, Availability, and Productivity* (Philadelphia: University of Pennsylvania, 1966).

[3] Clive Dewey, 'Agricultural Statistics of the Punjab 1867–1947', *Bulletin of Quantitative and Computer Methods in South Asian Studies*, vol. 2 (March 1974).

[4] Ajit K. Dasgupta, 'Agricultural Growth Rates in the Punjab, 1906–42', *The Indian Economic and Social History Review*, vol. 18, nos. 3 and 4, 1981.

[5] Satish Chandra Mishra, 'On the Reliability of Pre-Independence Agricultural Statistics in Bombay and Punjab', *The Indian Economic and Social History Review*, vol. 20, no. 2, 1983.

actually had a negative trend. In the case of individual provinces and commodities there is reason to believe that even the level of yields was inaccurate. The independent estimates of yield per acre and acreage which used statistically sound sampling techniques that Desai has gathered indicate a considerable amount of variance from the official figures at the provincial level.

The only attempted revisions of the yield per acre series was by Heston in his paper on Indian national income.[6] Heston argues that the trend in yield per acre was at least zero rather than negative like the official statistics indicate and that the yield estimates for the 1950s are more accurate estimates of the level of yields than the official estimates. Therefore, in his calculation of the national income of India for the period 1900 to 1947 he assumes that the trend in yield per acre was zero and the level of yields was that of the 1950s.

This paper examines the evidence on the accuracy of official agricultural statistics for the Punjab. It argues that the trends indicated by the official statistics are probably not very accurate and that the trends estimated from official statistics or using Heston's assumptions lead to an underestimation of output growth and the trend in yield per acre. It then adjusts the official statistics on the basis of available alternative estimates of output and yield per acre. Finally, the growth in agricultural output is disaggregated into a yield component, acreage component and cropping pattern component. This indicates that although the increase in irrigated acreage was the major cause of output growth new technology also played an important role.

The paper has three parts: first, there is a description of the way the data was collected; second, there is a discussion of the reliability of the official statistics; and third, the growth in output of Punjabi agriculture is broken down into the contribution of growth of irrigated land, unirrigated land, yield per acre, and shifts in cropping patterns.

Official Data Gathering Procedure

Output estimates for the main crops in the Punjab until 1920 were calculated using the following formula:

[6] Alan Heston, 'National Income'. In Dharma Kumar (ed.), *The Cambridge Economic History of India*, vol. 2 (Cambridge: Cambridge University Press, 1983).

Area × Normal Yield × Seasonal Factor = Output

The area was supplied by the village land revenue official (patwari) whose job included recording which crops were grown on each field in the village. The village acreage under each crop was collected and aggregated at the tehsil office, and then sent on to the district level revenue officials who aggregated them and sent them on to the provincial government.

The normal yield or standard yield 'is stated to be the average yield on average soil in a year of average character'.[7] The Punjab *Season and Crop Report* describes how it was determined:

In preparing this statement (of the normal yield) the yield fixed in the previous returns or assumed for assessment purposes and the results of the crop experiments made from time to time have been considered along with the opinions of local officers of the Revenue and Agricultural Department, who were consulted before these yields were finally fixed.[8]

The normal yield was established for each district for a five year period. The crop experiments were crop-cutting experiments which were executed at first by the subordinate officials of the Land Revenue Department, and then as the Agricultural Department grew, the agricultural assistants were also made responsible for a certain number of experiments each year. The results of these experiments were forwarded to the provincial level where results which were thought to be unrepresentative were thrown out. The remaining experiments for each district were averaged, and the result was the official annual average of the crop-cutting experiments. After five years these annual average yields were averaged and used to help determine the normal yield for the next five years. The results of the experiments which were done in the years 1923–7 were then used to calculate the normal yield for the years 1928–32. This normal yield with the condition factor determined the yields used to calculate official production statistics for the years 1928–32. The normal yields of wheat in Lyallpur and Hoshiarpur during the 1920s and 1930s examined by V. G. Panse, a statistician from the Indian Council of Agricultural Research,

[7] V. G. Panse, *Report on the Scheme for the Improvement of Agricultural Statistics* (New Delhi: Indian Council of Agricultural Research, 1946).

[8] Punjab, Land Records Department, *Report of the Season of Crops of the Punjab, 1946* (Lahore: Government Printing, 1947), p. i.

were always within 5 per cent of the averages of the crop-cutting experiments.[9]

The seasonal factor, which was also called the condition factor, was an estimate of the yield per acre expressed as a fraction or percentage of the normal yield. Each year revenue officials at the tehsil level would make an estimate of the season factor for each of the main crops. These seasonal factors would then be forwarded to the district level where they could be modified by the district officials. The district seasonal factor was then sent on to the provincial level where they once again were scrutinised and frequently modified. From these the Director of Land Records would set the official estimate of yield per acre in each district. The yield estimates were multiplied by the acreage to calculate the production of a crop, and the district production figures were then aggregated to calculate total production for the Punjab.

This system was changed in 1920 for wheat and cotton and in 1940 for sugarcane. Instead of estimating the crop as a percentage of a normal crop in the district, the official at the tehsil level estimated the yield of his area in terms of maunds and seers per acre. This estimate was then passed upward, averaged and possibly modified as before to get a district yield estimate. The normal yields continued to be published every five years, but were not explicitly used in the process of estimating yields or production. However, as Panse notes, 'it probably influences the forecasts (production estimates) as every official who is concerned with the preparation of forecasts is aware of what the normal is'.[10]

Another change which took place in the 1920s was the growth of the Agriculture Department. As agricultural extension officers began to spread into the countryside, they were expected to send yield estimates for their areas to the district level officers. The district officer compiled yield estimates for the whole district from the reports of the agricultural assistants and from his own observations. These were sent to the Director of Agriculture. In the 1920s he replaced the Director of Land Records as the official who examined these figures and the figures from the Revenue Department and then set the estimate of yields for each district for the year.[11] As the extension staff of the DAP grew, the number of crop-cutting

[9] Panse, p. 22.
[10] Ibid., p. 26.
[11] Ibid.

experiments and the number of districts covered by these experiments, grew rapidly. The Land Revenue Department was also increasing the number of experiments and districts covered. From 1930 onwards crop-cutting experiments were conducted in every district of the Punjab by both of these departments. Panse reports that in wheat, which had the most experiments of any crop, about 500 experiments a year were performed.[12]

The Reliability

Acreage of Crops

Panse's statement indicates the advantages of the method of collecting acreage data which was used by the Punjab government:

> The soundness of the method of complete enumeration of area under crops on the basis of the individual field inspection is unquestionable . . . It may be asked, however, with what efficiency the field work is done and whether areas may not be recorded by the patwari on casual reports from the cultivators and not on a personal inspection of the crop. With adequate supervision and checks, for which there is provision, there is no real difficulty provided the charge of the patwari is manageable.[13]

The most serious criticism of the area estimates has been by Dewey. His criticism is that the supervision and checks on the work of the village officers was inadequate. Also before the land revenue settlements of the 1880s and 1890s in the Punjab the quality of the patwaris was poor, and both the patwaris and the officers who were supposed to be checking them were related to powerful moneylending groups of landholders.[14] The situation improved gradually after the Department of Land Records and Agriculture was set up in 1884–5.

He believes that the period before World War I was the high point of efficiency in the Land Revenue Department, and hence the best period for accurate area statistics. After the war he reasons that the discipline of the Land Revenue Department declined because of personal grievances of the patwaris and the Nationalist movement. At the village level these two factors combined to cause

[12] Ibid., p. 22.
[13] Ibid., p. 15.
[14] Clive Dewey, p. 3.

patwari strikes immediately after the war. At department headquarters in Lahore the decline in importance of land revenue as a source of funds for the government and the distraction of the top officials by the Nationalist movement meant that district officers spent much less time checking the work of their subordinates.

Although the logic of this argument is quite convincing, there is little empirical evidence to support his case. He does quote the settlement officer of Lahore as saying that village statistics in the late 1930s were 'exceedingly unreliable'.[15] In contrast, Panse, who did an intensive investigation of the agricultural statistics of Lyallpur and Hoshiarpur Districts, finds only one fault in the acreage statistics; and this is in the handling of acreage of mixed crops. Thus, the weight of the empirical argument seems to be in favour of Panse and the accuracy of the acreage data.

Level of Yield Estimates

Most debates about the standard yield and condition factor have been inconclusive because there were forces biasing the yield estimates down at the same time as other forces seemed to be forcing the yield estimates up. The standard yield was determined by the Director of Land Records and later by the Director of the Agriculture Department for each district using 'the yields fixed in the previous returns or for assessment purposes, together with the results of the crop-cutting experiments made annually and during assessments'.[16] The weight placed on these various factors depended on the individual director. H. K. Trevaskis, a Director of Land Records, felt that the 1920s crop-cutting experiments when averaged produced a yield that was higher than the actual average on the yields. He explained: 'Such experiments would generally be made on land which could at least produce a fair crop, and they thus ignored the considerable areas of land yielding very little crop at all'.[17] The other factor that was considered when fixing a standard yield was the assessment yield. The assessment yield was set by the

[15] Ibid., p. 8.

[16] Great Britain Royal Commission on Agriculture in India, vol. 8, *Evidence Taken in the Punjab* (Calcutta: Government of India, 1927).

[17] Hugh K. Trevaskis, *The Punjab of India: An Economic Survey of the Punjab in Recent Years* (1890–1925), vol. 1 (Lahore: Civil and Military Gazette Press, 1931), p. 199.

Settlement Officer of the Land Revenue Department and determined the land revenue that farmers paid. Trevaskis says:

> But the accuracy of a Settlement Officer's crop estimates is inevitably marred by his bias in the direction of safety. If he over-estimates the gross product there is a danger of the settlement breaking down, if he underestimates no great harm ensues except the slight loss to government. His estimate is, therefore, like an engineer's estimate of the breaking strain of a bridge; it is essential that he should provide a large margin for safety. . . . For all these reasons, therefore . . . there is an inevitable bias in the direction of under-estimating the outturn.[18]

The reason they were so worried about the settlement breaking down was the expense of settlement operations which frequently took three years and a lot of manpower per district. Thus, there were logical arguments which support either raising or lowering the estimate of standard yields if the officials had strong opinions of their own on the matter.

Opinion was divided on the bias in the condition factor also. Dewey points out that opinion was mixed about the nature of the bias, but concludes that the estimates by the local revenue people were probably too low.[19] Since it was the local patwari and local farmers upon whom the tehsil level people based their condition factor reports, and farmers wanted low yields so that the land taxes would be lower. This must have biased the condition factor downward. However, when Panse made his crop-cuttings on a random sample of fields he asked local officials and farmers to estimate the yield in the standing crop. Both groups overestimated the actual yields. It was not until after threshing operations were over that the farmers started to under-estimate their crop.[20] It is, however, quite possible that the officials in this test made higher estimates than usual because they knew they would be checked by crop cuts.

It is possible to go beyond this debate and determine the direction of the bias in the official yearly estimates of the main field crops late in the British period. There are two sources of independent evidence on cotton. There is an Indian Central Cotton Committee (ICCC) study of village cotton consumption and statistics collected on the amount of cotton used in cotton mills or

[18] Ibid., p. 193.
[19] Dewey, p. 9.
[20] Panse, p. 41.

exported. Columns 3, 4 and 5 of Table 1 are based on that data. When officials of the Agriculture Department compared this to the official yield per acre estimate (Column 6), they realised that the official estimates greatly underestimated output.

In the case of sugarcane there is evidence from a survey of farmers' fields about the size of the yield increase due to new varieties. This suggests a 41 to 70 per cent increase in the yield of the planted crop due to the use of varieties introduced by the mid-1930s (see Table 2). Soon after this survey, two new varieties, which gave even higher yields on Department farms were introduced and spread rapidly. Sir William Roberts, the leading authority on Punjabi agriculture in the British period, estimated an 80 per cent increase in yields due to the Coimbatore varieties.[21]

The evidence of the cost of cultivation survey and the 50 per cent increase in official yield of sugarcane between 1938–42 and 1943–6 strongly suggests that in the 1930s and up to 1942 sugarcane yields were substantially underestimated.

In the wheat crop there were yield estimates based on crop-cuttings of a random sample of fields throughout the province. Because of the sample size, the sample design, and the care with which these crop cuts were carried out, these estimates provide the most accurate estimates of the yield per acre of any crop in the Punjab before Independence. The annual average of these yield estimates are presented along with the average official yield estimates for the same three years and the standard yield which applied to that period in Table 3. The actual yield from the random sample crop-cuttings was 7 per cent higher than the official estimates of the irrigated wheat yield and 18 per cent in the case of unirrigated wheat. This shows that in wheat also the independent evidence indicates underestimation by officials of the actual crop.

The only evidence on the yields of the other main crops of the Punjab—rice, jowar, bajra, maize, and gram—is the data on the yields of these crops in the East Punjab during the 1950s. Starting in 1952 with rice and then spreading to wheat and the rest of the crops listed above, the Punjab government began using crop-cuttings based on a random sample of yields to estimate the official yields of these crops. Between 1942 and 1956 there were no major changes in the technology or amount of inputs in these crops. The

[21] William Roberts and Kartar Singh, *A Textbook of Punjab Agriculture* (Lahore: Civil and Military Gazette, 1951), p. 308.

Table 1. Consumption of Cotton 1930–7

Years	Area in Cotton (000 Acres)	Baled Crop (400 lbs. bales)	Baled Crop Per Acre (mds. raw cotton)	Home Consumption Per Acre (mds. raw cotton)	Yield/Acre Implied by Consumption Estimates (mds. raw cotton)	Official Yield/Acre (mds. raw cotton)
	(1)	(2)	(3)	(4)	(5)	(6)
1930	2,208	766,300	4.95	1.23	6.18	7.76
1931	2,164	798,100	5.27	1.31	6.58	4.61
1932	2,160	615,700	4.07	1.33	5.40	3.73
1933	1,890	645,500	4.88	1.54	6.54	4.40
1934	2,449	1,194,600	6.97	1.20	8.17	5.67
1935	2,347	1,001,300	6.09	1.27	7.36	6.02
1936	2,803	1,335,900	6.81	1.07	7.88	6.53

SOURCE: Columns 1–5: Punjab, Department of Agriculture, *Report* (Lahore: Superintendent Government Printing, 1937), p. 82. Column 6 calculated from Gulshan Rai, *Agricultural Statistics of the Punjab 1901–2 to 1935–6* (Lahore: Board of Economic Inquiry, 1937).

Table 2. Cultivators' Yields of Sugarcane (Maunds of Sugarcane)

	Desi			Improved		
	1933–4	1934–5	1935–6	1933–4	1934–5	1935–6
Lyallpur		240	220		330	320
Jullundur	220	200	240	420	350	380
Gurdaspur	220	210	200	na	na	na

na: not available because there was no survey in the district that year.

SOURCE: Government of India, Central Marketing Department, *Report on the Marketing of Sugar in India and Burma* (New Delhi: Government of India Press, 1943), p. 21.

Table 3. Wheat Yield Estimates (Maunds/Acre)

		Irrigated	Unirrigated
R.S. Estimates	1944–6	13.22	7.06
Official Estimates	1944–6	12.31	5.98
Standard Yield	1942	11.96	6.52

SOURCE: Random Sample Estimates and Official Estimates: P. V. Sukhatme, *Report on the Wheat Estimation Survey in the Punjab 1943–4* (New Delhi: Indian Council of Agricultural Research, 1945) and same report for the 1944–5 and 1945–6 seasons.

Standard Yield: A weighted average of the district standard yields with the fraction of wheat acreage in each district used as the weight. District standard yield and wheat acreage from Punjab, Department of Land Records, *Report of the Season and Crops of the Punjab 1946* (Lahore: Government Printing, Punjab, 1947).

main cause of differences in yields between the 1940s and 1950s was the shift from the old method of determining yields to the new technique. The other factor that may have played some role was the weather. Some of the fluctuations due to weather are smoothed out by using 3 or 5 year averages. However, one bad year in either period could lead to incorrect conclusions about the size or direction of the bias.

Table 4 contains the official yield per acre estimates in two different time periods for the 13 districts of the old Punjab which went to India in 1947. In all crops except jowar the yield estimates from the crop-cutting survey are substantially higher than the yields estimated using the old method. In jowar the average yield from the 1950s was pulled down by a particularly bad year in 1956

Table 4. Official Yields of Various Crops in East Punjab Only

Crop	Acreage Covered as % of United Punjab	Average Yield/ Acre 1942–6 (maunds)	Average Yield/ Acre 1950s (maunds)	Yield 1950s/ Yield 1940s
Wheat	32	9.64	11.34	1.18
Rice	34	11.73	14.62	1.25
Jowar	55	2.89	2.34	0.77
			(2.60)	(0.90)
Bajra	64	2.97	3.89	1.31
Barley	70	6.83	10.44	1.53
Maize	66	9.99	13.06	1.31
Gram	67	5.09	8.83	1.74

NOTE: Column 1 shows the per cent of the total area under this crop in the United Punjab which was in these 13 districts in 1946.

Column 3 shows the yield per acre in the years from the beginning of the implementation of the new crop-cutting technique through the year 1956. After that year the boundaries of the state were changed, and yields for those 13 districts which were in the British Punjab are no longer available in the U.S. Thus, the period over which these yields were averaged varies from 5 years for rice, 4 years for wheat, jowar, bajra, barley and maize, and 3 years for gram.

SOURCE: Column 1: Calculated from William Roberts and S. B. S. Kartar Singh, *A Textbook of Punjab Agriculture* (Lahore; Civil and Military Gazette Ltd., 1951), p. 17 (a).

Column 2: R. L. Anand, *Punjab Agriculture, Facts and Figures* (Punjab: Economic and Statistical Advisor to the Government, 1957), p. 67.

Column 3: Punjab (India) Land Records Department, *Report of the Season and Crops* (Chandigarh: Controller of Printing, various years).

when the yield was only 94 pounds per acre. If that year is excluded, the average yield of jowar becomes 214—which is still lower than the earlier years but not by much. While the evidence does not prove that the data is biased, it does suggest that the yields in these 13 districts may have been underestimated.

TREND IN YIELD ESTIMATES

It is not possible to assume that the level of under- or overestimation of yields has remained constant in the Punjab; so there is little reason to believe that an estimate of the yield trends based on official statistics are accurate. For the Punjab, my hypothesis is that changes in the yield per acre reflected the decisions of administrators more accurately than the changes in Punjabi agriculture.

Two types of administrative changes in yield are recognisable in the Punjab statistics. The first is a general upward or downward shift of all standard yields due to the differences in interpretation of the agricultural data by the Land Records Department officials. The second is a shift in a specific crop of the normal yield or the official yield in directly estimated crops.

An example of the first type of change in yields is described in the Appendix of the *Agricultural Statistics of India 1914–15*:

The revisions (of standard yields) of 1902 and 1907 were made on the basis of very unscientifically selected and inadequately supervised experiments carried out by the district staff. . . . The present revision has been made in consultation with settlement officers in the case of districts of which the settlement is in the early stages, while in other cases the average yield has been worked out mainly from the area and yields given in the assessment reports. . . . There is no doubt that the yields now fixed, based as they are on the over-cautious estimates of settlement officers, are too low, but they are at any rate placed on a uniform basis. The result of the revision is a reduction of the yields of all the crops except rapeseed and sugarcane the averages for which have been raised.[22]

A revision of yields set the standard yield for the following five years and the revision referred to here was made in 1912. According to Dewey the Director of Land Records wanted to make this change in 1907, but it had been vetoed by the Lieutenant-Governor because the proposed yields were too low. However, the Lieutenant-Governor retired before the Director of Land Records and the latter got his way in 1912.[23]

When it became time for the next revision in 1917, the author of *Agricultural Statistics of India* writes:

In consultation with district and settlement officers and the Principal of the Agricultural College, Lyallpur and other officers of the Department of Agriculture, increases have been made where the results of crop experiments indicate that enhancement is required, provided that the number of experiments has been sufficient. . . . The present

[22] India, Department of Commercial Intelligence and Statistics, *Agricultural Statistics of India*, vol. 1 (New Delhi: Manager of Publications).

[23] Dewey, p. 9.

revision shows that a general increase in the provincial averages has taken place.[24]

Since these standard yields were multiplied by the condition factor to estimate the official yield estimates of all crops before 1920, these shifts in the standard yield should show up in the aggregate yield per acre. Figure I, taken from Blyn, shows the five year moving averages of yield per acre of all crops, foodgrains and non-foodgrains. The 1912 revision produces the expected decline in foodgrains and all-crop yields and the increase in non-foodgrains which reflects the increased standard yield of sugarcane, rape and mustard. The 1917 revision reverses the decline in foodgrains and helps non-foodgrain yields continue to grow. In 1917 foodgrain yields go back up and non-foodgrains continue to grow due to the upward shift of the new standard yields for the five years following 1917.

The second type of administrative shift in yields took place when officials became aware of new sources of data with which to check the official figures of certain crops rather than simply making new interpretations of the same data. The official yield series indicates two such cases—sugarcane and cotton. In these crops there is a significant shift upward in the official yields for which there is no explanation in terms of new technology or increased inputs.

The basic cause of the shift was pressure and research from the Indian Central Cotton Committee (ICCC). The ICCC conducted a survey to determine how much cotton was used in the villages in India for pillows, quilts, and other things.[25] Once this was determined they could add it to the amount of cotton which was ginned and pressed—data which was already being collected—and have a very good estimate of how much cotton was produced in a year. Their results were used by the Department of Agriculture to produce Column 4 in Table 1.

On the basis of this evidence the Agriculture Department decided that the standard yield after 1933 of 4.63 maunds of raw cotton per acre was far too low. Since 'it is felt that the estimates made by subordinate revenue and other staff are influenced to a considerable extent by what are known as the official standard

[24] *Agricultural Statistics of India 1919–20*, p. 344.

[25] Indian Central Cotton Committee, *General Report on Nine Inquiries into the Village or Extra Factory Consumption of Cotton in India 1933–6* (Bombay, 1938).

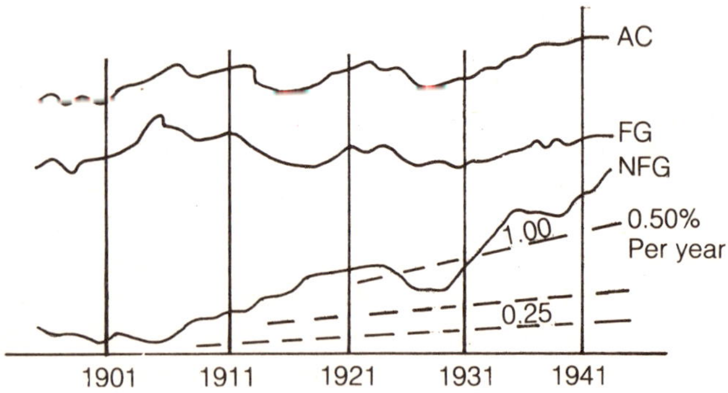

Figure 1. Greater Punjab Yield per Acre of all Crops, Foodgrains and Non-Foodgrains, Five Year Moving Averages, Semilogarithmic Scale.

SOURCE: George Blyn, *Agricultural Trends in India, 1891–1947: Output Availability and Productivity* (Philadelphia: University of Pennsylvania, 1966), p. 169.

yields,'[26] the ICCC funded a statistician to spend several months helping decide on a more accurate set of standard yields for the five year period beginning in 1938. He examined and checked ginning and pressing data, and used the ICCC study to calculate consumption. On the production side he examined the crop-cuttings, yields on DAP farms and yields from large private estates. On the basis of his work, the provincial average of standard yields was raised from 4.63 maunds to 7.25 maunds per acre for irrigated desi and irrigated American went from 4.74 to 7.04. This amounts to an increase in irrigated yields of 57 and 49 per cent for desi and American respectively.[27] The result was the increase in official estimates of yield per acre.

Official sugarcane yield estimates make a similar discontinuous jump in the 1940s. Table 5 gives the annual official estimate of yields and the annual average for two periods. As with the cotton crops, sugarcane yield was estimated directly in maunds per acre instead of using the condition factor and standard yield. Also, like cotton, there is a substantial shift upward in yields—the annual

[26] Punjab, Department of Agriculture (Lahore: Government Printing, 1939) p. 64.

[27] Ibid., p. 65.

Table 5. Irrigated and Unirrigated Sugarcane Yields 1938–46

Year	Irrigated Sugarcane (mds./acre)		Unirrigated Sugarcane (mds./acre)		% Cane Area Improved
1938	222	140		63	
1939	195		95		64
1940	228	231	100	133	na
1941	246		163		75
1942	260		168		na
1943	290		157		77
1944	303	334	176	206	83
1945	362		260		na
1946	381		232		na

SOURCE: Official Yields 1938–44: Gulshan Rai, *Agricultural Statistics of the (British) Punjab Supplement 1–5* (Lahore: Board of Economic Inquiry, 1938–45).

Official Yields 1945–6: Punjab, Department of Land Records, *Report of the Season and Crops* (Lahore: Superintendent Government Printing, Punjab, 1947).

Percent Improved: DAP *Reports*, various years.

average of the second period is 45 per cent higher than the first for the irrigated crop and 55 per cent higher for the unirrigated sugarcane. In the case of sugarcane there are two possible hypotheses to explain this increase. This first hypothesis is that this shift reflects an increase in yields in farmers' fields due to the spread of new high-yielding cane varieties. Second, there is the possibility that like cotton, sugarcane yields had always been underestimated and the shift was an attempt to correct this mistake.

Sugarcane is the one crop in which the new varieties introduced by the Agriculture Department were capable of producing very large gains in yield per acre. Table 2 shows that on farmers' fields in 1934–6, gains in yield of 41 to 74 per cent were being achieved using new varieties. Varieties Co. 313 and Co. 312, which were released in 1936, were particularly high yielding. So, it is possible that farmers were increasing their yields and that this change in yields was recorded in the figures above. The question is, did the spread of these varieties take place at the same time as the yield increase in Table 5? The Agriculture Department's estimates of area under high-yielding sugarcane varieties indicates that it did not. The last column in Table 5 gives their estimate of the percentage of the total sugarcane acreage which was planted with new varieties. If we assume that 100 per cent of the area was covered by new varieties in 1945 and 1946 and that the figures for 1940 and 1942 were 64 and 75 per cent, then the average area under improved varieties for the 1938–42 period would be about 68 per cent and the average for the 1942–6 period, 90 per cent. This means an increase of 22 per cent between the two periods. If the yield increased 80 per cent by replacing old varieties with new varieties as Roberts estimated and 22 per cent of the land changed to the new varieties during this period, total yield per acre would increase by 17.6 per cent explaining less than half of the increase in yields that actually took place. Furthermore, a look at the official yields since improved cane varieties were introduced in the early 1920s shows no relationship between improved varieties and yields.

Table 6 shows the annual average yield per acre of cane along with the average annual percentage of cane under new varieties. For the first four periods yields go down while the percentage under new varieties climbs and another important factor—the percentage of sugarcane land irrigated—was also going up. It is not until the period of the 1940s that yields start to rise. Thus, it appears that there is little evidence that the rise in official yields was a reflection of an actual rise in yields caused by new varieties.

The second hypothesis is that this increase in yields was an adjustment by officials to make up for earlier underestimates. In 1941, discussing the official estimate of sugarcane yields, the author of the DAP *Report* says:

> It is of interest to note that on the basis of this estimate (official outturn), the average yield of gur per acre would be only about 24 maunds per acre for the entire crop. When it is remembered that according to present estimates 75 per cent of the entire sugarcane crop in the province consists of improved Coimbatore varieties, the poorest of which even with the worst possible cultivation and treatment will outyield that average, the conclusion is obvious that the gur production in the province is apparently as hopelessly under-estimated as has been proved in the case of the yield of the cotton crop.[28]

This opinion was probably strengthened in 1943 with the publication of the *Report on the Marketing of Sugar* which was put together by the Central Agricultural Marketing Department to the Government of India. This report came to much the same conclusion as the Agriculture Department. It stated that new varieties should have increased yields before 1940, not lowered them, and

[28] Punjab, Department of Agriculture, p. 114.

Table 6. Average Annual Yields of Sugarcane and Per cent of Acreage under Improved Sugarcane Varieties

Year	Maunds/Acre	% Improved
1921–5	239	1
1926–30	223	10
1931–5	205	34
1936–40	206	58*
1941–4	257	78

NOTE: * Average of years 1936–9.
Average of years 1941, 1943, and 1944.

SOURCE: Yields 1921–40: India, Central Agricultural Marketing Department, *Report on the Marketing of Sugar in India and Burma* (New Delhi: Government of India Press, 1942), p. 286.

Yields 1941–4; Gulshan Rai, *Agricultural Statistics of the (British) Punjab 1940–1 to 1943–4* (Lahore: Board of Economic Inquiry, 1945), p. 9.

Improved Acreage: 1921–38: Indian Council of *Agricultural Research, Agricultural Operations in India* (New Delhi: Government of India Press, various years).

Improved Acreage 1939, 1941: DAP *Reports* (Lahore: Superintendent Government Printing, 1940, 1942).

Improved Acreage 1943, 1944: DAP unpublished annual reports.

that 'the case for the revision of the normal yields . . . deserves a close examination'[29] (also published data in Table 2). It seems likely that these comments reflect the slowly changing official opinion which eventually led to the shift in yield per acre in Table 5.

Sources of Growth

The purpose of this discussion of agricultural statistics is not simply to discuss their deficiencies; rather it is to find the sources of growth in agricultural production during the last forty years of British rule. In view of the uncertainty about the level and trend of crop yields, I have decided not to try to correct these series and then estimate a production function. The one previous attempt at fitting a Cobb-Douglas production function to the official data was not very successful. Raj Krishna first uses total output, 1914–46, as the dependent variable. But because of intercorrelation between the independent variables, the only significant coefficients he gets are for irrigated land and rainfall.[30] He has to drop the trend variable from his regression because it is so highly correlated to

[29] *Marketing of Sugar*, p. 21.

[30] Raj Krishna, 'The Growth of Aggregate Agricultural Output in the Punjab', *Indian Economic Journal* (July–September 1964), p. 56.

irrigated acreage. In order to test for growth in productivity he then uses output per acre as the dependent variable. His estimated equation is shown below (Equation 1) with the standard error in parentheses.

$$(1)\ \log (V/L_n) = C + \underset{(.31)}{.18} \log L_w + \underset{(.12)}{.28} \log W + \underset{(.0013)}{.0007}\,T \qquad r^2 = .35$$

where

V/L_n is output per acre;
C is a constant;
L_w is percentage of cultivated land that is irrigated;
W is rainfall;
T is the trend variable;
( ) is standard error.

This equation leads Krishna to conclude that there was no growth in productivity in this period.[31] However, he ignores the correlation between L_w and T which may account for their insignificance. He also ignores the data problems which have been discussed above which undoubtedly help account for the low r^2 of his estimated equation.

I have used the Minhas–Vaidyanathan technique of disaggregating the increase in output into the increase caused by several different factors. The data requirements of this technique are not as great as production function estimates because all that is needed is data for the starting and ending points of the period rather than an annual series. Because of the data problems mentioned above, I did not feel it was possible to correct the entire series.

The disaggregation is based on the Minhas–Vaidyanathan (MV) method as presented in Gotsch.[32] Let

$$(2)\ GVP_0 = A_0 \sum_{i=1}^{n} p_i C_{i0} Y_{i0}$$

and

$$(3)\ GVP_0 = A_t \sum_{i=1}^{n} p_i C_{it} Y_{it}$$

[31] Ibid., p. 57.

[32] Carl H. Gotsch, 'Regional Agricultural Growth: The Case of West Pakistan', *Asian Survey*, vol. 8, no. 3 (March 1968), p. 197.

where

GVP_0 = gross value of production in the base period
GVP_t = gross value of production in the terminal period
A_0 = total acreage in the base period
A_t = total acreage in the terminal period
Y_{i0} = yield per acre of the ith crop in the base period
Y_{it} = yield per acre of the ith crop in the terminal period
C_{i0} = percentage of the ith crop of total acreage in the base period
C_{it} = percentage of the ith crop of the total acreage in the terminal period
P_i = constant price weights for ith crop

then

$$(4)\ GVP_t - GVP_0 = (A_t - A_0) \sum_{i=1}^{n} p_i C_{i0} Y_{i0}$$
$$+ A_t \sum_{i=1}^{n} p_i C_{i0} (Y_{it} - Y_{i0})$$
$$+ A_t \sum_{i=1}^{n} p_i (C_{it} - C_{i0}) Y_{i0}$$
$$+ A_t \sum_{i=1}^{n} p_i (C_{it} - C_{i0}) (Y_{it} - Y_{i0})$$

For clarity in interpreting the results I have modified (3) slightly.

$$(5)\ GVP_t - GVP_0 = (A_t - A_0) \sum_{i=1}^{n} p_i C_{i0} Y_{i0}$$
$$+ A_0 \sum_{i=1}^{n} p_i C_{i0} (Y_{it} - Y_{i0})$$
$$+ (A_t - A_0) \sum_{i=1}^{n} p_i C_{i0} (Y_{it} - Y_{i0})$$
$$+ A_0 \sum_{i=1}^{n} p_i (C_{it} - C_{i0}) Y_{i0}$$
$$+ (A_t - A_0) \sum_{i=1}^{n} p_i (C_{it} - C_{i0}) Y_{i0}$$

$$+ A_0 \sum_{i=1} p_i C_{it} - C_{i0}) (Y_{it} - Y_{i0})$$

$$+ (A_t - A_0) \sum_{i=1}^{n} p_i (C_{it} - C_{i0}) (Y_{it} - Y_{i0})$$

The first term on the right hand side of Equation 5 is the increase in GVP when just the acreage is changed. The second term gives the yield effect and the fourth term gives the change due to a change in the cropping pattern. In contrast, the MV yield and cropping pattern effects are weighted by the acreage in the terminal year which exaggerates their impact. The third, fifth, sixth and seventh terms give the interaction effects. In the British period, yield and area data are available separately for the irrigated and unirrigated acreage of each crop. In order to get the most information out of this technique, I have calculated Equation 5 separately for irrigated and unirrigated output.

The base period is the five years, 1907–11 — the first five years for which yield estimates are available in the *Season and Crop Reports*. The final period is 1942–6. The crops included are wheat, desi cotton, American cotton, rice, barley, jowar, bajra, maize, and gram. The price weights are the average of the harvest prices of these crops for the years 1937–9. The official acreage figures were used for both periods because, as mentioned above, they are generally considered quite reliable.

The real problem as the first part of this chapter suggests is what yields to use. For the final period in four crops there is a relatively simple solution. In wheat, desi cotton, and American cotton there are independent estimates of yields which are superior to the official estimates. The yield of wheat as estimated by Sukhatme (Table 3) will be used and the standard yields for 1938 will be cotton. For sugarcane I have used the official yields from the period 1943–6 as these have apparently been adjusted by the government to take into account the improved varieties of cane. It is the yields of the other crops that cause the problems. There seem to be two possible choices. First, the lower bound group of yield could be used as the official yields for 1942–6. The second is an upper bound estimate of yields which come from multiplying the official yields of 1942–6 by the ratio of 1950s yields to 1940s yields of the East Punjab from Table 4.

In view of the discussion above on the unreliability of any trends from the official production figures, I am assuming that the yield for the beginning period is the same as the end except in crops where there is clear evidence of some change due to new technology, weather, or disease. The crops for which such evidence exists are wheat, desi cotton, sugarcane, and gram. The first three crops had increasing yields due to the introduction of improved crop varieties. The trend in the last crop was probably downward due to disease and weather problems. In northern Punjab in the late 1930s the gram crop was almost totally destroyed in several districts due to a fungal disease called gram blight.[33] Gram wilt was causing problems in the southeastern part of the province at about the same time.[34] There are no reports of serious outbreaks of these diseases during the 1940s but they probably continued to depress yields in certain areas.

In wheat I have used the Sukhatme estimates of the yields of the unimproved crop as the yields of irrigated and unirrigated wheat in the initial period. For sugarcane I have used the yield of unimproved varieties from the cost of cultivation survey for the irrigated crop and assumed that the percentage change in the unirrigated crop was the same as in the irrigated crop to get an estimate of the unirrigated crop yield. In desi cotton, the data from experiment stations and large farms in the Punjab was used to calculate the yield.[35]

[33] Roberts, p. 301.

[34] Ibid.

[35] Experiment station and large farm data were used to find the ratio of the yields of improved and unimproved. This ratio, the percentage of cotton under improved varieties, and the standard yield from 1938 were used in Equations 5 and 6 to get the initial yield.

(5) $Y_{38} = hY_I + (1\text{-}h)Y_U$

Y_{38} is the yield per acre of desi cotton in 1938
Y_I is the yield per acre of improved desi
Y_U is the yield per acre of unimproved desi
h is the ratio area under improved desi to total area under desi cotton

Equation 5 says that the yield of desi is a weighted average of the yields of improved and unimproved desi cottons. Since the ratio of improved yield to unimproved yield (r) is also available, the yield of unimproved, which is to be used as the initial yield, can be calculated with Equation 6.

(6) $Y_U = \frac{38}{(hr - h + 1)}$ where $r = Y_I/Y_U$

There is no way of knowing exactly how much gram yields declined due to these disease problems. As a result, I have arbitrarily decided to assume that the yield of gram was 10 per cent higher in the initial period.

The results of the disaggregation are in Table 7. Under Assumption 1 the GVP in the initial period was Rs 431 million. If the higher yields per acre are used, the initial GVP was Rs 502.5 million. The total increases in rupees are given in the last row of Table 7. They represent 47 and 41.5 per cent increases over the lower and higher initial estimates, but in terms of rupees there is very little difference in the quantity change. Therefore, the main effect of the different assumptions about yield per acre is to change the growth rate rather than the absolute quantities. Instead of a growth rate of 1.08 per cent per annum (assuming a semi-logarithmic growth path) with the lower yields, the higher initial yields imply a 0.92 yearly growth rate.

The rest of Table 7 answers the question of how much the GVP would have increased if the factor in the first column increased, but everything else was held constant. First, as expected the increase in irrigated acreage contributed more than any factor to the increase in output—between 74 and 79 per cent of the total increase. Thus, under Assumption 1, if the irrigated acreage increased to its 1942–6 level but the yield per acre, cropping pattern, and unirrigated land stayed at their initial levels, output would have grown by Rs 150.4 million. This is 74.2 per cent of the total Rs 204.2 million change that actually took place. Second, despite Krishna's conclusion that new technology did not contribute to growth in the Punjab, this table suggests that it did make an important contribution. The change in yield per acre which accounts for 10 to 15 per cent of the increase, was due to higher yielding varieties of wheat, desi cotton, and sugarcane. The change in cropping patterns was almost entirely the result of the introduction of American cotton by the Punjab Department of Agriculture. It was grown in only a few scattered plots in the initial period, but by 1944 it was grown on 1.8 million acres.[36] Yield, cropping pattern and their interaction term on irrigated and unirrigated land contributed Rs 38.0 million or 18.7 per cent of the increase under Assumption 1 and Rs 32.0

[36] Gulshan Rai, *Agricultural Statistics of the Punjab 1901–2 to 1935–6* (Lahore Board of Economic Inquiry, 1937), Supplement 5, p. 10.

Table 7. Disaggregation of Agricultural Growth 1907–16 (1937–9 Prices in the Punjab)

	Assumption 1				Assumption 2			
	Irrigated		Unirrigated		Irrigated		Unirrigated	
	Output Change (Rs Million)	% of Total Change	Output Change	%of Total Change	Output Change	% Total	Output Change	% Total
Area	150.4	73.6	–5.7	–2.8	164.0	78.7	–7.1	–3.4
Yield	24.9	12.2	5.7	2.8	22.6	10.8	–1.5	–.7
Cropping pattern	11.4	5.6	–1.4	–.7	13.1	6.3	1.2	0.6
Area and yield	15.0	7.3	–.2	–.1	13.6	6.5	0	0
Area and cropping pattern	6.8	3.3	0	0	7.9	3.8	0	0
Yield and cropping pattern	–3.0	–1.5	0.5	0.3	–3.4	–1.6	–.1	0
Area, yield and cropping pattern	–1.8	–.9	0	0	–2.0	–1.0	0	0
Total irrigated and unirrigated	203.6	99.6	–1.0	–.5	215.8	103.5	–7.5	–3.5
1907–11 GVP	431.0				502.5			
Grand Total Change	Rs 204.2				Rs 208.3			
1942–6 GVP	635.2				710.8			

million or 15.4 per cent of the increase under Assumption 2. Therefore, the Department of Agriculture research program seems to have produced significant results; and it is worthwhile to examine how these results were obtained.

Conclusion

The discussion of the methods for determining official yield per acre and crop acreage estimates indicate that this was quite an arbitrary process depending on the inclination of officials. The independent evidence on yield per acre shows that the trends and levels of the official yield per acre cannot be relied upon. This evidence contradicts the assumption of Krishna and more recently Mishra who assumed that there were no systematic biases in these series over time.

After adjusting the level and trends in these series, I have recalculated the rate of growth and the sources of growth. The results of this calculation do not change the aggregate growth rate much since some of the biases in yield per acre were upward biases and others were downward. The growth rate of total output remains about 1 per cent which is less than the growth in population during this period.

These adjustments do change the interpretation of the sources of growth. The increase in irrigated land remains the major source of growth but the interpretation of the role of new technology differs. Mishra concludes: 'Improved varieties of crops and new implements such as the Meston plough remained only isolated instances which did not materially affect overall yield rates.'[37] In contrast the adjusted data indicates that new varieties of wheat, sugarcane and desi cotton did increase yield per acre and that the introduction of a stream of new varieties of American cotton improved the value of the cropping pattern. In aggregate, they may have accounted for almost 20 per cent of the growth in output during this period.

[37] Mishra, p. 340.

Chapter 6

Trends in Crop Production in the Undivided Punjab: A Reassessment

[1988]

M. MUFAKHARUL ISLAM

In discussing the performance of the agricultural sector in British India and its different regional units, it has been usual for commentators to treat Punjab as an exceptional case. This is understandable, for Blyn's study on the subject, which is still the only one of its kind, shows that there was a marked disparity between the Punjab and India as a whole or any other individual province. While all crop output remained almost stagnant in British India (0.37 per cent year) from 1891–2 to 1946–7, in the Punjab it increased by 1.57 per cent. During the same period population increased at the annual rate of 0.67 per cent in India and 0.93 per cent in the Punjab. The disparity was even more marked in foodgrains output (0.11 per cent in India as against 1.1 per cent in Punjab). The nearest growth rate in all-crop output achieved in any province (Madras) was 0.98 per cent per year.[1] The Punjab's performance has suggested to several commentators that the foundation of the present-day Green Revolution in the two parts of the divided province was laid during the last half century of colonial rule. According to Clive Dewey:

> If one superimposes a map of agricultural India today on a map of Indian agriculture in 1900, one finds that the areas in which the Green Revolution is currently acclaimed – the Punjab and Gujarat – are those in which agricultural growth was always most pronounced. . . . Development economists, when they attribute the Green Revolution to the second five year plan, run a certain risk in ignoring this historical perspective.[2]

[1] George Blyn, *Agricultural Trends in India, 1891–1947. Output, Availability and Productivity* (Philadelphia, 1966), 99 and 119.

[2] Clive Dewey. 'The Agricultural Output of an Indian Province: The Punjab, 1870–1940' paper presented at the Institute of Commonwealth Studies. See also Xinru Liu, 'Small Land-holdings in the Punjab: The Historical Perspective', *Punjab Past and Present*, XVI–II (1982), 32.

This contention may well be justified, but the present paper argues that the Punjab's performance in crop production may not have been as spectacular or as dramatic as Blyn's pioneering work would lead one to believe.

The 'Undivided Punjab' treated in this paper (i.e. the British province as it was constituted in November 1901) differs from Blyn's 'Greater Punjab' in as much as it includes the North-West Frontier Province (N.W.F.P.). This may not mean a significant difference in the trend rates, however, for in 1901 the cropped area of the N.W.F.P. only accounted for 8 per cent of the total cropped area of the Punjab and the N.W.F.P. taken together—and it is likely that this weight declined in the subsequent years.

Blyn's Data Base and his Method of Adjustment

The need to reassess Blyn's study arises from the defects of his data and still more, the defects of the procedure he employs in estimating the production of certain crops not reported in his sources till 1911–12. The crop statistics are available from four main sources: *Punjab Revenue* (later *Land Revenue*) *Administration Reports*, the *Agricultural Statistics of India*, *Estimates of Area and Yield of Principal Crops in India* (henceforth *Estimates*) and the *Season and Crop Reports*. The *Revenue Administration Reports* contain district-wise data on individual crops from 1870–1 onwards. From 1887–8 a second set of data on the area under cultivation and production of wheat, cotton, indigo, mustard and sesamum is presented in separate appendices for the province as a whole. The sources and the method of collection of these two sets of data are not mentioned in detail but it is pointed out that the data in the first set are based on village papers and those in the second taken from the final forecasts. The first set is also available in the *Agricultural Statistics* from 1884–5. The second group of statistics on acreage and output of certain crops is published in the *Estimates* (as also in the *Agricultural Statistics*) from 1891–2. The number of crops covered in this series increased over time as follows: sugarcane 1898–9, barley, bajra, maize, jowar, gram 1911–12, linseed 1912–13, tobacco 1926–7 and rice 1939–40. The publication of the district acreage statistics (i.e. in the first set) in *Revenue Administration Reports* ceased in 1901–2, but the *Season and Crop Reports* took their place. Two important changes were introduced in this series from 1906–7. Firstly, district data on the production of the following crops were presented: wheat, rice, jowar, maize, barley, gram, cotton, rabi, oilseeds and sugarcane. Secondly, the acreage data referred to the areas sown with a crop (not harvested as in the past).

Blyn estimates the trends in cropped area, yield per acre and production on the basis of the data furnished in the *Estimates*, (i.e. those for the province as a whole based on final forecasts).[3] Only the acreage data of bajra, gram, barely, maize and rice (which are not reported in this series) are said to have been collected from the *Agricultural Statistics* and the figures for these crops are riddled with anomalies. Firstly, data on wheat acreage (as available from the *Estimates*) for the Greater Punjab differ considerably from those based on village papers in the first set of *Agricultural Statistics and Revenue Administration Reports*. The acreage data on wheat for the Punjab proper also differ from those given in the *Season and Crop Reports* from 1901–2. Again, the statistics on wheat production in Punjab proper as presented in the *Estimates* differ from those in the *Season and Crop Reports* from 1906–7. The discrepancy between the two series continues till 1922–3. Part of the difference in the acreage data during the period 1893–4 to 1905–6 was due to the fact that the data in the *Estimates* refer to the area sown whereas those in the other set apply to harvested area. Secondly, Blyn's data on sugarcane and cotton acreage and output do not agree with those available in the *Estimates* (Appendix A). The discrepancy continues till 1922–3 in the case of cotton and 1911–12 in sugarcane. Moreover, although Blyn estimates the trend rates of sugarcane from 1891–2, acreage and output data are not furnished before 1898–9. It is possible that he makes some adjustments in the data relating to sugarcane and cotton, as he does in the case of rape and mustard, but the specific procedure is not spelt out.[4]

The fact that Blyn's data are not comparable over time is a more important drawback. Acreage data of wheat and mustard relate to the harvested area prior to 1893–4 and sown area for all the subsequent years. For all other crops, up to 1905–6, the acreage statistics are those on area harvested and those of the subsequent years relate to sown area. Statistics showing the areas over which the harvest failed are not available for individual crops before 1906–7. But if we proceed on the basis of the proportion of total, failed area for the

[3] Blyn, 40.
[4] Ibid., 58.

period 1896–7 to 1900–1, it would appear that the acreage data are about 20 per cent lower for wheat and mustard during the first two years, and for all other crops during all the years up to 1905–6. This implies that Blyn's study overestimates the rates of change in crop acreage during the first two reference decades.

The same contention applies to trend rates for the output of minor cereals. Blyn estimates the output of gram, bajra, maize and barley for the period of 1891–2 to 1911–12 on the basis of the yield per acre of 'similar crops'. Crops taken as similar are, respectively, wheat, sugarcane, and sesamum.[5] Such a method overestimates the rates of change in the production of these crops in two ways. Firstly, as Blyn himself points out, irrigated area under these crops did not increase as much as the irrigated area under wheat.[6] Secondly, the acreage data of gram, barley, maize and bajra relate to those on harvested area prior to 1906–7 and sown area in the subsequent years, although the acreage data of wheat and sesamum are those on sown area for the entire period from 1893–4. This means that the output of gram, barley and maize is estimated at a lower level prior to 1906–7 because the yield per acre of wheat and sesamum is lower than it would have been if the 'failed' areas had been excluded. It is difficult to get any idea of the underlying trends in yield per acre, but if we go by the proportion of 'failed area' mentioned earlier, it would appear that production figures of these crops for the years prior to 1906–7 are about 20 per cent lower. Again, this would imply a certain degree of overestimation in the percentage rate of change.

Overall, it would appear that Blyn's study exaggerates the Punjab's achievements in crop production during the first two decades. If we compare rates of increase during these years with the subsequent reference decades (Table 1) we reach the same conclusion. Weather conditions were very unfavourable in 1891–2 and 1896–7 and exceptionally unfavourable in 1899–1900, but Blyn's study shows that the annual rates of increase in crop production were the highest

[5] Statistics on jowar and rice production in Punjab are not presented by Blyn in his Appendix tables. This implies that they are not included in his study. However, he mentions that estimated rice yield is based on wheat, 216. This would mean that rice production figures have been estimated by him for almost the entire period, because the relevant data were not reported in the *Estimates* before 1939.

[6] Blyn, 216–19.

Table 1. Percentage Rates of Change Estimated by Blyn

Crops	1891 to 1900	1896 to 1905	1901 to 1910	1906 to 1915	1911 to 1920	1916 to 1925	1921 to 1930	1926 to 1935	1931 to 1940	1936 to 1945	Average
Area											
FG	00	2.74	2.98	1.08	– .10	.45	– .03	– .08	– .14	1.82	.87
NFG	1.92	3.35	1.85	– .11	0.32	2.71	1.35	.72	1.12	– 1.19	1.20
All	.36	2.81	2.88	.94	.07	.82	.17	– .02	.13	1.47	.96
Yield											
FG	.77	1.72	– .01	– 1.28	– .18	.17	– .39	.84	1.21	.23	.31
NFG	– .87	– .14	1.43	1.65	1.92	.55	.20	3.37	1.03	2.20	1.13
All	.57	1.71	0.21	– .63	.34	.45	– .29	1.97	1.64	.28	.62
Output											
FG	1.06	4.12	2.92	– .16	– .05	– .60	– .61	0.56	1.23	2.50	1.10
NFG	2.07	3.72	3.68	1.88	2.15	3.34	.26	3.02	3.24	.69	2.40
All	1.20	3.89	3.08	.52	.56	1.26	– .39	1.73	1.86	1.98	1.57
Population	.70	.30	– .09	– .09	.37	1.58	1.29	1.94	1.59	1.58	.93

NOTES: FG = foodgrains: NFG = non-foodgrains; All = All crops.

SOURCE: = George Blyn, *Agricultural Trends in India, 1891–1947* (Philadelphia, 1966), Appendix Table 5B, 332.

during these early years. The last decade witnessed considerable increase in area sown with high yielding varieties, a phenomenal increase in the price level and the 'Grow More Food' campaign, but production—according to Blyn—increased at less than 2.0 per cent per year. Thus, the height of the trend rates of the first two decades is in doubt, not only because of the nature of the data on which it is based, but also because it is inconsistent with the rate of change in the subsequent years.

Revised Trend Rates

As mentioned earlier, the *Season and Crop Reports* contain data on the cultivated area of each crop from 1901–2 and the production of all important crops (wheat, barley, bajra, rice, maize, rice, gram, oilseeds, sugarcane and cotton) from 1906–7 onwards. This series has several advantages over the *Estimates*. Firstly, the method of estimating crop acreage and output and the agency responsible for preparing the estimates remained more or less the same over the entire period. Secondly, cropped area, yield per acre and total out-turn are shown under two heads: irrigated and unirrigated. Thirdly, the statistics are furnished for every district, thus making it possible to get some idea of regional variations in the performance of the agricultural sector. Fourthly, there are no gaps in the data except in the case of tobacco output. Finally, the *Season and Crop Reports* make it possible to include two crops (jowar and rice) excluded in Blyn's study. In other words, the statistics available from this series should give us a better view of agricultural trends in the Punjab than the alternatives used by Blyn.

Average annual rates of change in crop acreage, yield per acre and crop production estimated on the basis of data available from the *Season and Crop Reports* are presented in Table 2. The method of crop aggregation and the weights given to individual crops are the same as in Blyn's study. The methods of estimating the trend rates are also similar.[7] But the results are quite different. We get much lower rates of increase in foodgrains output and its two determinants: cropped area and yield per acre. The rate of increase is a little higher in non-foodgrains, but for all crops taken together the average

[7] In this paper trend rates are estimated by fitting an exponential equation of the type $\log Y = a + bt$.

Table 2. Average Annual Rates of Change

Crops	Area			Yield			Output		
	(*a*)	(*b*)	(*c*)	(*a*)	(*b*)	(*c*)	(*a*)	(*b*)	(*c*)
AC	0.43	0.51	0.96	0.36	0.54	0.62	0.79	1.10	1.57
FG	0.31	0.43	0.87	0.11	0.01	0.31	0.42	0.41	1.10
NFG	1.08	0.70	1.20	1.55	1.56	1.13	2.64	2.10	1.40
MC	0.26	–	–	0.00	–	–	0.26	–	–
Wheat	0.36	–	–	0.28	–	–	0.63	–	–

NOTE: AC = All crops; FG = Foodgrains; NFG = Non-foodgrains; MC = Minor cereals (jowar, bajra, gram, barley and maize); Trend rates under (*a*) are those estimated in this paper, those under (*b*) refer to the average of the rates estimated by Blyn for the decades beginning 1906 and 1916, while those under (*c*) are his estimates for the entire period 1891–2 to 1946–7.

rate of change as estimated by Blyn is reduced by nearly half. Consequently, population growth is shown to have exceeded crop production.[8] The disparity widens in the case of food production. Such lower rates of change in all-crop output estimated in the present paper strengthen the contention that the inclusion of the data for the period 1891–2 to 1905–6 introduces an upward bias in the performance of the crop production sector in Punjab agriculture. Further evidence reinforcing the same contention is provided by the remarkable similarity between these trend rates and the average of those estimated by Blyn for the seven reference decades beginning 1906–16 (Table 2). Non-foodgrains output seems to have expanded at a faster rate when we base our estimates on the data available from the *Season and Crop Reports*, but despite this the rate of increase in all-crop output is a little lower than that estimated by Blyn.

Obviously this pattern implies that in the present paper foodgrains have more weight than in Blyn's study. This difference may be due to two factors. Firstly, Blyn does not seem to include rice and jowar in the foodgrains category. Secondly, it is possible that the inclusion of the N.W.F.P. in his study further increases the weight of the non-foodgrains.

[8] Blyn's figures (Appendix Table 5B, 332) suggest that population in Greater Punjab increased by 1.2 per cent per year during the last seven reference decades beginning 1906–16.

Reliability of the Estimated Rates of Change

Should the trend rates presented in this paper—or any other paper—be taken seriously? If the range of error in the relevant statistics did not remain uniform over time, reliable trend rates cannot be estimated. Clive Dewey has argued that this was the case in the Punjab. He concedes that area statistics are generally reliable, but contends that it is questionable whether the degree of underestimation in the yield statistics did remain constant. He suggests that the subjectivity of the agricultural statistics induced conservatism, leading to an increase in the degree of underestimation, so that the growth of agricultural output was greater than Blyn supposed.[9] A detailed discussion of the questions which have been raised in the debate[10] is beyond the scope of this paper, but if we consider some of the more relevant facts the rates of change may not appear to be grossly underestimated.

Among the inputs which cause or facilitate improvement in crop yield significant progress was made in the Punjab in respect of two: irrigation and improved varieties of seeds. Irrigated area under the crops included in this study expanded at 1.2 per cent per year and, during the decade 1937–8 to 1946–7, total irrigated area accounted for 52 per cent of the total cropped area in the province. Secondly, improved varieties of wheat, cotton and sugarcane were evolved at the research centres, and the area sown with these seeds expanded rapidly from the 1920s. Thus, in 1938–9, about half of the wheat area, 64 per cent of the area under sugarcane and, in 1945, 70 per cent of the cotton acreage were sown with these seeds.[11]

Such impressive gains in irrigation and the use of new seeds naturally create the expectation that the rate of improvement in

[9] Dewey, 'Agricultural Output', 2.

[10] Clive Dewey, 'The Agricultural Statistics of the Punjab, 1867–1947', *Bulletin of Quantitative and Computer Methods in South Asian Studies*, no. 2. (March 1974); '*Patwari* and *Chaukidar*: Subordinate Officials and the Reliability of India's Agricultural Statistics' in *The Imperial Impact: Studies in the Economic History of Africa and India*, ed. C. Dewey and A. G. Hopkins (London, 1978). S. C. Misra, 'On the Reliability of Pre-independence Agricultural Statistics of Bombay and Punjab', *Indian Economic and Social History Review*, XX (2) (1983); and C. E. Pray, 'Accuracy of Official Agricultural Statistics and the Sources of Growth in the Punjab', *Indian Economic and Social History Review*, XXI (3) (1984).

[11] For wheat and sugarcane see *Report On the Operations of the Department of Agriculture, Punjab* (annual) 1938–9, 71 and 77. For cotton see William Roberts and S. B. S. Kartar Singh, *A Text Book of Punjab Agriculture* (Lahore, 1947), 437.

yields per acre should be higher than those estimated in this study, especially in the case of foodgrains. There were, however, certain developments which probably had adverse effects on crop yields during the period under review. Firstly, soil fertility may have been affected by the fact that the proportion of land annually left fallow to enable it to recover its productive power decreased over time.[12] Secondly, working in the same direction was another development more serious in nature: the problem of water logging in the irrigated tracts of the province. In 1946–7 it was found that 2.3 million acres, or 24 per cent of the area under canal irrigation were affected by water logging in the thirteen districts of the Pakistani Punjab.[13] Thirdly, the proportion of land cultivated by the sharecroppers or tenants-at-will increased from 32 per cent in 1890 to 48 per cent in 1932,[14] and this is likely to have increased in the subsequent years. As Clive Dewey has argued, cultivation by such tenants may not necessarily have reduced efficiency,[15] but contemporary observers were almost unanimously of the view that tenants-at-will cultivated less efficiently than owners.[16] Fourthly, almost all the improved cottons were valued for the better quality of their staple rather than their higher yields. Moreover, the quality of the new seeds deteriorated after several years' use.[17] Finally, it was estimated that whereas the number of ploughs per 100 acres remained constant (at eight) the number of plough-cattle declined (from 19 to 14) during the period 1904 to 1935.[18] This suggests that the intensity of ploughing declined or at best remained constant over time.

[12] Fallow land declined by 0.5 per cent per annum during the period 1912–13 to 1935–6. For details see Hirashima Shigemochi, *The Structure of Disparity in Developing Agriculture* (Tokyo, 1978), 34.

[13] Punjab Board of Economic Inquiry, *Agricultural Statistics of the Punjab, Pakistan* (Lahore, 1950), 14–15. Out of the total waterlogged area 13 lakh acres were being cultivated.

[14] Dewey, 'Agricultural Output,' 9.

[15] Ibid., 10.

[16] Thus, according to H. Calvert, 'These tenants (at-will) generally take less care in preparing the land for crops, plough it less often, manure it less and use fewer implements upon it than owners.' For details see his *Wealth and Welfare of the Punjab* (Lahore, 1936), 206. The same view was taken by D. Milne, Director of Agriculture, Punjab. For details see *Report of the Royal Commission on Agriculture in India*, vol. VIII, *Evidence taken in the Punjab* (London, 1927), 189.

[17] Milne's testimony to the Royal Commission, ibid., 242. See also T. G. Kessinger, *Vilyatpur 1848–1968* (New Delhi, 1979), 120.

[18] Board of Economic Inquiry, Punjab, *Agricultural Statistics of the Punjab, 1901–2 to 1935–6* (Lahore, 1937), 27.

If these facts are borne in mind, it is difficult to believe that the annual rate of improvement in cash crop yield was an underestimate. Indeed, we might even suggest that if there is an error at all, it is on the side of overestimation. In this connection it may be mentioned that the entire area under oilseeds continued to be sown with traditional seeds. Moreover, there was little expansion of the area under the American varieties of cotton during the first fifteen years of the period under review.

With regard to the foodgrains, virtually nothing was done to evolve new seeds for pulses and minor cereals like bajra, maize, gram and jowar. None the less, the irrigated area under cereals and pulses expanded at 1.0 per cent per year, and during the last decade accounted for 40 per cent of the total area under these crops. Yield per irrigated acre was considerably higher than yield per non-irrigated acre. We should then expect a better rate of improvement in the yield of these crops. One would tend to take the same view if only the trend in wheat yield is taken into consideration. Irrigated acreage under this crop increased by 0.82 per cent per year and, as mentioned earlier, by the late 1930s about 50 per cent of the wheat area was sown with HYV. Still yield improved by only 0.28 per cent per annum. Should it then be suggested that the margin of error in foodgrains yield increased over time? Or should we attribute the relative stagnation in yield to the possibility that the adverse factors mentioned above operated more than proportionately in the case of foodgrains? Obviously nothing definite can be said on these questions. Perhaps, some allowance has to be made for a certain degree of underestimation in foodgrains yield rate, but it is clear that the adjusted rate of increase in all-crop output would not be as high as 1.57 per cent per annum. In this connection it may be mentioned that very little progress was made in the use of HYV of wheat during the first two decades.

To summarise and conclude, given the nature of the crop statistics of the first two reference decades and his method of estimating the crops not reported in the *Estimates*, Blyn's study exaggerates the rate of growth of crop production in Punjab during these years, and this, in turn, introduces an upward bias in the time trends for the entire period, 1891 to 1947. This presumption is strengthened by the rates estimated on the basis of crop statistics available from the *Season and Crop Reports* for the period 1906–47. It is possible that these statistics underestimate the foodgrains output rate of increase, but the underestimation is not likely to be very marked.[19] It is, therefore, doubtful whether the performance of Punjab's agriculture during the last half century of colonial rule was as dramatic as we generally suppose.[20]

[19] Growth rates of agricultural output in Punjab have also been estimated by Chander Prabha, 'District-wise Rates of Growth of Agricultural Output in East and West Punjab during the pre-partition and post-partition Periods', *Indian Economic and Social History Review*, VI (1964) and Raj Krishna, 'The Growth of Aggregate Agricultural Output in the Punjab', *Indian Economic Journal* (December 1964). Chander Prabha uses data from *Season and Crop Reports* for the period 1906–7 to 1945–6 and arrives at an annual growth rate of 0.92 per cent. The growth rate estimated by Raj Krishna (for the period 1913–14 to 1945–6) is 1.1 per cent per year.

[20] This paper arises from my current research on the impact of irrigation on crop patterns and tenurial relations in undivided Punjab (1887–1947) and my earlier examination of the crop statistics of Bengal. For the latter see my *Bengal Agriculture, 1920–46: A Quantitative Study* (Cambridge, 1978).

Appendix A. Crop Statistics from Different Sources

Years	Wheat		Cotton		Sugarcane	
	(*a*)	(*b*)	(*a*)	(*b*)	(*a*)	(*b*)
1891–2	7,768	6,224	547	540		
1892	8,646	7,123	582	948		
1893	9,717	8,265	1,005	1,125		
1894	9,264	8,052	1,164	1,161		
1895–6	7,094	6,893	1,170	1,177		
1896	6,792	6,584	1,064	1,128		
1897	8,872	8,013	1,070	789		
1898	7,942	7,729	759	988	417	351
1899	5,953	6,366	763	145	380	344
1900	9,810	8,766	1,134	1,080	370	355
1901	6,671	7,227	988	1,027	406	352
1902	7,730	6,995	1,203	1,194	361	309
1903	9,567	7,766	1,185	1,205	376	321
1904	9,414	7,712	1,502	1,698	382	326
1905	10,388	8,572	788	2,020	181	173
1906	9,647	9,100	1,261	1,413	279	278
1907	7,393	8,272	1,318	1,474	394	392
1908	8,397	9,002	1,448	1,562	369	366
1909	8,676	9,142	1,277	1,436	417	404
1910	8,885	9,981	1,250	1,385	400	387
1911–12	9,726	11,018	1,463	1,582	298	285
1912–13	8,767	9,309	1,443	1,575	367	360
1913	8,473	9,588	1,825	2,053		
1914	9,915	11,336	1,688	1,857		
1915	8,992	10,246	827	902		
1916	9,467	10,737	1,074	1,163		
1917	9,926	11,271	1,643	1,800		
1918	7,684	8,536	1,418	1,555		
1919	8,813	9,953	2,071	2,269		
1920	7,751	8,781	1,957	2,142		
1921	8,789	9,981	1,149	1,239		
1922	9,620	10,870	1,273	1,417		

NOTES: Data under (*a*) are those available from *Land Revenue Administration Reports* prior to 1901–2 while those under (*b*) are taken from the *Estimates*. For the period prior to 1901–2 the statistics relate to the Greater Punjab and those for the subsequent years are for Punjab proper. As mentioned in the text, statistics on sugarcane acreage are available in the *Estimates* from 1898–9. After 1922–3 there is no difference in the two sets of statistics for wheat and cotton. In the case of sugarcane the statistics are the same from 1913–14. All figures are in thousand acres.

Chapter 7

Long Term Trends in per Acre Wheat Yields in North India, 1827–1947: An Evaluation of Old Controversies with Some Fresh Evidence

[Hitherto Unpublished]

ASHWANI SAITH

Introduction

Subscribers to the 'classical' and 'nationalist' schools within modern Indian history contend that the nineteenth century was, at best, a period of agricultural stagnation.[1] Blyn's (1966) research on crop- and region-wise agricultural trends then forms the basis for the conclusion that this stagnation was transformed into a perceptible decline in the twentieth century. On the other hand, the 're-interpretationist' and 'official' schools contest this characterisation. Neale (1962), Morris (1963; 1968) and the United Provinces Government *Report on Agriculture* (1926) argue that the nineteenth century was a period of substantial expansion in agricultural productivity, with impressive increases in physical yields per acre of crops; Neale, ambivalently, and Heston (1973) categorically, reject Blyn's evidence suggesting agricultural deterioration in the period to 1947. That such polarized positions can persistently be maintained about such an important—and essentially quantitative—variable, exposes the shaky statistical foundations of this debate on the magnitude and character of agrarian

[1] For a convenient summary of the central issues in the debate, see Morris (1963) and contributions by Bipan Chandra, Raychaudhuri, Matsui and Morris in *The Indian Economy in the 19th Century, A Symposium*, Delhi, 1969; for variants of the 'nationalist' theme, see Naoroji, D. (1901), Dutt, R. C. (1950, 7th ed.), Govt. of India, *Zamindari Abolition Committee Report*, vol. I, 1948; for the 're-interpretationist' and alternative variants, see Morris, M. D. (1963, 1968); Neale, W. C. (1962), Heston, A. W. (1973), United Provinces Government, *Report on Agriculture*, 1926.

expansion in the nineteenth and twentieth centuries.[2] This weakness arises in part, of course, from the paucity of time series data, and from the inherent constraints to its systematic interpretation on account of the inevitable problem of non-comparability of alternative sources. Unfortunately, however, even such statistical material as has been used in this debate has often suffered from an outright misinterpretation of the raw data sources, from an unscientific treatment at the technical stage. There would thus appear to be room in the present state of the debate, to accommodate an effort at identifying and evaluating discernible long-term trends in wheat yields per acre in North India for the period 1827–1947.

An analysis of wheat yield trends is likely to be particularly revealing. Firstly, wheat was the most important cereal crop in most parts of North India, and featured very prominently in the internal, as well as the export trade. It was more profitable than the inferior cereals, and therefore is likely to have received preferential treatment from cultivators with regard to the application of inputs than most other crops, except, perhaps, sugar-cane.[3] Secondly,

[2] More recently, a parallel exchange has developed over the comparison of crop yields per acre (and other related variables) between Akbar's time and the 1960s. Using evidence from the *Ain-i-Akbari*, Ashok Desai (1972) has argued that crop yields per hectare were considerably higher in Akbar's time on similar qualities of land. This finding is moderated by Moosvi (1973); but even after correcting the earlier (official revenue-tied) yields for deliberate overestimation by government officials wanting to inflate the land revenue demand on *zabt* lands, Desai's basic conclusion remains valid. Citing Habib's (1963) evidence from the *Ain*, Heston (1977) 'rightly takes both of us [Desai and Moosvi] to task for an incredible slip in compiling our comparative tables . . . where we both inadvertently took the *man* (*maund*) of Akbar's time as equal to 82.3 lbs instead of 55.32 lbs' (Moosvi, 1977, p. 397). Correction 'shows that no significant change in productivity per unit of area for the major crops . . . can be postulated' between 1595 and the 1890s (Ibid., p. 400). However, this is still consistent with Desai's original contention that yields in the 1960s were lower than the 1595 levels if the official statistics for the 1891–1960s can be accepted. Heston (1977) challenges this, using essentially the same arguments he deploys against Blyn's (1966) work using official statistics.

[3] Thus, while Blyn is forced into estimating the yield of six minor foodgrain crops and rice in the less important growing regions partly on the basis of wheat yields, he queries:

> Is it reasonable to expect that the forces which gave rise to increasing wheat and sesamum yield per acre would also have had a similar effect on

while trends in total outputs and availabilities are crucial for a study of the overall level of consumption of the population, trends in physical yields per acre, more than in any other single variable, are likely to reflect more accurately the net effect of changes in the underlying social, as well as technical cultivation conditions in North Indian agriculture. This would be all the more applicable to long-term trend analysis, when the weather and climatic variations could reasonably be expected to balance out, leaving the net trends only marginally affected.[4] It must, of course, be clearly recognized that such tendencies towards improvement as might be discernible on the basis of wheat yields analysis would greatly exaggerate the tendencies in the inferior grains, which are likely to fare systematically worse (in a trend sense) than wheat. This point is of obvious significance when translating conclusions derived for wheat into generalisations applicable to the entire agricultural, or even the foodgrains sector.

In the context of wheat cultivation in North India, there exist three major sources of statistics on yields per acre. These are:

(i) Official Statistics on Area and Yield: These are available in the form of a regular time series from 1891 in *Agricultural Statistics of India* and underlie the Blyn study.

(ii) Irrigation Department Statistics: The Irrigation Department maintained a regular series of statistical returns on the area and the value of crops raised on the land under canal irrigation. Using suitable price indices for the districts which are serviced by the respective canals, one can

---

the minor foodgrains and in the unreported rice regions? It seems doubtful that the forces raising wheat yield per acre would have had like effect on the minor grains. Much of the rise in wheat yield per acre during the early part of the period was due to the increased proportion of acreage irrigated but it is hardly likely that the minor grains would have been subject to such a force, especially in the early part of the period (in the later part of the period for which data were available there appears to have been little change in the proportion of minor foodgrain acreage irrigated. A small part of the wheat yield per acre increase in the early part of the period was due to use of improved seed; only 5 per cent of the acreage was reported in this category as of 1922–23. For the minor grains, however, even as late as 1937/38 less than one per cent was reported under improved seed. Blyn (1966, p. 217)

[4] See Blyn (1966, pp. 234–6).

form indices of the yield per acre for each important crop in the different canal command areas.[5]

(iii) District Settlement Reports: Every land revenue Settlement Officer was required to formulate fairly precise notions regarding the productivity of the different varieties of soil in his district in order to be able to fix the land revenue demand of the State. The more conscientious officers actually conducted a large number of controlled crop-cutting experiments, thus generating data on yields per acre, the reliability of which exceeds that of any other comparable data put out by official agencies.

The evidence available in the District Settlement Reports (DSRs) and in the Irrigation Reports has not been utilised systematically before, and therefore special interest attaches to the type, and reliability of evidence that can be extracted from these DSRs about long-term trends in wheat yields.

In Section 2, we will very briefly review Blyn's exhaustive empirical study of crop- and region-wise agricultural trends during 1891–1947 based on the official statistical sources for areas and yields—noting especially the trends in foodgrains and wheat in British India and the United Provinces. Subsequently in Section 3, we will shift the focus to yield trends in the nineteenth century and introduce the basic 're-interpretationist' thesis. Thereafter, in Sections 4 and 5, we will examine the statistical basis of this thesis through a careful evaluation of the raw data and the processing methods employed by this group. A detailed attempt will be made to collate and analyse wheat yield data available in the DSRs for Muzaffarnagar and Bareilly districts over the entire period with a view to extracting benchmark statistics on wheat yields. Special attention will be paid to ensure comparability of such benchmark data. The conclusions with regard to nineteenth and twentieth century wheat yield trends in these two districts will be reported in the final section, where we will also tentatively attempt to ascribe the

[5] These statistics are available in the *Annual Reports of the Irrigation Revenue Department* of the United Provinces Government from 1876–7 onwards, and thus pre-date the Official Series. After the start of the Official Statistics, the per acre yields implicit in the Irrigation Department returns seem to correspond to the 'normal' irrigated yields for the crops, as derived for the construction of the Official Series. However, different canal areas do display different 'normal' yields for the same crop.

observed yield trends to different component sources, viz., irrigation, and other factors making for yield increases. The implications of our findings for the continuing debate on the nature of agrarian change under British rule will be briefly stated.

Heston versus Blyn on Twentieth Century Agricultural Deterioration

In order to provide an appropriate perspective, selected statistical evidence from Blyn's study has been reproduced in Tables 1, 2 and 3. From the point of view of our analysis, the following observations might be pertinent.

(*a*) Over the entire period, foodgrains yield declined annually by 0.18 per cent, the rate of decline being –0.44 per cent in the period since 1921; the non-foodgrains yield rose over the entire period by 0.86 per cent per annum, the rate of increase being 1.15 per cent per annum since 1921.

(*b*) A similar pattern, though slightly moderated, is evident for the United Provinces.

(*c*) If we consider the crop-wise trends, we find that at the British India level, wheat yield increased over the period at an average annual rate of 0.38 per cent. The increase in the period up to 1915 was as high as 1.25 per cent, while in the period from 1921, the rate declined to 0.02 per cent per annum. It is significant that the rate of increase of wheat yields is higher than that for any other foodgrain in the entire, or any sub-period, with the sole exception of maize for the 1921–46 period. This corroborates our presumption that whatever rising trends in what yield might be discerned from our subsequent analysis, these are likely to overstate considerably the tendencies (if any) towards improvement in the yields of the inferior foodgrains.

(*d*) Table 3 shows that while the wheat cultivation area in the United Provinces remained essentially stable over the entire period—especially after the first decade—the yield per acre rose steadily until the 1911–20 decade, and thereafter declined, coincidentally, to exactly the first decade level by the last decade of the period, this level being the lowest for any reference decade in the entire period. From the peak decade to the last decade, the wheat yield per acre declines

Table 1. British India and Regional Aggregate Yield per Acre: Average Trend Rates of Change, and Change in Reference Decade Rates of Change (%)

Regional Crops	10 RD Av. Per Year	Change in RD Rates, Per RD	First 4 RD Av. Per Year	Last 4 RD Av. Per Year
British India				
All-crops	0.01	–0.09	0.47	–0.02
Foodgrains	–0.18	–0.12	0.29	–0.44
Non-foodgrains	0.86	0.02	0.81	1.15
Greater Bengal				
All-crops	–0.34	–0.12	0.08	–0.48
Foodgrains	–0.55	–0.11	–0.11	–0.74
Non-foodgrains	0.59	–0.09	0.74	0.78
United Provinces				
All-crops	0.15	–0.05	0.38	0.16
Foodgrains	–0.02	–0.18	0.57	–0.31
Non-foodgrains	0.24	0.13	–0.34	0.91
Madras				
All-crops	0.65	–0.18	1.24	0.19
Foodgrains	0.35	–0.17	0.99	–0.03
Non-foodgrains	1.25	–0.19	1.58	0.58
Greater Punjab				
All-crops	0.62	0.04	0.47	0.90
Foodgrains	0.31	–0.01	0.30	0.47
Non-foodgrains	1.13	0.24	0.52	1.70
Bombay-Sind				
All-crops	0.28	0.04	0.54	0.35
Foodgrains	–0.11	–0.06	0.43	–0.41
Non-foodgrains	0.92	0.88	0.10	2.08
Central Provinces				
All-crops	0.08	–0.32	1.97	–0.91
Foodgrains	0.05	–0.33	1.12	–0.84
Non-foodgrains	0.77	–0.32	1.60	–0.02

SOURCE: Blyn (1966), pp. 165–6.

at 0.73 per cent per annum. Thus, on Blyn's evidence, based on the official statistics, average wheat yields per acre rose between 1891–1900 and 1911–20, and thereafter declined steadily.

Table 2. British India Yield per Acre of Crop Aggregates and Individual Crops: Average Trend Rates of Change and Change in Reference Decade Rates of Change (%)

Crop	10 RD Av Per Year	Change in RD Rates per RD	First 4 RD Av. Per Year	Last 4 RD Av. Per Year
All Crops	0.0	–0.09	0.47	–0.02
Foodgrains	–0.18	–0.12	0.29	–0.44
Rice	–0.24	–0.15	0.39	–0.57
Wheat	0.38	–0.20	1.25	0.02
Jowar	0.00	–0.17	0.64	–0.63
Gram	–0.26	–0.19	0.52	–0.88
Bajra	0.06	–0.07	0.35	–0.24
Barley	–0.12	–0.30	0.71	–1.11
Maize	0.21	–0.10	0.88	0.10
Ragi	0.12	–0.11	0.29	–0.10
Non-foodgrains				
Sugarcane	0.73	–0.01	1.03	1.20
Cotton	0.95	0.02	0.93	1.27
Jute	0.14	–0.22	0.86	–0.30
Tea	1.43	–0.02	2.22	1.59
Tobacco	0.17	–0.14	0.72	–0.24
Groundnut	0.23	–0.29	0.73	–0.61
Rape-Mustard	0.19	–0.01	0.48	0.31
Sesamum	0.29	–0.12	0.58	–0.03
Linseed	–0.10	–0.26	1.05	–0.80
Indigo	0.47	–0.28	1.28	–0.09

SOURCE: Blyn (1966), pp. 151–2.

Heston (1973) and Neale (1962) have argued that such conclusions based on the official sources reflect more the methodological or statistical biases inherent in the estimation procedures rather than the real trends in cultivation conditions in agriculture.[6] The official formula for the estimation of the physical yield per acre of a crop, Y_t, was: $Y_t = SY \quad SCF_t$, where SY represented the 'Standard Yield per Acre' for the crop, and SCF_t the 'Seasonal Condition Factor' of the crop in year t in relation to the standard yield, equal to the proportion of the current to the standard yield. SY was a constant in each district for at least five years at a time. It was not

[6] For a fuller account, see Blyn (1966, Ch. 2).

Table 3. Wheat – Long-Term Trends in the United Provinces

Yield (tons)	Acres	Y/A (lbs/acre)	Y/A 5 year average	Yield (tons)	Acres	Y/A (lbs/acre)	Y/A 5 year average	Yield (tons)	Acres	Y/A (lbs/acre)	Y/A 5 Year average
1891				1911				1931			
2,035	6,502	701		3,032	7,578	896		2,610	7,748	755	
2,354	6,307	836		2,938	7,382	891		2,713	7667	793	
1,853	6,675	622	673.4	2,221	6,406	777	882.6	2,537	8,453	672	752.4
1,470	6,334	520		3,042	7,301	933		2,523	7,549	749	
1,591	5,177	688		2,700	6599	916		2,498	7,053	793	
1896				1916				1936			
1,851	4932	841		3,061	6,764	1,014		2,468	7 484	739	
2,250	5,985	842		2,889	7,248	890		2,780	7 810	797	
2,277	6,349	803	828.6	2,304	5,444	948	922.6	2,694	8 520	708	783.0
2,410	6,203	870		2,996	7,037	954		3,167	8 109	875	
2,385	6,790	787		2,362	6,557	807		2,826	7 935	796	
1901				1921				1941			
2,402	6,462	833		2,685	6,873	875		2,571	7373	731	
2,972	6,910	963		2,574	6,984	826		2,685	7,546	797	
3,230	7,789	929	823.4	2,640	7,182	823	800.6	2,526	7,672	738	719.0*
1,897	7,706	551		2,419	7,368	735		2,646	7,892	751	
2,429	6,479	841		2,287	6,884	744		2,305	8,056	641	

1906				1926				1945		
2,164	7,044	688		2,492	6,714	831		2,349	8,020	656
1,675	4406	851		2,361	7,467	708				
2,124	5,695	835	858.2	2,480	7,112	781	828.4			
2975	6,491	1,027		3,309	7,182	1,032				
2919	7342	890		2,686	7,612	790				

SOURCE: Blyn (1966), p. 259

unambiguously defined[7] but referred implicitly to the modal yield on average quality land in years of unexceptional climatic conditions. It was based on evidence from the District Settlement Reports, crop-cutting surveys and the informed judgement of district and provincial officials in the relevant agencies. SCF—reckoned in terms of *annas* out of a rupee of 16 *annas*, and therefore referred to often as the *annawari* estimates—was based on village-level reports filed regularly by *patwaris* and *chaukidars* which were then collated and adjusted by the district officials in the light of the latter's judgement of the crop condition in the district, a similar process subsequently occurring at the provincial level. Thus, SCF was effectively revised at two levels by Government officials. Furthermore, provincial officials could alter or originate SY or SCF (Blyn, 1966, p. 44). Both the components of the officially estimated yield were therefore subject to considerable errors arising out of ambiguities at the conceptual, as well as the measurement levels.[8] Some major ones might usefully be stated.

(*a*) *Sub-normal 'normal' Standard Yields*: With regard to the 16 *anna* normal SY, Neale (1962, pp. 144–5) and Heston (1973, pp. 317–18) levy the oft-quoted charge that crop-reporters implicitly made reference to a less-than-16-*anna* 'normal' instead of the officially assumed 16 *anna* one.[9]

[7] The full definition(s) of SY as can be found in various issues of *Estimates of Area and Yield of the Principal Crops in India* is:

That crop which past experience has shown to be the most generally recurring crop in a series of years; the typical crop of the local area; the crop which the cultivator has a right (as it were) to expect, and with which he is (or should be) content, while if he gets more he has reason to rejoice, and if less he has reason to complain; or in other words, it is the 'figure which in existing circumstances might be expected to be attained' in the year if the rainfall and season were of an ordinary character for the tract under consideration, that is neither very favourable nor the reverse! Briefly, it is stated to be 'the average yield on average soil in a year of average character'. This normal or average yield will not necessarily correspond with the average of a series of years' figures, which is an arithmetical average. (*Estimates*, 1940–1; p. 46).'

[8] Measurement accuracy was generally better in the Temporarily Settled Regions where the land revenue demand had to be revised frequently. United Provinces data, therefore, (with the exception of Benares Division) could be regarded as being less unreliable on this count.

[9] Thus, for wheat in the Province of Agra during 1880–1 and 1899–1900, the reported SCF varied as follows:

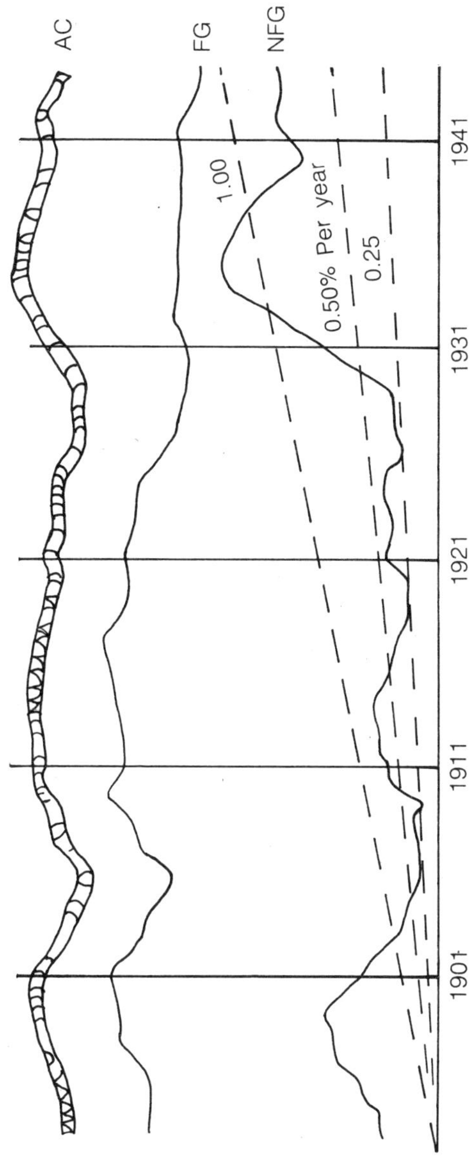

Figure 1. United Provinces Yield per acre of All-Crops, Foodgrains, and Nonfoodgrains, Five Year Moving Averages, Semilogarithmic Scale

'However, crops apparently were never better than "normal", for one does not find reports of "18-*anna*" or "20-*anna*" crops. The system therefore effectively suppressed reports of increased yield and over the years undoubtedly had the effect of depressing yield statistics' (Neale, 1962, p. 144). While an under-representation of 16-*anna plus* SCFs would be expected if in fact there *was* a declining trend in yields, a complete absence of such reports does indicate the existence of a sub-normal 'normal'. However, while this could be expected to lower the absolute level of the base yield (assuming that SY did not make a compensating adjustment), it could not be expected to suppress an increasing trend until this increase exceeded, on average, 33.33 per cent of the base yield.[10] However, on average, the observed SCF trend is *downwards*, thus suggesting that Neale's objection is inoperative.

(*b*) *Patwari Pessimism*: A related charge to the earlier one is that the *patwaris* and *chaukidars* were inherently pessimistic by nature and therefore under-reported the good harvests and exaggerated the bad ones.[11] Such behaviour would once again affect the

									Average
SCF (in *annas*)	9	10	11	12	13	14	15	16	12.35
Frequency	1	2	4	3	5	3	1	1	20

Source: Annual Reports of the Revenue Department of the N.W. Provinces

This tendency was well-known to the district and provincial officials of the time and is widely referred to in the official publications of the period. Thus: 'There seems in fact to be little doubt that in many cases, 100 is taken to represent a bumper, rather than an average crop, and that an average crop would not be returned as yielding more than 85 or at the most 90 per cent of the supposed normal' *(Season and Crop Report*, United Provinces Government, 1905–6, p. 3). The implicit presumption is that there was a psychological barrier preventing village-level crop reporters from registering 16-*anna plus* SCFs.

[10] This assumes that the implicit operative 'normal' is 12-*annas* as suggested by our 20-year run, and that the crop-reporters would run into their psychological barrier once the average 16-*anna* level was attained. Thereafter, the trend would be suppressed into a zero rate of growth path.

[11] For one instance of this, see the oral evidence of D. B. Meek to the *Royal Commission on Agriculture in India*, vol. I, Pt II. A variation on this theme is provided by the *Season and Crop Reports* for U.P. 1904–5, where the *patwari*'s pessimism is assumed to be non-symmetrical: 'The tendency to regard the *normal* as the *maximum* is still strong among the estimating staff: it does not vitiate the returns so seriously when the crops are substantially below the normal, but when the normal is reached or exceeded it comes strongly into play'. (Ibid., p. 3).

absolute level of the yield, but not its trend features. An assumption of an increasing degree of pessimism over time is necessary to generate a declining trend in yield; indeed, if following Neale or Heston, it is assumed that the 'true' trend was a rising one, then a correspondingly stronger assumption concerning the rate of increase of the *patwaris*' pessimism over time would be required to convert such an *assumed increasing* trend into the actually *observable declining* one.

There exist several other reasons why the sub-normal 'normal' and the *patwari*-pessimism could not reasonably be expected to generate a declining trend in yields spuriously. Firstly, there could be situations where the crop-reporters would inflate the SCFs. Tiwari (1951) argues in the context of the United Provinces that 'the supervisor *Kanungo* avoids making too low estimates and the tendency to over-estimate increases with poor crops. This is due to the fear of displeasing his superiors' (p. 89). Secondly, it has generally been assumed so far that the reporting biases in SCFs did not affect the nature of the bias in SY, the other component in determining yields. This assumption is untenable. The SYs were in general set higher than the average of the reported yields per acre (Blyn, 1966, p. 47; cf. Indian Council on Agricultural Research, *Sample Surveys for the Estimation of Yield of Food Crops, 1944–9*, 1951, p. 5). This would have compensated for (a constant level of) the *patwari's* alleged pessimism. Also, as Blyn argues, 'both standard and seasonal condition factor were ultimately set by the same district or provincial officers. It would seem likely that exaggerated standards would be offset by lower condition estimates in that circumstance' (p. 47); and all the more so, since there was an acute awareness of the *patwari's* under-reporting bias at both the district and the provincial levels where officials had the discretionary powers to make suitable adjustments in the aggregation process.[12] Furthermore, over this period, SYs were regularly re-estimated in many districts on the basis of crop-cutting experiments and fresh data.

[12] To this, Heston (1973, pp. 317–18) makes a curious and naive reply: 'even if the below average condition factors in fact tended to offset the excessive standard yields, it was a spurious result, because officials responsible for the judgement on the nature of the crop in a particular year were not necessarily aware of the standard yield assumed for a normal year'. It was not the crop reporters who were expected to 'correct' the over-estimated SY through reporting a compensating low SCF, but the district and provincial officials who, given the SY, generated an adjusted aggregate SCF.

This re-estimation was independent of the previous years' reported SCFs, and should thus have identified any trend change in yields. That SYs were more often revised downwards rather than upwards over this period suggests that yields were unlikely to have been systematically increasing.

More recently, Heston (1973) has launched a fresh critique of the conclusions about yield per acre trends derived, as by Blyn, from official statistics, viz., 'the finding that the condition factor apparently declined over a substantial portion of the period 1900 to 1947' (p. 318).[13] Heston's attack on this deterioration conclusion is two-pronged. He argues 'that in the period 1886–1947, there were biases in the official yields per acre—particularly an upward bias from 1886 to 1897 and a downward bias from about 1937 to 1946—in several areas of India' (Ibid., p. 304). Let us consider each in turn.

Base-Period Statistical Discrepancy Upward Bias: In 1897, the Bombay *annawari* system changed its 'normal' level from 16 *annas* to 12 *annas*. Thus, an 8 *anna* SCF after 1897 would be converted into 0.75. SY as against 0.50. SY as in the period before 1897. This would, of course, impart a downward bias to the base period reported yields. However, in 1897, a new SY figure was adopted (presumably to compensate for an earlier over-estimation of SY), which was 38 per cent below the original SY (Ibid., p. 319). This would imply that the same 8 *anna* crop originally converted into 0.50. SY would after 1897 be converted into 0.75.(1.00 – 0.38).SY = 0.465.SY. This implies a statistical or procedural over-estimation of yield in the base period (1886–97) of (0.50/0.465).100 = 7.53 per cent.[14] It needs to be noted here that this argument applies not

[13] Heston's empirical arguments are based on the Bombay experience. But it is perhaps typical of his cavalier misuse of the historical method to assert that 'until more research is done, we can only say that all of the factors that we have suggested operated in Bombay, were operative in other parts of British India as well' (p. 329). This assertion is all the more unfortunate since Heston's work is marred by several inconsistencies and errors. His conclusions are therefore likely to be false at a general level, for Bombay, or for the United Provinces, as will be argued in the following paragraphs.

[14] Since Blyn's study period starts from 1891, this over-estimation of 7.53 per cent would apply to the first 6 of a 57 year period and cannot therefore be expected to significantly affect any of Blyn's over-all conclusions on its own.

to the reported SCFs, but to the procedure adopted to convert these into final yield statistics.

End-Period Politically Motivated Downward Bias: The statistical system for estimation of crop yields was the by-product of the Land Revenue Administration, and was used to set the pitch of land revenue collection. Heston argues that ever since 1907 (when a new regulation was promulgated tying revenue remissions to the nature of the harvests as measured by the SCF) 'there were increasing pressures on local revenue officers to accept lower condition factors' (Ibid., p. 327). This political factor operated with greater force in the period after 1937, when in the face of no-rent campaigns, local administrators placed a higher premium on political stability than on land revenue, which in any case, had declined in importance as a source of revenue. They therefore filed artificially low SCFs so as to increase revenue remissions, thereby lowering the tax burden on the cultivators.

Heston thus contends that Blyn's conclusions on declining yield trends are spurious as they can be adequately explained in terms of the simultaneous operation of these two biases at the two ends of the study period.[15] He then seeks to corroborate this line of reasoning through two separate exercises. Firstly, in a statistical exercise, he posits a positive linear relationship between rainfall levels and the observed SCFs, and on the basis of the pattern of the residual term derived from a large set of simple regressions, argues that the observed SCFs deviate from the predicted ones in the base and end periods in a manner which suggests to him that the above biases were in fact in operation. This exercise is riddled with contradictions and also betrays Heston's innocence of the elementary principles underlying ordinary-least-squares regression analysis; for economy of space, we will ignore this exercise and not pursue its results in the text.[16] Secondly, he cites a couple of reasons why

[15] 'There is no evidence for Bombay that suggests that the reported declines in yields per acre during the period 1886–1947, correspond to the agricultural history of the period—to administrative and political history yes, but to reality, no'. (Ibid., p. 328).

[16] 'Since one of the principal, if not the only reason save pests and disease, for fluctuation in the condition factor is the weather . . .' (Heston, 1973, p. 323), Heston specifies the following linear relationship between SCF and the average level of rainfall, RF:

trend yields could have been increasing. We will consider these in the final section of this essay alongside other similar evidence concerning the underlying determinants of trend yields. Let us, however, return to Heston's two biases and examine their validity in general, as well as specifically from the point of view of their applicability in the United Provinces.

$$SCF^{i}_{t} = \hat{a} + \hat{b}.RF^{d}_{t} + \hat{u}^{i,d} \qquad (1)$$

where

SCF^{i}_{t} is the average seasonal condition factor over the time period, t, for the ith crop, averaged out at the provincial level;

RF^{d}_{t} is the average rainfall level over the time period, t, for the dth district;

$\hat{u}$ stands for the estimated error term, using OLS methods;

and $i = 1, 2,...,5$; $d = 1, 2,...,19$; $t = 1, 2,...,6$. See Table 4.

Thus, there could be 95 such estimated relations, though Heston is restricted to 74 cases as 21 crop-district combinations are non-existent. His basic hypothesis is that 'in periods 2 through 5, the revenue yields (*sic*) and the rainfall are related in the expected manner, but that in the last decade before Independence the condition factor declined more than was warranted by changes in the rainfall' (Ibid., p. 324). As it happens, (1) yields very weak results: $b > 0$ in only 52 cases, but 'very few of the relations were statistically significant; in addition, most of the relationships were weak' enough for Heston not to report the 't' or the R^2 statistics. But this weak result 'we suggest, is because the condition factor was subject to administrative influences that outweighed influences of the season . . .' (p. 325ff.) in t(1) and t(6). Heston therefore gathers the 148 estimated error terms for these two periods together, and finds that while 72 of these terms are strongly negative, only 19 are strongly positive, and to him, 'the results of this analysis certainly suggest that the condition factor in both the periods 1887–97 and 1937–46 was unusually low'.

There is little in this exercise that is correct. Firstly, it is not clear why u(t1) should be negative. Heston says 'the reason for period 1 is the change in the number of annas considered normal'. But this change did not affect the reporting of the SCFs, but the conversion of these into absolute yield figures in conjunction with the standard yields. Thus, as Heston himself notes, an 8 anna crop is still called and reported as an 8 anna crop after 1897, though now it implies 8/12 = 0.75 of the SY rather than 8/16 = 0.50 of the SY. Secondly, even if negative residuals for t(6) are obtained, it cannot be taken to mean, as Heston does, that the 'political-administrative influences' hypothesis is valid, since relation (1) is totally misspecified in the first place. Thirdly, with regard to the specification of (1), there are several mistakes: (*a*) *State* level crop SCFs are related to *district* level rainfall levels; (*b*) the critical importance of the seasonality of rainfall requirements, where this seasonality is also

Table 4. Average Condition and Rainfall Factor for Major Crops in Bombay and Index of Average Total Rainfall for Each District, 1886–1947

Crop/ District	1886–97	1898–1906	1907–16	1917–26	1927–36	1937–46	Total or Average
	(1)	(2)	(3)	(4)	(5)	(6)	(7)
Crop			A. Condition Factor				Acreage
Rice	72	72	82	79	86	74	1,989
Wheat	67	55	68	74	70	63	1,404
Jowar	63	56	66	63	71	58	8,005
Bajra	64	59	65	63	71	62	3,925
Cereals	65	59	68	66	73	62	15,325
Cotton	61	62	73	70	65	62	4,117
Total:	64	69	69	67	71	62	19,440
District			B. Rainfall (1886–96 = 100)				Base Rainfall in inches
Ahmedabad	100	76	94	86	127	102	31.6
Kaira	100	74	77	71	93	80	38.9
Panch Mahals	100	78	96	87	129	97	41.1
Broach	100	74	85	74	75	84	42.8
Surat	100	64	87	82	100	104	47.0
Dhulia	100	77	77	93	96	93	26.0
Jalgaon	100	83	106	89	123	110	28.8
Nasik	100	76	97	78	103	83	31.7
Ahmednagar	100	75	91	91	108	93	25.5
Poona	100	78	103	82	98	99	27.0
Sholapur	100	82	83	86	92	82	30.1
Satara	100	76	94	75	101	96	44.2
Belgaum	100	93	105	94	101	104	50.8
Bijapur	100	80	76	74	90	88	26.2
Dharwar	100	105	132	135	144	112	24.2
Thana	100	86	89	85	97	102	105.7
Kolaba	100	84	86	83	94	83	94.6
Ratnagiri	100	92	95	113	97	99	100.5
Kanara	100	98	90	93	103	97	123.9
Average	100	82	93	88	104	95	

SOURCE: Heston (1973), p. 322.

Since the first bias is of marginal significance, it will be ignored in the text[17] in favour of a more detailed investigation of the second, political bias. Since the period of declining yields begins in Blyn's study from the 1910–20 decade, this bias will need to have operated from well before the 1937–46 period stressed by Heston. But could this bias be expected to have been operative in reality at all?

Before revenue remissions were granted, the average outturn would have had to be 8 *annas* or less. This would imply an extremely poor crop, and even in a fairly bad year would be beyond the hoodwinking misreporting that Heston says took place. If the crop was, say, 9 *annas* in fact, there would be the incentive for *zamindars* to have it reported as 8 *annas* or less and such an under-statement would probably fall within the range of official credibility; but what would the local official do about a 10 or 12 *anna* crop?[18] Thus, the

crop-specific, is totally ignored. It is no surprise that (1) then yields insignificant results. (c) Heston definitionally ignores and excludes from (1) all other determinants of yields which could display trend features. (For a discussion of these, see Blyn, 1966, Ch. 8, pp. 179–212.) Indeed, if the observed SCFs first rise and decline over the entire period, *and if* RF is correctly specified in (1) so as to remove the above-mentioned mistakes, *and if* the *excluded* 'yield-determinant' variable also displays a trend similar to that of SCF, and if RF etc fluctuations balance out in the long term, then the residual term could also be expected to display negative residuals in the first and last time periods. It is only if such residuals are observed even after the *inclusion* of the other trend determinants that Heston's exercise could have any potential validity; as it stands, it rests on a vacuous tautology.

[17] Blyn was not unaware of shifts away from the original 16-*anna* 'normal' and made explicit adjustments in the trends to eliminate discontinuities in the trend arising out of this, or other factors related to changing estimation procedures (Blyn, 1966, pp. 47, 48, 48ff. 64–5). Thus, substantial adjustments are necessitated for Madras for 1916–7, when changes in estimation procedures were introduced by the Director of Agriculture, G.A.D. Stuart. (See Stuart, 1919.) However, Blyn makes no adjustment for the 1891–7 period for Bombay. For our purposes, we need to note that the United Provinces retained the 16-*anna* 'normal' throughout the period, and hence is not vulnerable to Heston's first bias (Blyn, 1966, p. 48ff).

[18] The Board of Agriculture was alive to this 'danger of estimates prepared for statistical purposes being coloured by questions of suspension and remission of revenue. We consider that there has too frequently been in the past a tendency on the part of both primary and other reporting agencies to report an incorrect crop, *when the crop approaches a point at which questions of suspension and remission appear likely to arise*.' Proceedings of the Board of *Agriculture*, 1919, p. 32; quoted by Blyn, 1966, p. 48 (Emphasis added).

over-all effect of the political reporting bias would be a slight exaggeration of the extreme downward fluctuations over the period during which the bias was operative; but the net effect on the trend yield could all too easily have been imperceptible.[19]

The underlying motivation, according to Heston was to lower the effective burden of revenue *collection* from the landowning classes. This motivation could not have been particularly strong[20] in the period 1907–29, since this period saw a sharp increase in agricultural prices which drastically reduced the real burden of 'temporarily-settled' (for 30 years or so) land revenue demands.[21] Indeed, the State attempted to recover some of this loss through systematically increasing irrigation and other charges in step with price increases. On the other hand, for the subsequent depression period, there was in fact a serious concern to mitigate the landowners' losses on account of price decreases, but inevitably, such revenue remissions (which were in magnitude far more important than those granted on account of natural calamities, etc.) were

[19] It can be confirmed that the bias was inoperative in the United Provinces: the total remissions granted on account of natural calamities, etc., exceeded 3 per cent of the total land revenue demand in no more than five years in the 18 year period from 1929–30 to 1946–7, and in virtually all the other years the figure was a fraction of 1 per cent. This does not form a grant significant enough to bear the weight of Heston's argument. (Figures derived from the *Revenue Reports* of the U.P.)

[20] But even granting that the Government wished to lower the tax burden on the landowning classes out of political expediency, how could it best go about it? Heston would have us believe that in reality, it was left to the local revenue officers to employ this device of under-reporting the SCFs in order to soften an otherwise rigid (or insufficiently variable) assessment and collection policy. The central and provincial authorities are therefore assumed either (1) to be against such remissions but (i) gullible and unaware of being hoodwinked, or (ii) aware of the under-reporting, but inert; or, (2) for such remissions, but (i) incapable of granting them directly, or (ii) not wanting to adopt such a generous stance overtly. None of these alternatives is very complimentary about the efficiency or rationality of the decision-making procedures of the Revenue Department; yet one of these must underlie this charade. In the first case, the local Revenue officials are assumed to be acting against the Regulations and mis-reporting consciously so as to correct for what they regard as an incorrect policy—i.e. they are *all independently* following a 'second-best' course. On the other hand, why is it that the Government does not accept the *true* outturn figures, and then make even greater political capital out of explicitly reducing revenue collections?

[21] See Datta, *Report of an Enquiry into the Rise of Prices in India* (1915); Misra, B. R. (1942, p. 260).

index-linked to the downward fluctuations in the *prices, not the outturn*, in the agricultural sector.[22]

Neither is Heston convincing when he argues that all this was done to keep the 'no-rent' campaigns out of the districts. Revenue remissions would benefit the landowning classes, but it is widely recorded that such remissions were, in fact, only marginally (if at all) passed on to the tenants and sub-tenants.[23] Since it was the latter classes which formed the explosive elements in the 'no-rent' and earlier, rural campaigns, revenue-remissions would have constituted an exceptionally inefficient policy instrument for buying rural political stability. Indeed, the 1920s and the 1930s witnessed the dismantling of the so-called 'Oudh Policy', with the Government becoming increasingly insensitive to the interests of the *zamindar* and *taluqdar* class. The central politico-economic issue in these decades was not the alienation of the State's land revenue in favour of the *zamindars*, but rather the alienation of the *zamindars*' landownership rights in favour of the tenants under them.[24]

A related charge of politically motivated under-reporting of the SCFs over this period has also been levied by Neale (1962, p. 145, ff(d)): 'It would also have been good nationalist politics in the 1920s and 1930s to understate output and thus reflect badly on the Imperial administration.' This assertion is even less substantiable than Heston's; its implausibility is evident in its implicit assumption that the statistical and revenue systems were in the hands of the Nationalists, for as we have noted earlier, village-level reports were 'averaged' in turn at the district and the provincial levels by 'responsible' officers, many of them European. (See U.P. Government, *Report on Agriculture*, 1926, pp. 83–7.) Indeed, it would appear more plausible to assume that the Government in power would wish to control the statistical system to generate as favourable a picture as could possibly be made credible within the

[22] Indeed, to the extent that revenue remissions were also based on the official price expectations held for the following year, under-reporting the outturn would probably generate inflationary expectations, and therefore reduce the revenue remissions. However, it would probably be more accurate to describe the revenue-remission process as being of the *ex-post* compensation type.

[23] For a fuller discussion of this range of issues, see A. Saith, Ph.d. thesis (Cambridge, 1978), Ch. 2.

[24] Ibid.

constraints imposed by the generally observable objective realities of the period. The political bias could therefore as easily operate in the opposite direction.

What conclusions can we elicit from the foregoing analysis? The first major point which emerges is that while the estimates of yield can easily be faulted for their imprecision and inaccuracy with regard to *the absolute levels* of yields, as well as the *amplitude of fluctuations*, there seem to exist no over-riding grounds for rejecting as systematically false whatever *trend features* the yield-per-acre series displays. Heston's, and Neale's objections are clearly more objectionable than the data they criticise, and we may, with a reasonable degree of confidence, accept the conclusions derived by Blyn and others from official statistical sources, as initial working hypotheses. However, the debate does leave a residue of legitimate doubt arising from the ambiguities underlying the conceptual and measurement aspects of the 'standard yield', particularly at the more aggregated levels. The debate therefore also points to the imperative need to conduct independent investigations: firstly, attempting to construct benchmark data on yields (and other variables) using statistical material at a much more disaggregated level, where the data collection methods and their weaknesses can be directly scrutinized; and secondly, of trends in the underlying determinants of crop yields per acre utilising all statistical and other material pertinent for such an enquiry. In the rest of this Appendix, a modest effort will be made at conducting such investigations in the context of the Muzaffarnagar and Bareilly districts of the United Provinces for the period 1827-1947. Such a descent to the district level is, of course, necessitated by the non-existence of the official yield series for the U.P. before the 1880s, so that any evaluation of 19th century yield trends involves a dependence on district level evidence.

The Re-interpretationists' Thesis on Nineteenth Century Trends in Yields

'The classical view sees the nineteenth century as an era of stagnation and possibly, even of steady deterioration.' But this nationalist interpretation 'suffer(s) from internal contradictions which become quickly apparent when exposed to the touchstone of the simplest economic tools' (Morris, M. D, 1963, p. 608).

Bemoaning the inadequacies of recent Classical scholarship,[25] Morris argues 'that there is good reason to suspect that average output per acre and per man rose during the nineteenth century' (Ibid., p. 612). Let us investigate the statistical evidence underlying Morris's re-interpretation.

In 1926, under the orders of the provincial government, a *Report on Agriculture in the United Provinces* (henceforth, *UPG Report* (*1926*) was prepared for the Royal Commission on Agriculture in India (1928). 'It is commonly asserted' the Report says 'that the produce per acre has been steadily decreasing. Old men say so today and old men, according to the settlement reports, said so a hundred years ago'.[26] (Ibid., p. 117). As a rebuttal to these charges, the *UPG Report (1926)* produced the following Table 5 pertaining to Muzaffarnagar District, and contended that 'these figures conclusively show that there has been an increase rather than a decrease in the produce per acre in the last eighty or a hundred years' (Ibid., p. 117). Subsequently, Neale used the same table to argue that 'it is clear that the nineteenth century was a time of increasing prosperity if still a time of absolute poverty' (Neale, 1962, p. 143);[27] and that there was 'an increase of three-quarters in physical product per acre'. In turn, Morris, in one of his periodic re-interpretations of nineteenth century Indian economic history cites 'Neale's data on Muzaffarnagar', viz., Table 5 from the *UPG Report (1926)*, to argue

[25] '. . . in recent decades the results of scholarship committed to the Classical view seem rather disappointing . . . there have been few if any attempts to test the validity and/or the internal consistency of any of the canonical themes. Historians have tended merely to add more descriptive material . . . Economists . . . typically have not used their analytical tools either to elicit the mechanisms of the system or to explore the theoretical implications of the propositions advanced' (Morris, 1966, p. 190). These charges might well be well-founded, but they impart a special interest to a consideration of the analytical methods employed by the proponents of the anti-Classical view.

[26] Both generations of 'old men' could of course have been telling the truth; see fn.2.

[27] In general, Neale argues that 'the history of agriculture in the United Provinces appears to have two periods: one of growth during the nineteenth century and one of stagnation, if not decline in the twentieth' (Neale, p. 143). His position therefore straddles the two camps, agreeing with the re-interpretationist school for the nineteenth century, and with the nationalist position for the twentieth. The latter can be ascribed to Neale's dependence on Tiwari's (1951) study for trends in U.P. agriculture in the twentieth century. Typically, Morris ignores Neale's conclusions for this period.

Table 5. Comparison of Certain Past and Present Figures for the District of Muzaffarnagar

	Outturn (lbs per acre)											
				Wheat			Barley				Percentage of cultivated land	
	Rice	Sugar	Bajra	Irri-gated	Unirri-gated	Average	Irri-gated	Unirri-gated	Average	Gram	Irrigable	Double cropped
1827–40	530	420	350	1,000	620	650	770	600	610	460	18	4
1897–1921	900	640	450	1,280	840	1,100	1,500	1,000	1,120	810	60	23

	Value of outturn per acre	Rent per cultivated acre	Revenue per cultivated acre	Rent as percentage of outturn	Revenue as percentage of outturn	Population per cultivated acre	Estimated size of average holding
1840	8.1	2.6	1.6	32	20	*0.89	17.0
1824	81	10.8	2.6	13	3	1.31	11.5

* Taken from a footnote to Mr Mansel's settlement report of Agra in 1841.
Calculated on the assumption that the percentage of cultivators to population was the same in 1840 an in 1924.

SOURCE: *U.P.G. Report* (1926), p. 117.

that in Muzaffarnagar, productivity rose by 900 per cent between 1840 and 1924, and since population per acre over this period rose by only 47 per cent, value productivity per person rose by 580 per cent. Using these figures with the officially recorded levels of rent and revenue per acre, Morris asserts that 'the example challenges those who glibly assume that all gains were transferred into the hands of the landlords and the State' (Morris, 1968, p. 350) and 'that with rising productivity an increasing debt may be consistent with a declining burden on income received'. (Ibid., p. 371). On this evidence rests Morris's speculative re-interpretation that increasing debt did not impose a sufficient constraint on cultivator's net savings and investments.

The *UPG Report (1926)* uses current data for the later period, but for the earlier one, relies on the evidence of Thornton's 1840 Land Revenue Settlement Report for Muzaffarnagar District (henceforth, *Thornton* (*1840*)). In the following section, we will scrutinize this data, the methods by which Thornton generated them, and the subsequent uses to which it has been put by the United Provinces Government, Neale and Morris.

Wheat Yields per Acre in Muzaffarnagar District: An Analysis Based on the Evidence in the DSRs.

Let us begin by a few introductory remarks on the type of yield-data available in the DSRs. The weakness of the official aggregate time-series data on yields places a special premium on such evidence. Since most of the United Provinces were throughout the period covered by Temporary Revenue Settlements, there exist for most districts, a set of three or more DSRs, each separated by the duration of a settlement, viz., approximately 30 years. The data available is naturally not really comparable across districts, and even the bench-mark data on any one district have to be interpreted with one sceptical eye on the methods of the collection of data. The basis of the revenue assessment was the capability of the landowners to pay revenue, as estimated with reference to the net rental worth of the landowners' estates. However, since reported rents were subject to wide concealments, and since many estates were owner-cultivated and therefore had no direct rental statistics available, the revenue demand was implicitly based on the Settlement Officer (S.O.)'s estimate of the produce per acre on the estate. The procedure followed by the S.O. was to undertake a careful and exhaustive survey of the district and classify soil types, geographical features, extant and potential irrigation, and on the basis of all this information, to formulate standard rates for different 'circles' within the district. Thereafter, upon a consideration of each individual estate in the district, local variations from the relevant standard 'circle' rates were applied to suit the particular circumstances of the estate, or of its owners. A crucial element in this was the estimation of the fertility of the soil. Most often, the S.O. relied on the rent and revenue papers of the local *patwari*, other subordinate staff and upon the enquiries made of the more 'reliable' zamindars to arrive at the estimates of the yield per acre of different crops. However, some of the more industrious and conscientious S.O.s actually designed and conducted scientific crop-cutting experiments to estimate the yield rates. In rare instances, there exists evidence about the crop-cutting yields as generated by different generations of S.O.s in the same district but for different Settlements. Two such districts are Muzaffarnagar and Bareilly. For obvious reasons we will refrain from inter-district comparisons or from making any generalisations to the level of the Division or the Province, but will attempt to compare bench-mark statistics for each district at the different points in time at which the DSR statistics on yield are available. Of course, special interest attaches to the Muzaffarnagar data, since it is on the strength of this district that M. D. Morris, Neale, as well as the UPG, make the 're-interpretation' of nineteenth century agricultural trends. In the rest of this section, we will focus exclusively on Muzaffarnagar evidence, and make a brief evaluation of the Bareilly data in the following section.

The average physical yield per acre of wheat (or any other crop) could have risen over the period for two broad factors: (i) A shift from unirrigated to irrigated wheat cultivation could have raised the *average* yield while yields on irrigated as well as unirrigated lands remained constant. We shall refer to this as the 'shift increase'. (ii) Independently of the shift effect, yields per acre on either type of land could have been rising for other reasons, viz., improved seeds or methods of cultivation, greater use of manures, more intensive application of labour, etc. Such a yield change will be referred to as an 'intrinsic increase'. Thus, a *shift* increase can almost exclusively be attributed (in the Muzaffarnagar context), to the exogenous provision of canal water without implying any additional initiative on the part of the cultivator; an *intrinsic* increase, however, would have to reflect an increased application of inputs or superior organisational forms under which the cultivator operated, and would therefore more accurately reflect an improvement in the cultivation conditions of the cultivators on the ground. In the following paragraphs, we will therefore look out particularly for intrinsic increases. We will try to see to what extent the change in the average can be accounted for by the shift effect; the residual change will then be attributable to the intrinsic effects. We will concentrate, wherever meaningfully possible, on wheat, which was Muzaffarnagar's major crop produced on the better land for markets outside the district; and indeed, it is for this crop alone that the more reliable data exist. Let us then return to Table 5, and to the main conclusions derived from it by the UPG, Neale and by Morris, as stated on pages 229–30.

Table 5 provides figures for physical productivity increases as well as for increases in the value of the outturn per acre. The first task must be to investigate, on the basis of the evidence provided and the available data on price movements over this period, whether these two sets of figures are consistent with one another.

The Value Data

We will first attempt to derive implicit indices of increases in physical yields per acre (of the shift and intrinsic types) adopting as our starting point the value data set out in Table 5. Let us proceed in a step-wise fashion.

Step I: Adjustment for Double-Cropping: The value of out-turn per acre rises from a base value of 100 to 1,000, but this needs an adjustment for double-cropping, which rises in index terms to 123/104 = 118.3. Using this, the adjusted level of the index of out-turn per cropped acre is 1,000/118.3 = 845.3. Applying this to the corrected base value of output per acre of Rs 7.8, we derive a value per acre of Rs 65.85 for the end period, compared to the Rs 81.0 in Table 5.

Step II: Adjustment to Exclude Sugar-Cane Values: Since we are primarily interested in foodgrains (and especially wheat) yields, we will make a deduction in both the base and the end-period values for the contribution made by the sugar-cane crop to the value per acre. This adjustment yields a figure of Rs 6.11 per acre for the value of crops other than sugar-cane, and Rs 23.94 as the corresponding value in the end period.[28] As an index, therefore, the value per acre of non-sugar-cane crops rose to (23.94/6.11). 100 = 391.8 in the end period.

Table 6. Price Index Numbers

	1840	1923–4	1924–5
Wheat	100	398	567
Barley	100	355	442
Gram	100	262	397

The 1840 price data is implicit in *Thorton(1840)*; for the other years, prices are U. P. harvest prices from *Wages and Prices in India.*

Step III: Price Deflation for Construction of Non-Sugar-Cane Volume Index: Prices for the other major food crops, viz., rice, urad, moong, jowar and bajra are not available for the base period, but since the prices of the latter two cereals were ruling at exceptionally high levels in the end period, we could not be far wrong in using the wheat price index for deflating the index of per acre values of non-sugar-cane crops. Indeed, our choice of 398 as the deflator is the one most favourable for the derivation of a result showing *rising* physical yields per acre. Deflating, we get 391.8/398.0 = 98.4 as the end period index value of the *volume* of output per acre. Hence, if within the group of non-sugar-cane crops there were no shifts in cropping patterns, the average yield per acre of such (essentially foodgrain) crops could be said to have fallen by - 1.6 per cent over this period.

Step IV: Correction for Cropping Pattern Shifts: However, cropping pattern shifts within non-sugar-cane crops did occur: wheat area rose from 26 per cent in 1840 to 40 per cent of the total area by

[28] From *Thornton (1840)* we know sugar-cane occupied 4 per cent of the area with a per acre value of Rs 48.1 in 1840, so that its exclusion yields a per acre value of [7.8 - (48.1). (0.04)] / (0.96) = Rs 6.11. Similarly, the *Lane DSR for Muzaffarnagar (1921)* shows an increase in the sugar-cane crop percentage to 12.47 and the value per acre to Rs 360, and a similar calculation yields Rs 23.94.

1921 (*Thornton* (*1840*); *Lane DSR* (*1921*)). However, sugar-cane areas rose from 4 per cent to 12.5 per cent, so that the wheat-cropped areas as percentages of all non-sugar-cane area are 27.1 per cent in 1840 and 45.7 per cent in 1921. Wheat per acre values would of course be higher than the other crops in the non-sugar-cane group and hence the results of Step III yield overestimates of physical yield increases. Using end period values, the value per acre of wheat is 55.2 per cent greater than the average value per acre of rice, barley and maize.[29] Using this figure in conjunction with the adjusted wheat cropping percentage ones, it can readily be calculated that had physical yields of all non-sugar-cane crops stayed constant, this increased emphasis on wheat would have increased the constant-price volume per acre index to 108.93 in the end period with 1840 = 100. The Step III index of 98.4 therefore needs to be deflated by this value to arrive at a corrected index number representing the increase in the physical yields of the non-sugar-cane group of crops. The new index number is thus: (98.4/108.93). 100 = 90.33. Hence, the conclusion is that the average physical yields of non-sugar-cane crops *fell* over the period by 9.67 per cent.

Step V: Separation of the Shift and Intrinsic Effects on Yields: Let us now try to decompose this average decline of 9.67 per cent over the period 1840–1924 into its component shift and intrinsic changes as defined on pages 231–2 we know from Table 5 that the *irrigable* area rose from 18 per cent to 60 per cent over this period; from the

[29] The table below gives the value in rupees per acre of wheat, and three other foodgrains (rice, maize and barley) which are prominent in the irrigated areas. The table is based on the data on per acre crop values by Canal for the U.P. as published in the statistical appendices to the *Irrigation Revenue Reports* for the relevant years. EJC and UGC refer to the Eastern Jumna and the Upper Ganges Canals, which both run through Muzaffarnagar district.

	1922–3		1923–4		1924–5	
	EJC	UGC	EJC	UGC	EJC	UGC
(i) Wheat	65.0	56.0	61.0	53.0	76.0	69.0
(ii) Rice, Barley, Maize	42.2	37.7	44.7	30.4	51.7	40.4
Ratio: (i)/(ii)	1.54	1.49	1.36	1.74	1.47	1.71
Average Ratio = 1.552						

SOURCE: *Annual Reports of the Irrigation Revenue Department, United Provinces Government* (for the years cited).

Thornton (1840) and *Lane (1921)* DSRs we can improve upon this by using the *irrigated* area figures of 10.5 per cent and 52 per cent in 1840 and 1921. The factor by which irrigation raises yields is calculated conservatively as 1.5 on the basis of the figure for both periods in Table 5. Then, it is evident that with the 1840 level as 100, the increase in irrigation alone could have been expected to raise the physical volume index to 119.7, *ceteris paribus*, in the end period: the observed index as calculated in the last Step is 90.3. When this average index is deflated by the shift effect index, we get the index of intrinsic yields as (90.3/119.7) ×100 = 75.4 for the end period with 1840 = 100. Hence, our overall conclusion after all these necessary corrective steps is that while the average physical yields of the non-sugar-cane crops declined over the period by 9.7 per cent, there was a fairly strong positive shift effect of 19.7 per cent, which however, was more than counterbalanced by a powerful negative intrinsic effect of –24.6 per cent.

But these results, based on the value figures of Table 5, flatly contradict the physical productivity figures provided in the other part of Table 5, all of which show physical increases of 60 to 75 per cent. Could it not be that the value data are at fault, and not those on physical yields per acre? Let us check.

The only data that is available on the values of outturn per acre is for the canal irrigated areas published annually in the *Irrigation Revenue Reports*. These are not presented by districts, but rather by Canals, and the relevant values for the two canals, the Ganges Canal and the Eastern Jumna Canal which feed Muzaffarnagar are presented below for the years 1922–3 to 1924–5.

This yields an overall average of Rs 81.90 per acre. This corresponds quite closely to the value of Rs 81 per acre assumed in Table 5. These figures lead us to question the validity of the comparisons in Table 5, for the value of Rs 81 is unquestionably an overestimate as the *average* value of output per acre in *all* Muzaffarnagar. (The 1840 figure of Rs 8.1, it will be recalled, represented the over-all value of output per acre in *both* the irrigated as well as unirrigated tracts). The overestimation is both on account of the far greater emphasis on high-value crops along the canal areas, and also on account of the higher yields per acre on canal irrigated land as compared to unirrigated land. Hence, the corrected yield in the value data would become even more depressed and therefore even

Table 7. Value of Output per Acre in Rupees in Canal Irrigated Areas

	Ganges Canal	EJC
1922–3	68.83	81.09
1923–4	81.03	87.41
1924–5	77.62	95.37
	75.83	87.96

more incompatible with the direct yield per acre evidence presented on the top half of Table 5. Let us then scrutinize the data on the physical yields per acre in Table 5.

The Physical Yields Data

(A) *The Base Period* (*1827–40*): The data for the base period are extracted by the *UPG Report (1926)* from Thornton's extraordinarily thorough Settlement of Muzaffarnagar District under Regulation IX of 1833. This Settlement commenced in 1833 and was finalised in 1840, and was based on the produce rates derived by Thornton through the use of two alternative procedures. These were:

(i) *Zamindars*' rental papers for an area of 413,650 acres were examined. The reliability of these records is defended by Thornton and the UPG on the grounds that (*a*) rents were almost everywhere in kind, and 'every cultivator was an expert at estimating the outturn' (*UPG Report* (*1926*), p. 117). (*b*) According to Thornton, 'An appeal to experiment (of cutting a small portion, threshing and weighing it on the spot) is the allowed privilege of the cultivator and is constantly made use of' (*Thornton* (*1840*), p. 18). (*c*) 'It is extremely unlikely that the *zamindars* deliberately falsified their books thirteen years before the settlement took place, or that like the modern *bania*, they kept two sets; Mr Thornton's settlement was the first scientific settlement and the *zamindars* would have no previous knowledge of the methods which he was to follow' (*UPG Report* (*1926*), p. 117). Such data was scrutinized for the period 1827–40, and the period averages are used by the UPG in Table 5.

(ii) The other procedure used by Thornton to corroborate these results was to resort to crop-cutting experiments conducted over different soil types. These experiments covered 11,419 acres, which represents as much as 17.43 per cent of the total cultivated area.

Although there are no explicit references to this fact, it appears that the sample was suitably stratified so that each soil type was represented in the sample in the same proportion that it formed of the total cultivated area in the district.

The evidence in Table 8 refers to wheat only, and (I = Irrigated; UI = Unirrigated) has been calculated from the Statements appended to *Thornton (1840)*. The correspondence is not exact but it is sufficient to make the averages derived by Thornton acceptable even by modern statistical survey standards.

These figures are clearly likely to be more accurate than the entries on the registers of the landlords, but the latter were used by Thornton for the Settlement partly because they represent averages for a longer period, and partly also to establish the moderate nature of his Settlement.

Indirect evidence points to the crop-cutting 1840 yields as being under-estimates. From Cadell's data on the prices of wheat in Muzaffarnagar since 1818 (*Cadell* (*1873*), pp. 21–2), it is evident that the year 1840 had the highest prices of wheat in the entire period from 1818 until 1860 (when prices were sharply influenced by the great famine), and since in the earlier period prices were quite responsive to the local harvests, the figures for the crop-cutting sample of 1840 are likely to be under-estimates rather than otherwise, of the average levels of yield of that period.

A comparison of the Crop-Cutting yields (CC) and the Rent Register yields (RR) would be appropriate, in order to investigate the existence of any bias. The only direct comparison possible is for the overall average yield per acre of wheat on all types of soil, irrigated and unirrigated. The Rent Registers give a yield for 1827–40 of 652.9 lbs per acre, while the Crop Cutting yield averages out to 793.9 lbs per acre. In Table 9, the RR figures are compared with the CC yields.

There exist strong grounds for believing that Thornton's RR estimates are seriously under-estimated, not on account of the intentional manipulation of the statistics by the *zamindars*, but on account of the survey and calculation procedures employed by Thornton. A substantial critique is developed by Cadell in his *Settlement Report of 1878 of the Ganges Tract of Muzaffarnagar District* (henceforth, *Cadell, 1878*), and we will limit ourselves to eliciting the relevant objections.

Table 8. Muzaffarnagar: per cent Distribution of Sample and District Wheat Area by Type of Soil

Soil Type	From Crop Statement for Total Cultivated Area	From Thornton's Crop Cutting Sample
Meesum I	8.11	8.91
Meesum UI	6.83	4.58
Rouslee I	7.70	4.04
Rouslee UI	49.91	58.84
Dakur I	0.98	0.25
Dakur UI	4.39	2.31
Bhoodah I	0.00	0.13
Bhoodah UI	22.08	20.94
	100.00	100.00
Total Area under wheat	65,515 acres	11,419 acres

Table 9. Muzaffarnagar: Wheat Yields in lbs/acre

Year	Method	I	UI	Average
1827–40	RR	1,000	620[30]	650
1840	CC	1,217	725	794

(a) Soil Classification: Although the averages ascertained by the RR method for each type of soil might have been correct, the final average could still be underestimated if the weightage of the inferior soils (as estimated by the survey procedures) was over-estimated. There is considerable evidence that this was indeed the case.[31]

[30] The UPG also reports these irrigated and unirrigated RR yields in Table 5 but typically without disclosing their source; certainly, no such figures are available directly in the Settlement Report proper.

[31] Thornton himself informs us that 'In the measurement now going on in the Muzaffarnagar district all such doubtful cases [of soil classification] are classed under the inferior denominations' (Quoted in *Cadell* (*1878*), p. 30). This may have moderated the assessments, but it also had the side effect of lowering the estimated yield figures. Cadell himself notes (ibid., p. 42) that 'A final and convincing proof of the inadequacy of the rates assumed for the circles to the south [where this underclassification of soils was most widely observed] is given by their application to the soil areas of the better villages, as recorded in the papers of the old settlement. The result shows that the better

(b) So also, the proportion of the land that was manured (referred to as *meesum*, or *misan*), was heavily under-reported in the soil tables.[32]

(c) Another factor which could possibly depress the reported RR yields is one also operative in Bareilly district, as will be seen later. Even though the greater proportion of the land in Muzaffarnagar was under kind rents, it would be true to say that the cash-rented lands would have a higher proportion of the high-value crops, as the better land was more strongly represented in the cash-rented areas. Hence, by limiting the enquiry to the kind rent areas, the overall yield for the district would be under-reported, and more seriously so for wheat, which was definitely a favoured superior crop.

For these reasons, one can arguably reject the RR estimates and adopt the CC ones, noting that on the evidence of the wheat prices data (as a proxy indicator of wheat output fluctuations) even these are likely to be under-estimates rather than otherwise for the period.

The insertion of the Crop-Cutting yields in place of the lower Rent Register figures into Table 5, of course alters the comparative picture considerably; but the *end period data* remain to be scrutinised. Before that, however, it is necessary to follow up evidence which is chronologically prior to 1924.

(B) *The Interim Period*

(i) *The 1866 Settlement Report*: S. N. Martin's Settlement of 1866 was not made operational, but this report makes the point that 'A comparison of the elaborate table appended to Mr Thornton's Report printed in 1841, with the returns now prepared by the

villages were assessed without any reference to these rates, which in some cases give little more than half of the rental that was assumed.' This would have the effect of artificially raising the proportion of the total land ascribed to the inferior soils, thereby depressing the average yield calculated on the basis of these incorrect weights.

32 Cadell notes that 'many crops which are never grown without manure were cultivated in fair proportions in land entered as unmanured' (*Cadell (1878)*, pp. 42–3). This was seriously the case with a vital crop, sugar-cane; 'In the whole tract under review the percentage of sugar-cane was 8, and that of *misan,* instead of being 26 as Mr Thornton's proportions required, remained at 18, so that more than 20,000 acres which ought to have been *misan* were recorded *rausli*; and even this estimate is too small . . .' (*Cadell (1878)*, p. 47).

Settlement Officers, shows that there has been little, if any, improvement in the amount of produce—very little change in the system of tillage. The proportion then and now of the crops remains much the same' (*Martin DSR* (*1866*), p. 4). Although no data are presented, valuable information is provided with regard to the results of crop-cutting experiments, and their comparison with the estimates entered in the landlords' and village accountants' papers—the latter being generally under-estimated.[33]

(ii) *Cadell's DSR on the Ganges Tract in Muzaffarnagar District, 1878*: The S.O., Alan Cadell, conducted a most thorough enquiry into Thornton's survey and settlement methods, and in turn himself, through crop-cutting experiments, ascertained the yield per acre of 14 important crops for the year 1878, classified according to five soil types (of which two were irrigated) over three circles. As the soil types carry somewhat different names, they have been aggregated suitably so as to generate groups of soil types which would be similar to those used by Thornton. These would yield a more meaningful comparison than a direct one of gross averages. (The latter are 794 lbs per acre in 1840, and 807 lbs per acre in 1878—hardly a significant difference). In Table 10, comparable soil qualities are considered.

A further comparison is also possible on the basis of the state-

[33] 'Mr Thornton's elaborate enquiries showed that the amount of produce according to appraisements made in the presence of European Officers was considerably higher than that entered in the papers of the landlords and village accountants. Mr Martin's experiments show a similar difference. An attempt has been made in the course of the Settlement now in progress to ascertain what the produce actually is by cutting the crop off a certain area, and weighing it after it has been threshed and winnowed. The result of this test was an enormous excess of produce above all previous estimates. This last test cannot be taken as the basis of a general average; the operation had to be superintended by European Officers. The Officers available were few. The area examined was therefore so small that no general conclusion could be drawn. Though the instructions were, that average fields and average crops should be selected, it is quite possible that the amount of produce was above the average. Again, it was of course necessary that the whole operation should be completed in one day; the weight of the grain may therefore have been very much more than it would have been had the usual length of time between cutting and weighing intervened, during which the grain loses weight considerably by drying. But this and all similar experiments tend to prove that the yield of the land is considerably greater than it is represented to be' (*Martin DSR* (*1866*), p. 4).

Table 10. Muzaffarnagar: Wheat yields in lbs/acre in the Nineteenth Century

Soil Type	DSR 1840	DSR 1878
Wet Rausli	1021	1063
Dry Rausli	750	773

Table 11. Muzaffarnagar: Wheat Yields on Better Quality Soils

Soil Type	Yield in lbs/acre	Year	Method
1. Thornton's Misan Irr.	1321	1840	CC
2. Cadell's Wet Loam	1247	1878	CC
3. Cadell's 'distinctly good villages'	1359	1878	Native experts

ments extracted by Cadell from reliable 'selected *zamindars* and *patwaris* of distinctly good villages'. This can perhaps be compared with the yield entries against Thornton's *Misan* irrigated land, and also with Cadell's 'Wet Loam', which the best quality registered in 1878.

On this evidence again, there is little evidence to believe that the yield per acre of wheat had risen by any discernible amount (*Cadell DSR* (*1878*), pp. 21–2).

(iii) *Irrigation Revenue Reports—1881–2 to 1883–4*: From 1876–7, the Irrigation Department regularly published estimates of the value per acre of the output grown on the various canals in U.P. Continuous data by canal are available for the entire period under consideration, but it is only for the three years 1881–2 to 1883–4 that the yields per acre can be directly calculated without recourse to the price data. As such, these figures are more reliable and are reported in Table 12. Compared with the earlier estimates of irrigated wheat yields, Table 12 tends to corroborate the essential stability of intrinsic yields in the interim period up to the early 1880s.

(C) *The End Period* (*1897–1921*):

Let us again return to the seminal Table 6. The UPG's figures for the end period, 1897–1921, are obtained internally from the Agricultural Department, but we can trace their origin indirectly.

Table 12. Wheat Yields (in lbs per acre) in Canal Irrigated Areas

Year	Ganges Canal	Eastern Jumna Canal
1866*	N.A.	1060*
1881–2	1163	1096
1882–3	1231	1105
1883–4	1092	955
Average:	1162	1052
Overall Average = 1107 lbs./acre.		

SOURCE: *Irrigation Revenue Reports*, U.P. Govt., 1881–2, 1882–3, 1883–4.

* Estimated by the local irrigation officials on the Eastern Jumna Canal especially for Muzaffarnagar District; reported in *Martin DSR, 1866.*

Table 13, sets out the 'normal' wheat yields for Muzaffarnagar District, and it turns out that the average *'normal'* irrigated and unirrigated yields for the period 1898–1922, viz., 1280 and 840 lbs/acre, respectively, are exactly the figures used by the UPG in Table 6. The overall average reported, and used for the basic comparison, is 1,100 lbs per acre.

The UPG's use of the 'normal' yield figures in the basic comparison is clearly inappropriate, as these figures are over-estimated and do not represent the *actual* yields for the periods. The extent of the over-estimation can be calculated from Table 14, which also sets out all the other figures for making as accurate a comparison as is possible between the 1840 and the 1897–1921 benchmarks.

Before entering into a discussion of these alternatives, we need to note a few relevant points concerning the End-Period average yield figure in *Comparison B*. This figure, from *Wheat Stats*, is also derived from the official statistics of the Agricultural Department, but gives the *actual* average yield rather than the inflated so-called 'normal' yield for Muzaffarnagar. *Wheat Stats*, reports an average irrigated wheat area percentage of 65 per cent for the period 1913–21: and from the U.P. Government's End-Period figures in *Comparison A*, we find that the yield of wheat on irrigated land is 52 per cent higher than on unirrigated land. Using these two statistics, the end-period average of 879 lbs/acre has been decomposed into the irrigated and the unirrigated figures of 995 and 663 lbs/acre in

Table 13. 'Normal' Yields of Wheat in Muzaffarnagar District (in lbs/acre)

Years	Irrigated	Unirrigated	Muzaffarnagar District Actual Average Wheat Yield Using the Condition Factors as well*
1989–1902	1250	800	
1903–7	1250	850	
1908–12	1300	850	
1913–17	1300	850	(860)
1918–22	1300	850	(931)
1898–1922	1280	840	
Over-all Average = 1100 lbs. / acre			

SOURCE: *Crop Statistics of U.P.*, vol. II, pp. 474–5; U.P. Govt. 1967.

* These *actual* wheat yield period averages have been taken from *Wheat Statistics of India*, Directorate of Economics & Statistics, Ministry of Food and Agriculture, Government of India, 1972; Table 7.70 (henceforth, *Wheat Stats.*) Figures not available for 1898–1912 period.

Used by *UPG Report (1926)*: see Table 6.

Table 14. Alternative Comparisons of Long-term Wheat Yield Changes

Period	Irrigated Yield	Unirrigated Yield	Average Yield
Comparison A: Source – U.P. Government: see Table 6 for Base, and Table 13 for End Periods			
Base: 1827–40	1000	620	650
End: 1897–1921	1280	840	1100
Percentage Increase	+28.0	+35.5	+69.2
Comparison B: Source – Present Study: see Table 10 for Base, and Text for End Periods			
Base: 1840	1217	725	794
End: 1913–21	995	663	879
Percentage Increase	–18.2	–8.6	+10.7

Comparison B. This procedure should not create any discernible distortion in the comparison. Unquestionably, however, the *Comparison A* end-period 'normal' yield figures are quite inadmissable. (The implicit over-estimation of the irrigated, unirrigated and the average yields is 28.6 per cent, 26.7 per cent and 25.1 per cent respectively). Again, with regard to the Base-Period, we have noted the manner in which Thornton's 1840 Settlement generated significant under-estimates of yields per acre, not on account of the mis-reporting of the zamindars, but rather because of the inherent procedural biases of the survey methods by which the wheat yield data was gathered and averaged. We saw how the crop-cutting data was more reliable, though even then rather under-estimated, judging by the fact that Muzaffarnagar wheat prices were the highest in the entire four decades centring on 1840. Hence, *Comparison B* is again preferable to *A*, which under-estimates the base-period irrigated, unirrigated and average yields by 17.8 per cent, 14.5 per cent and 18.1 per cent respectively. We will therefore discard the U.P. Government's *Comparison A* in favour of *Comparison B*, which, arguably, is the most accurate comparison that can be generated on the basis of the available data.

Not surprisingly, radically different conclusions follow from the two alternative comparisons. Thus, the UPG would argue that both irrigated as well as unirrigated yields rose substantially (by 28.0 per cent and 35.5 per cent respectively); and that on account of the shift-effect due to increased irrigation, the average yield rose by as much as 69.2 per cent. The valid *Comparison B*, however, reveals that both irrigated and unirrigated yields were declining, with the irrigated decline being greater, at -18.2 per cent than the -8.6 per cent decline in unirrigated yields. However, as the percentage of wheat area irrigated rose from 13 per cent in 1840 to as much as 65 per cent in 1921, the shift effect dominates the over-all outcome, and throws up an *average* yield *increase*, but of only 10.7 per cent.

The plausibility of the *Comparison B* findings can be confirmed indirectly. Firstly, it is widely recorded that while the canals increased yields in the previously unirrigated lands, such increases did taper off, and were then reversed on account of the problems of water-logging, alkalinity and over-cropping associated with canal flow-irrigation. These factors are discussed at length in Chapter II and also in Appendix. In this context, it is significant that *Comparison B* shows a greater decline in the irrigated yields. This also ties in with the observation made by the Royal Commission on Agriculture (1928) that soil fertility on unirrigated land in India had reached a floor level even before the nineteenth century: 'A balance has been established, and no further deterioration is likely to take place under the existing conditions of cultivation' (quoted by Blyn (1966), p. 189). However, unirrigated yield declines could still occur on account of a deterioration in the conditions of cultivation. It is being argued that while canal irrigation led to a discontinuous once-for-all increase in the yield level, it also generated stronger deterioration tendencies subsequently than those prevalent in the unirrigated tracts.

Secondly, the plausibility of *Comparison B* can be further confirmed by testing one of its implicit corollaries. Since we argue that the *average* increase is positive on account of the irrigation shift effect (while the intrinsic effects are negative on both irrigated as well as unirrigated lands), it should be the case that once this shift effect becomes inoperative, that the *average* yield trend should also become negative. (This assumes that there was no simultaneous, sufficiently compensating improvement in the conditions of cultivation on account of other, independent factors.) As it happens, the percentage of wheat area irrigated in Muzaffarnagar district does stabilize completely around its 65 per cent level of 1921 in the post-1921 period until the tube-well expansion period is reached in the late 1960s. Hence, if our interpretation of *Comparison B* is tenable, we should expect the average yield of wheat to decline over this post-1921 stagnant irrigation phase. Table 15 on average yields confirm this expectation unequivocally.

At this stage, it must be recalled that on the basis of the step-wise corrections applied to the *value-data* of Table 6, we had concluded that there had been a decline in the average physical yields of the non-sugar-cane crops by 9.7 per cent over the entire reference

Table 15. Average Wheat Yields (in lbs./acre) in Muzaffarnagar District: 1921–48

Period	Average Wheat Yield	Wheat Area Irrigated (%)
1921–2 – 1930–1	892	62*
1931–2 – 1940–1	839	62
1941–2 – 1948–9	821	64
1949–50 – 1958–9	799	64

Source: *Wheat Stats*: Table 7.70

* Excludes 1923–4 on account of climatic abnormality
Results based on Crop-cutting Surveys: all others based on *annewari* system.

period. However, our finding from *Comparison B* in Table 14 shows that on the basis of the *physical-yields data*, the average *wheat* yield *rose* by 10.7 per cent. This contradiction is, however, more apparent than real. The crop coverage of the two sets of data is not identical, and on the basis of the evidence in Blyn (1966), and also on *a priori* considerations, we can expect the wheat yield trends to overstate improvements (if any) in the non-wheat cereals. Since wheat comprised less than one-half of the entire non-sugar-cane group, the 'discrepancy' would be explicable if the inferior cereals also had such inferior trends in relation to wheat. However, this proposition is not really testable on the basis of the data available. To the extent that this suggested explanation is deemed not to apply, we have to choose, as it were, between the value, and the physical-yields data sets. In such a situation, there can be no doubt that the physical data set would be the more reliable since the value data is generated by using the physical-outturn data in conjunction with the available price data in order to generate the final value figures. It is additionally reassuring to note that the value data and the physical-yields data generate conclusions about *intrinsic* yield effects which are of similar orders of magnitude: the value data on non-sugar-cane crops implies an average intrinsic yield decline of –24.6 per cent while the physical-yield data on wheat implies intrinsic declines of –18.2 per cent, –8.6 per cent and –14.8 per cent for irrigated, unirrigated and (weighted) average wheat yields, respectively, implying that a large part of the 'discrepancy' arises from differential irrigation shift effects in wheat, and inferior cereals yields.

(D) *The Interim Period Again: Dating the Decline in Intrinsic Yields*

From the evidence considered for the *Interim Period* earlier, it was concluded that wheat yields on individual soil types did not exhibit any noticeable decline up to the early 1880s. When the *End Period* data is juxtaposed on this, the inference must be that intrinsic yields began declining sometime between 1880 and 1921. Let us return to this period to try to date the period when intrinsic yields began to display a declining trend.

Unfortunately, on this period, the data are rather scanty, and Miller's Settlement Report for Muzaffarnagar District for 1892 is not very forthcoming from our point of view.[34] However, data on wheat outputs and areas are available by 'circle' (groups of districts) for the United Provinces for the period 1891 to 1912 in the *Datta Price Enquiry Report* (1915), vol. III. We have derived an annual yield series for wheat for the 'North and West Circle' (which includes Muzaffarnagar District), and then used five year moving averages to even out the year-to-year fluctuations, and finally, divided the period into two halves. The average yield for the first half, 1891–1901 is 955.4 lbs/acre, whereas for the second half, 1902–12, it works out to 878.7 lbs/acre, thus showing a decline of about 8 per cent over the two decades. Again, assuming as before that irrigated yields are 52 per cent higher than unirrigated ones (see Table 6), and assuming that 60 per cent of the wheat crop was irrigated in 1891–1912 (viz., the Muzaffarnagar percentage), an average yield of 955.4 implies an irrigated yield of 1092, and an unirrigated one of 728 lbs/acre. These figures for 1891–1901 are not too dissimilar from Thornton's crop-cutting figures for 1840 as reported in Table 10. On this rather slender evidence, the start of the decline in intrinsic yields can be dated to the first decade of the twentieth century. This conclusion, however, is tentative, and the decline could well have begun in the last two decades of the nineteenth century.

Wheat Yield Trends in Bareilly District

One other district for which reliably comparable records are available over this period is Bareilly where there exists, as a benchmark, the evidence of Henry Boulderson's 512 crop-cutting experiments conducted in the years 1828–9 and 1830–1.[35] Our task is made

[34] There is only a marginal reference to trends in crop yields. 'A comparison of the crop statistics of the present Settlement with those of Mr Cadell's or Mr Martin's does not point to any marked improvement in cultivation, or, indeed, . . . to any marked change in the agricultural methods of the district' (*Miller DSR* (*1892*), p. 42).

[35] Thornton himself made a reference to this data, but observed that the difference in soil qualities between the two districts would probably explain the observed differences in yields (*Thornton* (*1840*), p. 32). The impossibility of using such district soil-specific yield figures for cross-district comparisons was also noted by Cadell who said 'that the average of his [Thornton's] estimates is of no use for comparison with other districts, unless the proportion of dry and sandy land is similar' (*Cadell* (*1878*), p. 22). We will therefore shun a comparison with Muzaffarnagar, and will concentrate once again on gleaning evidence on yields from subsequent DSR's on Bareilly.

Table 16. Wheat Yields in Bareilly District

Year	Yield in lbs/acre
1828–31	1,046
1878	928
Per cent change	–11.3

lighter by the very considerable effort of S. M. Moens who presented in his very thorough DSR of 1874, the results of both Boulderson's as well as his own, crop-cutting experiments. We will again concentrate on wheat, on the justification that any improvement in the cereals would manifest itself first of all in wheat, and only then, if at all, in the inferior cereals. Unfortunately, Moens does not present the soil-specific yield rates for his own, or for the earlier experiments, so that all we have for a comparison is the overall *average* yield derived by these officers on the basis of these experiments. The results are given in Table 16

S. H. Fremantle's DSR of 1903 does not permit of the 1942 DSR any firm conclusion about improvements in agriculture. The crop-cutting experiments do not afford material for comparison as they do not specify that they were conducted on the same field for both benchmarks, and the S.O. prefers the data implicit in the commutation rates in the rent registers as being the one most likely to bear comparison. On this data (for Circle I, Nawabganj Tehsil), it is shown that the yield of wheat was 691 lbs./acre in 1870, and 806 lbs per acre in 1942. However, Lewys-Lloyd discounts the conclusion that this reflects a significant improvement, for he argues that 'the greater difference between the wheat produce figures may be explained by the fact that some of the better wheat-growing fields in 1870 were cash-rented and so did not enter into the Settlement Officer's estimate of average production. . .' (*Lewys-Lloyd* (*1942*), p. 4). If anything, he argues the case for a constancy of yields over time.

Lloyd, however, chooses to ignore the official evidence (also given in *Wheat Stats*) on wheat yields in Bareilly district from 1911–12 onwards. In Table 17 below, we have presented the average decadal values for wheat yields per acre. Alongside is given the average proportion of the wheat acreage irrigated. Using this information, and applying an irrigation yield-shift factor of 1.5, we estimate for the first decade, the irrigated and unirrigated wheat

Table 17. Twentieth Century Wheat Yield Trends in Bareilly District

Years	Average Observed Yield in lbs/acre	Irrigation per cent	Expected Yield*	Index of Actual/Exp.
1911–12 to 1920–1	860	36.7	860	100.0
1921–22 to 1930–1	738	16.7	788	93.7
1931–32 to 1940–1	690	22.7	809	85.3
1941–42 to 1948–9	595	26.0	821	72.5
1949–50 to 1958–9	613	11.6	769	79.7

* Figures represent the average base period yield of 860 lbs/acre. Corrected only for the changes in the irrigation percentage for wheat.

Estimated from crop-cutting experiments.

yields separately. Thereafter, the following exercise has been undertaken: these yields, and the respective decadal irrigation proportions, are used to derive average *expected* yield figures for the other decades (on the implicit assumption that the only variation in yields would be on account of variations in the percentage of wheat area irrigated). These *expected* yields are then compared with the *observed* actual yields figures: if the actual is above the expected, it implies that even after taking into account the impact on the average yield of the changed percentage of wheat area irrigated, the yield per acre has risen, and vice versa. As can be seen in Table 17, the expected yields are well above the actual averages for all the subsequent decades—implying, that even after accounting for the depressing influence of falling wheat irrigation on average yields, the yields per acre still fell in comparison to the first decade. The last column of Table 17 shows that the index number (of actual yields as a proportion of the expected yields), declines steadily by more than one quarter over the period 1911–12 to 1948–9. The latter level is below that in 1878 which, in turn, is below that in 1828–31.

One can question the comparability of the settlement reports and the official statistics, but undeniably, the trend in each subperiod is downward: up until 1878, marginally; but in the period after 1911–12, the arguments *a priori* of Lewys-Lloyd notwithstanding, vary significantly.

The high probability that agricultural improvements would not be undertaken was attested to by Moens in 1874.

My experiments show . . . how very large is the margin for possible improvement in produce by scientific agriculture. I doubt, however, whether any improvement will take place. Our landlords as a rule are useless honey-eating drones. Their only idea of 'improving' a village is raising its rents; while the cultivators, from whom alone any real improvement could come, can get nothing but a bare subsistence—all their profits being swallowed up by the interest on their debts for seed, food, purchase of cattle, and marriage expenses . . . Till lately it was the *asami* who was in demand to cultivate the land, now population is pressing on the land, and the people *must* cultivate to live; they have no other source open to them: competition must set in, the rents must rise, and poorly off as the cultivator now is I fear he will be worse off hereafter.' (*Moens; Bareilly DSR, 1874,* pp. 101–2)

That agricultural improvement was not, in fact, undertaken is stated by Lewys-Lloyd in his DSR of 1942. The only significant improvement he cites is expectedly in sugar-cane, where the *desi* variety has been largely replaced by an improved one yielding an additional 20 per cent, but there are no references to improvements in the foodgrains. On the contrary, Lloyd cites reasons for believing that cultivation inputs might have declined in quality and quantity: smaller grazing areas and the lower proportions of land under fodder crops leading to a declining animal population, and this along with restrictions on the movement of night soil from urban areas, has lowered the availability of manure for cultivation; the extension of the cultivated area has led to a greater use of inferior land with a lower productivity.

Bareilly district thus experiences a process quite similar in character to that in Muzaffarnagar, viz. one of a trend decline in yield in the twentieth century; with the conditions for this decline already quite mature by the 1880s.

Concluding Observations

At the outset, the warning must be sounded that the evidence we have dealt with is from disparate sources—not all of them as uniformly reliable as might be desired. This is as inevitable as it is unavoidable in the given context. However, the collective weight of the data, even when suitably discounted and conservatively interpreted, leads us to reject the reinterpretationist thesis that the nineteenth century saw an increase of physical crop yields per acre of up to 75 per cent. The UPG's basic data, i.e. Table 6, is questionable; and its gross exaggeration[36] of the extent of improvement can plausibly be ascribed to the compelling political motivation of emphasizing the 'improvements' under British rule to the Royal Commission on Agriculture in India. Neale, and even more so, Morris, who appear as keen as the UPG to establish this, are willingly gullible, or guilty of poor historiography, or both.

Our independent evaluation, based on a wide range of official source material suggests the following conclusions with regard to trends in crop yields, especially wheat:

(*a*) *Intrinsic* wheat yields display a general stability up until the early 1880s.

(*b*) Intrinsic yields begin to decline around 1880–1900, and this declining trend continues unabated throughout the entire subsequent period until 1948.

(*c*) While canal irrigation continues to be extended until about 1920, the *average* wheat yield displays an increasing trend; this originated from the *shift* effect on yields, viz., through the fact that irrigated wheat yields are substantially higher than unirrigated ones.

(*d*) After the 1920s, when the canal irrigation extension factor is no longer operative, the decline in the intrinsic yields begins to show itself in declining *average* wheat yields; i.e. the negative intrinsic effect now dominates the weak shift effect.

(*e*) In the context of the UPG, Neale and Morris's comparisons for 1840–1921 based on Table 6, we find that necessary corrections yield conclusions opposite to theirs. The corrected value date show that the average physical yields index of non-sugar-cane crops declined by 9.7 per cent before, and by 24.6 per cent after, excluding the influence of increases on irrigation; on the basis of the physical yields data, the conclusion emerges that the intrinsic wheat yields on irrigated and unirrigated lands declined over the period by 18.2 per cent and 8.6 per cent respectively, though the average increased by 10.7 per cent through a very high increase in the percentage of wheat area irrigated.

[36] Even the U.P. Government Officers involved with the drafting of this *UPG Report(1926)* were aware of this fact. Cf. Oral Evidence of Mr A. E. Parr, Dep. Director of Agriculture, to the *Royal Commission on Agriculture in India*, vol. VII, p. 129.

The first general conclusion, therefore, is that in contrast to earlier stability, a progressive deterioration in the basic technical and/or social conditions of cultivation set in towards the end of the nineteenth century.

This conclusion is consistent with Blyn's evidence on wheat yield trends for the United Provinces which show that *average* wheat yields rose steadily over the period 1891 to 1911–20, and thereafter declined secularly through until 1948, the end of the reference period. This would be quite explicable in terms of the operation, until the 1920s, of the shift effect on wheat yields arising out of an increased irrigated to sown area ratio. After the commissioning of the Sarda Canal in the late 1920s, the irrigation shift effect petered out and this can account for the declining *average* wheat yield from 1921–30, when negative intrinsic effects begin to dominate, as in the case of Muzaffarnagar.

In his critique, Heston admits 'I am offering no evidence that yields per acre did not decline'; yet, he asserts that the reported crop yield decline over the period 1886–1947 does not correspond to the agricultural history of the period (*Heston* (*1973*), p. 328). Indeed, the question of the correspondence between the calculated statistical yield trends and the reported and documented trends in the underlying determinants of crop yields is of great importance. Can we then offer such independent support for our listed conclusions? We have argued that the decline in the *average* yields after 1911–20 is attributable to the end of the expansionary phase of canal irrigation; the crucial factor therefore is the calculated decline in the *intrinsic* yields after 1880–1900. What explains the timing of this turning point in trends in intrinsic yields? Let us briefly consider the more important influences.

(i) The turning point corresponds to the period when available land margins were reached in North India, and cultivation became intensive. Increasingly, fodder and grazing lands were taken up for crop cultivation,[37] and the consequent decline of livestock numbers, and hence of manure supplies within the rural sector, could only have been detrimental for crop yields. Alongside this, the proportion of fallow to cultivable land also began to shrink, with obvious implications for the yield capacity of the soil.

[37] For a detailed discussion of these tendencies in North India, see Klein (1974).

(ii) Since the area under wheat was increasing over the period, it is likely that the additional areas were less fertile—thus lowering the average fertility of irrigated and unirrigated lands separately. This effect is likely to have been operative in Muzaffarnagar, though Table 3 shows that it has limited applicability for U.P. as a whole.

(iii) The jointly-cultivating *bhaiyachara* communities were recognized as being more efficient in cultivation than individual *zamindars* or tenants.[38] Over the period under question, the *bhaiyachara* communities were the victims of the legal processes of the land administration[39] and the share of land owned by non-cultivating classes rose significantly. The decline of the former, if not the rise of the latter,[40] could be expected to have a negative impact on crop yields.

[38] Thus, for Muzaffarnagar District, *Martin DSR (1866)*, p. 4, records 'the perceptible difference between the condition of estates held by proprietory communities and those owned by individual landlords and cultivated by tenants-at-will'. Again, in the context of the newly introduced 'owners' rate' on the Agra Canal, the *Irrigation Revenue Report* (1876–7, p. 24B) observes: 'The working of the owners' rate has undoubtedly had the effect of retarding the development of irrigation in *villages belonging to large zamindars*' . . . 'The most noticeable feature in the working of the owners' rates is the rapid extension of irrigation in *villages owned by Bhaiyachara communities*. Where the land belongs to a large zamindar the increase, if any, is slight' (emphasis in the original).

[39] See Stokes, E. (1975). Such transfers were continuing apace until the end of the nineteenth century.

[40] There is virtually no hard statistical evidence on these issues, but in the context of the North-Western Provinces, the astute E. C. Buck observed: 'The new zamindars whom our laws have created, and who now own so much of the land are, as rule, disinclined to sink money in such improvements [as wells]. They transfer the responsibility to cultivators, and their sole object seems to be to take as much out of the land as they can, and to spend as little on it as possible; whilst the majority of the old proprietors are unable to set aside large sums out of their incomes for such improvements. The cultivators, on the other hand, . . . had not till recently sufficient permanent interest in the land to encourage them to sink their savings in the construction of masonry wells . . .' *Note on Wells*, E. C. Buck; Evidence on the N.–W.P. to the *Famine Commission, 1881*, Pt. III, App. III, p. 128. In the context of land transfers through indebtedness in the first quarter of the twentieth century, the *U.P. Provincial Banking Enquiry Committee Report, 1928–9*, takes a different stance: 'So far as the transfers have been to agriculturist purchasers, the change was almost certainly for the better. So far as the transfers were to non-agriculturist purchasers the change was not necessarily for the worse' ibid., vol. I, p. 128.

(iv) By-products of the tenancy protection legislation initiated in the 1880s were, firstly, to make the landowner apprehensive of allowing the tenant to construct a well, or to effect any other such tangible improvement on the land that would assist the tenant in any subsequent legal fight against the landlord for occupancy rights to the land;[41] and secondly, for the landlord to keep a high turnover of tenants on the same land so as to frustrate the accrual of permanent tenancy rights through continous occupation. This would undoubtedly have pre-empted such improvements as the tenants might have been capable of making.

(v) Again, after the 1860s–1880s Settlements, it was felt that landlords investment in land improvements, etc., was a cue for increased land revenue demands by the State.[42] This could have been a significant deterrent in a situation where usury investment was a strong competitor to productive ones. Moens[43] aptly characterizes the landlords as 'useless honey-eating drones'; but the dominance of their usurious activities could only have been strengthened by these disincentive effects operating on productive investments through the land revenue system.

(vi) There were widespread reports by the Irrigation Revenue Department as well as by District Revenue Officials that after a lapse of a few years canal areas showed a declining yield per acre, in the absence of additional manuring to compensate for the loss of soil elements due to flow irrigation; and also on account of the over-cropping resulting from the availability of flow irrigation. Severe water-logging and salinity problems emerged in the canal command areas, and Muzaffarnagar had more than its share of both

[41] There are frequent references to this effect in the official records, e.g. 'Uncertainty of tenure and defects of tenancy law have in the past prevented well sinking by tenants. Even a fairly enlightened zamindar like the Raja of Mursan would not allow his occupancy tenants to make *pakka* wells, though his action was illegal.' Evidence of the Collector of Ghazipur district to the Indian Irrigation Commission 1901, *Report, vol. IV, Selected Evidence*, pp. 250–1; for similar evidence on Lucknow District, ibid., p. 267.

[42] Such effects are widely reported by District Officials, and the following report of the Settlement Officer of Kheri and Sitapur Districts to the Irrigation Commission is typical. 'Most Settlement Officers will agree that, so far as there is a defect in our settlement system, it is that a man who works up his village at the end of the settlement is liable to find that his revenue will be enhanced more than that of the person who has left it alone' ibid., p. 264.

[43] Quoted on p. 46.

canal irrigation and such negative side-effects, which became apparent around 1870.[44]

(vii) In the context of the efficiency of the utilisation of canal irrigation, the increasing sub-division and especially the parcellisation of holdings could only have had a negative effect.[45]

There are few positive factors to set off against all the above negative ones. Thus improved seeds and chemical fertilisers were irrelevant for the period and crops under study. There were some mechanical implements in use on some zamindar farms, but these owed their profitability to labour displacement rather than to any net output expansion effect. However, both Morris and Heston have centred their counter-arguments on factors pivoting on trends in population growth. Let us consider these briefly.

(*a*) Following Morris (1963), Heston (1973, p. 330ff.25) asks: 'If there was a decline in per capita availability of foodgrains, would you expect the increase in population that India experiences especially during the period after 1921, which was also the period when population growth increased and yields per acre most decreased.' Morris makes a similar argument. Both implicitly posit a direct one-to-one relation between population and economic growth. However, population growth may or may not be associated with,

[44] In the Muzaffarnagar context, it is significant that Martin (1866) does not regard this topic as a major one; Cadell (1873, 1878) gives it great prominence. Since the second canal feeding Muzaffarnagar district, viz., the Upper Ganges Canal became operational in 1854, the negative impact of the side-effects could be expected to have been at full strength after the 1870–80 period. There were no counter-measures worth mentioning. On these aspects, see also: Whitcombe, E. (1972) and Klein (1974).

[45] See: RCA 1926, *Main Report*, Ch. V; and village level evidence, though not for the United Provinces, in Mann (1917), Diskalkar (1960), Pandit (1969); for Pimpla Saudagar in Maharashtra, and Kessinger (1975) for 'Vilayatpur' in Punjab. See also, Blyn (1966, pp. 211–12) and Farmer (1960). Farmer argues that fragmentation might not hinder, but even assist intensive rice cultivation. However, rice was a minor crop on the canal irrigated areas in comparison to wheat and sugar-cane which dominated cropping patterns. Other negative externalities of heavy parcellisation were seen to obstruct agricultural improvements even by the 1880–1900 period. Thus, in his evidence to the Irrigation Commission (1901), a District Collector observes: 'The great difficulty in the way of that [increasing the number of embankments] is that the land is very much sub-divided among many villages. In each village there are a very large number of co-sharers and you can never get these men to combine' *Report*, vol. IV, p. 257.

be caused by, or cause economic growth by some uniform universal law. And Morris conveniently shifts his ground in the context of his nineteenth century reinterpretation where he argues that growth occurred because 'the economy was not burdened by a high rate of population expansion' (*Morris* (*1969*), p. 611).[46] However, increasing population and poverty are quite explicable within a socially and economically rational decision-making framework if one examines the micro-economics of fertility behaviour; large families are maintained as this increases the chances of survival for the whole unit (*Mamdani, 1975*).

(*b*) 'Since most studies show that more workers per acre produce more output per acre in Indian farm studies, one might also suspect that as Indian agriculture became more intensive over the period, yields per acre would rise' (*Heston* (*1973*), p. 328).

Citing Sen (1962, 1964) for this cross-sectional result, Heston follows Boserup (1965) and claims that a similar effect would have been operative over time as the land-man ratio declined. This argument rests on a misconception. Neither Sen (1965) when expounding the wage-gap explanation of farm-size productivity differentials, nor other contributors to this debate ascribe the entire observed productivity differential to the wage-gap; indeed, the greater part of the differential could be explained in terms of the differences in other complementary factors of production. When viewing the process over time, several other questions arise. Firstly, it is not workers, but work hours per acre which is the relevant variable. It is entirely conceivable that while the workers/land ratio increased, that of work-hours/land flattened out as the marginal productivity of work-hours declined. Secondly, over time there would be shifts in the land-labour based cross-sectional production function that Heston appears to have in mind.

It has been argued here and elsewhere that such shifts were systematically downwards over the period, and easily dominated the labour intensity effect. With such downward shifts, it is possible that the flat section of the production function would be reached even more quickly, as the quantity and quality of complementary factors declined. Thirdly, after about 1880, the DSRs report a

[46] For an effective critique of Morris's position, see B Chandra, (1968, pp. 43–5).

relative shortage of land rather than tenants, leading to the onset of competition rents which left the tenants in general with little above subsistence requirements. This would clearly have reduced the capacity of the tenant to affect any improvements in cultivation practices. And given their near universal indebtedness, tenants might not have had the incentive to apply marginally productive units of labour when the returns, low as they might have been, would accrue in large part to their creditors.

What then is the over-all significance of our findings? They show clearly that contrary to the re-interpretationist thesis, yields per acre made a negative contribution to economic expansion in the United Provinces in the period after 1880–1900, and no discernible positive contribution before then. Hence, the increase in the value of output per acre over the period can be attributed to the impact of irrigation extension, which increased average yields through the shift effect, but also increased per acre values through shifts in the cropping patterns in favour of the high-value crops. The implication is inevitable, then, that canals generated an internal regional dualism within the United Provinces, though even the high-value per acre commercialized canal areas experienced secular declines in intrinsic yields subsequent to the introduction of the canals. An investible surplus, therefore, was created in the canal regions. The crucial questions therefore, are: who got the surplus? How was it extracted and transferred? What was done with it?

References

Desai, A. V. (1972) 'Population and Standards of Living in Akbar's Time' *Indian Economic and Social History Review*, IX, 1 (Henceforth, *IESHR*).

Diskalkar, P. D. (1960) *Resurvey of a Deccan Village: Pimpla Saudagar*, Bombay.

Heston A. W. (1973): In this volume.

Heston A. W. (1977) 'Standard of Living in Akbar's Time: A Comment' *IESHR*, XIV, 3.

Klein I. (1974) 'Population and Agriculture in North India 1872–1921' *Modern Asian Studies*, 8, 2.

Mann H. H. (1917) *Land and Labour in a Deccan Village—I: Pimpla Saudagar*, Bombay.

Misra B. R. (1942) *Land Revenue Policy in the United Provinces*, Benaras.

Moosvi S. (1977) 'A Note on Professor Alan Heston's "Standard of Living in Akbar's Time—A Comment" ' *IESHR*, XIV, 3.

Morris M. D. (1963) 'Towards a Reinterpretation of Nineteenth Century Indian Economic History' *Journal of Economic History*, XXIII, 4.

— (1968) 'Towards a Reinterpretation of Nineteenth Century Indian Economic History' *IESHR*, V, 1.

Neale W. C. (1962) *Economic Change in Rural India*, New Haven.

Pandit, D. (1969) 'The Myths Around Sub-Division and Fragmentation of Holdings: A Few Case Histories' *IESHR*, VI, 1

Stuart, G. A. D. (1919) 'The season Factor in Crop Statistics' *Agricultural Journal of India*, XIV.

Chapter 8

Quantitative Estimate of Agricultural Output in Chotanagpur

[Hitherto Unpublished]

P. P. MOHAPATRA

Any attempt at a quantitative estimate of reasonable accuracy, for agricultural production, in the Chotanagpur division has to take into account the appalling state of the sources of basic data. The sources for a continuous series of agricultural production, in the pre-independence period are limited to two Government publications: the annual *Season and Crop Report* and the *Report on Agricultural Statistics*, which were published by the Director of Agriculture, Bihar (from 1912 onwards and before that by the Director of Agriculture, Bengal).[1]

Bihar being a part of the permanently settled region, suffered from all the disadvantages which attended upon a lack of a regular revenue collecting machinery at the grass roots level. In the Raiyatwari and Mahalwari provinces like the United Provinces, Madras or Punjab and Deccan, there were village agencies which along with the work of revenue collection, also collected statistical data. In case of Bihar and Bengal the usual agency for the collection of statistical information was the village *chowkidar*.

The Chowkidar gave a rough idea of acreage and production to the inspector/*thanedar* of the police station who in turn took some sort of an average of them, not necessarily the arithmetic mean, using his own knowledge about the condition of the standing crops. This average was submitted to the district officers through the subdivisional officers. The district officers similarly averaged the statistics given by the thanedars. The average thus arrived at, which was often modified by the district officers, was then submitted to the Director of Agriculture. The result of this elaborate

[1] *Report on Crop Survey in Bihar 1944–48*, Patna, 1950, p. 6. (Hereafter *Report on Crop Survey*).

system of successive guesses was frequently fantastic if not altogether stereotyped. The lack of enthusiasm in the permanently settled regions for accurate crop estimation persisted throughout the colonial period, inspite of a succession of famines and acute distress which visited these areas. Unlike in Ryotwari regions (where Government revenue collections were determined to a great extent on the basis of accurate revenue statistics) there simply was no incentive in the permanently settled areas for estimating the crop statistics.

Unfortunately, there being no other source of comparative length or continuity, we have to make do with these faulty statistical basis. The first step in using them of course is to determine the source and extent of error in the crop statistics.

The *Season and Crop Report* was published annually from 1890 onwards. It provided information on (*a*) acreage of particular crops (*b*) the normal yield (*c*) the condition factor of the standing crop. The last two on multiplication gave the yield per acre of particular crop which when multiplied with the acreage figure gave the total yield of the crop.[2]

The total information on crops were thus of the following kind:

$$Y_n = A_n \times C_n \times N_n$$

where Y_n = Total yield of a particular crop n

A_n = Acreage under crop n

C_n = Condition factor expressed as a percentage of the normal yield of crop n.

N_n = Normal yield of crop n.

In each of the three factors on the right hand side of the equation, there were glaring errors. Let us discuss them one by one.

Acreage

The acreage of crops published prior to the commencement of Survey and Settlement operation in the districts were misleading to say the least. The difference between the figures published by

[2] Apart from these information, *Season and Crop Reports* published the harvest price of the crops and the rainfall statistics of the year as well as the land use pattern, i.e. the net and gross area under cultivation, under forest, under fallow, etc. We could not find the whole series of *Season and Crop Reports*. The basic series that we have used is for the period 1901–48.

the *Season and Crop Report* and the *Survey and Settlement Reports* were often very large, rendering the figures exceedingly questionable if not altogether useless.[3] The Survey and Settlement operation commenced in Chotanagpur division in 1902, in Ranchi district, and continued till 1925 when the whole of Chotanagpur division was covered.

It is only with the publication of the *Survey and Settlement Reports* that we find any reliable estimate of gross acreage under cultivation of different crops. Thus, per force, given the absurdity and arbitrariness of the earlier figures we would have to abandon the acreage figures published before the Survey and Settlement operations in various districts. This means that effectively, for any accurate estimate we would have to sacrifice a large portion of our time span.

Assuming that the figures published by the Agriculture Department were adequately revised after the publication of the Settlement figures, our trouble still does not end. The acreage figures should adequately reflect the year to year variation in sown acreage. Good weather conditions should predictably lead to increase in the sown acreage of favourable crops or conversely bad weather conditions must lead to a decline in the sown acreage. Further, it should also reflect the extension or contraction of acreage of crops, enabling us to determine shifts in crop composition both in the short and long term. However the official statistics in the post-settlement period do not reflect any of these changes; instead there was a conservative stereotyping of settlement figures. Therefore, if we except Ranchi, a district which was re-surveyed in 1927–35, the

[3] Thus K. L. Datta who was enquiring into the rise of prices in India, mentions the capricious nature of acreage figures in Chotanagpur division. In the earlier years, i.e. in the 1890s the acreage figures appear to have been pitched too high in all the districts except Manbhum where they were too low. In Ranchi the figures up to 1899–1900 were clearly overestimated. In 1900–1, the high figures attracted the attention of the district officer who reduced them more or less arbitrarily by about a half. This was further reduced in the following two years to about 1/3rd of the initial figures. Then again from 1903–4 onwards, the low figures were jerked up by about half—again through pure guesswork. The Survey and Settlement figures published in 1909–10 show the under-estimation to be more than 100 per cent. In Manbhum in the year 1897–8 the Collector raised his estimate by about 100 per cent purely through guess work without assigning any reason for doing so. Datta concluded that 'The figures are thus entirely unreliable'. K. L. Datta, *Report on the Enquiry into the rise of Prices in India*, Calcutta, 1917, vol. II, p. 306 fn.

acreage figures of all other districts remained practically unchanged till 1948, when the complete enumeration method was adopted for acreage statistics in the official reports.

A comparison of the official figures for 1945–8 with those published in the *Report on Crop Survey*, showed that there was severe under-enumeration in the official statistics, the degree ranging from 9 to 80 per cent for the districts (except for Ranchi). For the Division as a whole the official figures under-enumerated by about 20 per cent.[4] The error was neither uniform nor systematic. For the Division as a whole, the acreage figures were biased upward till around 1920, and downward after that.

If such is the case, we are precluded from correcting the official series by using the point revision method adopted by M. M. Islam.[5] The advantage of Islam's method was that by applying only one revision factor, a revised estimate of acreage/crop yield could be obtained. But the disadvantages are in the assumptions namely that the percentage fluctuations of the official series around the trend line are held to reflect the real annual variations. Secondly, the revision factor is estimated only at the end of the period and that too at only one point in time. One can easily visualize a situation where the official series through a process of adjustments either steadily diverges from the actual acreage or converges on it. That is to say, the amount of revision necessary could be either decreasing or increasing over a period of time rather than remaining constant. In that case the single revision factor estimated at the end of the period would tend to either over-estimate or under-estimate the earlier portion of the series.

Normal Yield

If the acreage estimates are often subject to the whims of the officialdom, the estimates of yield of crops are even more unreliable. The figure of the yield was fixed under the advice of the Director of Agriculture at a definite figure as 'normal or standard',

[4] The complete enumeration method was officially adopted in 1948, but between 1944 and 1948 the Bihar Government tried out this method under the guidance of P. C. Mahalanobis; the results of these surveys were embodied in the *Report on Crop Survey*.

[5] Islam, *Bengal Agriculture 1920–1946* (Cambridge, 1978). Islam adopted a revision factor which was the ratio of the official figure to the complete enumeration figure and multiplied it to the whole official series. His assumption is that of a systematic and unidirectional bias in the official figures.

and was varied each year by applying for each district a percentage indicating how far the crops of the year falls below or rises above the normal. The method used for estimating the normal yield was often not any better than an inspired guess. This is how J. A. Hubback described it:

An officer of some standing visits the tracts of whose yield he is required to form an estimate, and selects a fairly large area, usually 1/10th of an acre as constituting an average crop. This he cuts and carries and in due course threshes and weighs. If he has time, he makes two or more experiments, but it is obvious that he cannot usually manage to make a large number of experiments. The objection to this method is that firstly, it depends entirely, for the accuracy, on the ability of the officer to select a so called average field. Secondly, there is no possibility of estimating the probability of such statistics being acurate. . . . The method is comparable to estimating the average income of the population of a town by watching the streets for a few days and then picking at a man, who looks to be in average circumstances and discovering what his income is.[6]

The normal or standard yield was determined for a district through an insufficient amount of crop cutting and thus did not satisfy the need of statistical accuracy. It was also subjected to periodic changes, when new crop cutting experiments were made. The amount of variation from year to year was often large. The following table shows the variation in standard yield for various districts in case of cleaned winter rice and autumn rice.[7]

Table 1. Official Normal Yields (in maunds of cleaned rice/acre)

	Winter Rice			Autumn Rice		
Districts	1904–8	1919–33	1934–48	1904–8	1919–33	1934–48
Ranchi	14	6	10	9	9	8
Palamau	12	6	10	10	10	8
Hazaribagh	15	7	10	10	10	8
Manbhum	15	14	10	10	10	8
Singhbhum	15	14	10	10	10	8

SOURCE: *Season and Crop Report of Bengal & Bihar* for relevant years.

[6] Note on crop cutting experiments for rice fields in Bihar and Orissa by J. A. Hubback. *Report of Indian Economic Enquiry Committee* (1925), vol. III, p. 492.

[7] The figure for cleaned rice was determined by applying a standard conversion factor to the paddy yield. The standard conversion factor was assumed to be 63 per cent for Bihar and Orissa which was found to be too low by 7 per cent

The absurdity of these figures is evident from the fact that autumn rice yield was higher for the period 1919–20 to 1931–2 for some of the districts as compared to the winter rice yield. It was well known that winter rice yields were always higher than autumn rice yields in any normal year. Yet year after year the Department of Agriculture did not hesitate to make its yield estimates on the basis of these statistically unsound and often rankly absurd figures.

The settlement officers also conducted crop cutting experiments to determine the average yield of various classes of land. With a few exceptions, they suffered from all the errors that were inherent in non-random and small sized samples. But if the Settlement figures of crop yields were to some degree reliable in case of the paddy crops grown on the low land, the crops grown on the up land were often given short-shift and these figures had only conventional value rather than any semblance of statistical import.

Random crop cutting was introduced in Bihar for a few crops, from 1945 onwards and from 1949–50 it was adopted fully for all crops.

Condition factor

The final element in the crop yield is the condition factor which is an index of the state of the harvest for any particular year. The Department of Agriculture published it as a percentage of the normal yield but the information was actually collected by the 'annawari method' in which the harvest was expressed as a fraction of a rupee, in terms of 'annas'. It was by far the most subjective of all the factors that went into the yield estimate, and was roundly condemned by all concerned as the most unreliable.

All that is done at present is for the local police officer to make a guess to which in succession the SDO, the DO and the Director of Agriculture guess again. Hence the existing statistics of rice production are I believe, the result of applying to a fairly accurate figure of area, an arbitrary standard of normal yield and a pure guess of the condition of the year.[8]

Apart from the subjective factor involved in the estimation for condition of crops, there was some uncertainty as to what should

by the Rice Marketing Report in 1940. See *Report on the Marketing of Rice*, New Delhi, 1941.

[8] J. A. Hubback, vol. III, p. 492.

be considered a normal or 100 per cent crop. The standard practice was that the 16 anna crop was taken to be a bumper crop. For some districts of Bihar a 12 anna crop was taken to mean a normal crop and for other districts a 14 anna crop was stated to be the normal crop.[9] It is doubtful if these qualifications were sufficiently understood in the lower echelons of crop statistics collecting machinery.

But inspite of the evident probability of error in the guess work about condition factor of the crop, this perhaps was the only index which did not go wrong by a large margin. In 1925, A. C. Dobbs stated that the figures of yield of the season were perhaps only 10 per cent off the mark while the variation in acreage from year to year and the 'normal yield' were perhaps 20 per cent or more inaccurate.[10] During the discussion on the reliability of the crop statistics in 1942, the Commerce Department (Price Control) maintained that the errors of estimation of the yield per acre were relatively unimportant compared to the errors in measurement of area.[11]

Is it then possible to check whether the crop condition figures were a product of subjective fancy of the collection machinery or had some basis in actual state of the crops? In this connection, one is reminded of the Heston–Desai debate as to the reliability of the *annawari* condition factor.[12] The debate took place in connection with the relatively more reliable crop statistics of Bombay Presidency where the machinery for collection of crop statistics was of a different nature than in the permanently settled regions of Bihar and Orissa. Nonetheless, certain important points emerged from the debate. Heston's original contention was that the condition factors of most crops were consistently lowered due to Revenue considerations even when the rainfall figures did not support such pessimism. Secondly, there seemed to be statistically insignificant correlation between the rainfall and the condition factor. Desai in turn argued that there could not be possibly any revenue consideration in the lowering of the condition factor. This point was taken by Heston later. Secondly, Desai contended that the relation between rainfall and condition of the crop was non-linear and thus

[9] See George Blyn *Agricultural Trends in India 1891–1947: Output, Availability and Productivity*, Philadelphia, 1966, p. 48 fn. 15.

[10] Evidence of A. C. Dobbs, *Report of the Indian Economic Enquiry Committee*, vol. II, p. 432.

[11] *Report on Crop Survey in Bihar* , p. 7.

[12] See Heston (1973), (1978) and Desai (1978) in this volume.

Heston was barking up the wrong tree when he searched for a linear correlation between the two. But Desai himself gave no explanation for the progressive decline of condition factors from the high figures of the 1890s. Secondly, the range in which rainfall affects the crop yield, could be determined only if the condition factors represented the true yield. Otherwise, the linear function is as good a guess as the non-linear one. The problem could be solved of course if an exact non-linear function could be devised on the basis of a series of actual yields, which could than be retro-fitted to the whole series.

The possibility of a statistical verification of the reliability of condition factor in relation to the rainfall is thus the only significant point to emerge from the debate. The problem of choosing an appropriate mathematical relation between the two of course, remains.

We tried to find out the correlation between condition factor of rice and rainfall. First, we have taken a weighted average of condition factor of winter rice and autumn rice (weighted by their acreage in the *Settlement Reports*). Secondly, we have taken two indices of rainfall: the rainfall during the growing period of rice, i.e. June to September and the *Hathia* rainfall of the month of October and November. In case of Chotanagpur, rice cultivation, was crucially dependent on sufficient sub-soil moisture throughout the growing season, adequate rainfall during the transplantation period and some precipitation during the flowering period of rice (Hathia-rains).

The factor which affected the rice harvest most would be any prolonged break in the monsoon, or an abrupt cessation of it. Thus even if the total rainfall during the period may be more than the normal amount, the break in the precipitation would prove disastrous for the harvest. Unfortunately our indices would not adequately capture the relative distribution of rainfall during the monsoon. Moreover, crop failures need not only be on account of inadequacy of water supply. Pests and even abnormal weather conditions like frosts, hailstorms, etc., would also affect the yield figures.

Given these limitations and also our ignorance of other parameters affecting the crop-yield we would thus have a very strong *ceteris paribus* assumption—a high level of correlation between the condition factor and rainfall indices should not be expected.[13]

[13] During 1949–63, the relation between the rainfall and actual crop cutting yields at the divisional level was positive (0.5), the $R^2 = 0.25$.

Results of these correlations are given below for the rice crop alone.

Analysis of the Results

First at the aggregate level of the whole division, the condition factor of rice (weighted average of CF of all districts) is significantly correlated with the two rainfall indices, for the whole period (1890–1948) ($\bar{R}^2 = 0.24$) and the 2 tail 't' test shows that each of the regression coefficients is also significant.

The picture at the disaggregated level is not so uniformly significant. Only in the case of Ranchi district do we find the correlation to be significant and high enough to justify our test of reliability ($R^2 = 0.26$). Could it be that there is a significant trend element, which has vitiated the results? However, only in the case of Manbhum district is there a significant downward trend. When we extract the trend from the series, there is a significant jump in the level of correlation. It means then that at least in case of Manbhum, the fluctuations in the condition factor of rice, if not the trend, between 1901–48, is significantly correlated with the rainfall indices. But in case of all other districts we could not find any significant linear trend of the form $y = a + bt$.

It is possible that the rainfall indices we have chosen, do not explain any variation in the condition factor, because of misspecification. The condition factor of rice in each district and for the division as a whole is a weighted average of the condition factor of winter rice and autumn rice. It is possible, given the different cultural practices of winter rice and autumn rice that the conditions which favour autumn rice are not always favourable for winter rice and vice versa. So we ran a set of regressions for the winter rice condition factor as dependent variable and the two rainfall indices. The results are interesting. Except for Singhbhum district, the rest of the districts which showed a low correlation earlier, have a significant increase in the level of correlation as well as in significance. It thus clearly shows that the condition factor of winter rice more accurately reflected the variation in rainfall than the weighted average of the condition factor of autumn rice and winter rice.

The condition factor of winter rice for Singhbhum shows a steep decline in the level from 1933 onwards. In so far as the period till 1930 is concerned, again the level of correlation between the condition factor of rice and the rain fall indices became significantly higher again.

A similar test of reliability of condition factor for crops other than rice cannot be carried out, given the widely varying water requirement of each of the crops.

Proposed Method of Correction

In order to devise an estimate of actual agricultural output we propose the following method of correction of official statistics:

ACREAGE

Since the error in the official statistics is neither uniform nor systematic in nature, it was found impossible to use them as the basis for the construction of an alternative estimate. Instead, we have estimated acreage figures at the divisional and district levels by using two sets of accurate estimates a) those published during the survey and settlement period and b) those published under the complete enumeration method at the end of our period. The annual figures of the intervening period have been interpolated by using an exponential growth curve of the form $\log y = a + bt$. For the period between 1890 and the settlement period the acreage figures have been estimated by extrapolating backwards the growth curve for the later period. In calculating the growth rate, the mid-points of the survey period and the complete enumeration period (1950 as mid-point of 1946–53) have been used as reference points. In the case of Ranchi district, which was resurveyed in 1927–35, two different growth curves have been estimated, and the earlier of these extrapolated back to 1890. Since Singhbhum district was enlarged after 1947, the terminal acreage here refers to 1945–7 only.

The above method of estimation is not without problems. To begin with there was the problem of the non-simultaneity of various surveys and the non-comparability of the method of enumeration. The three component parts of Singhbhum district, Porahat, Kolhan and Dhalbhum were surveyed at different periods between 1902 and 1918; but a single year had to be chosen in order to estimate the district time-series. Further, the method of estimating crops on the uplands by the first survey officers, and that adopted during the complete enumeration at the end of our period differed from each other. An upland field was occupied by a different crop every year, and then left fallow for a period. The Survey and Settlement reports published two sets of acreage figures for upland crops. The *gross* acreage figure referred to the normal area devoted to the crop through the entire crop cycle, which when divided by the fallowing cycle gave the *net* acreage under each crop. In the complete enumerations however, only the actual area under each crop in any given year was enumerated. These differences have been reconciled to a certain extent by using only the net figures of upland crops during the survey and settlement period. In the case of Ranchi district there is an additional problem since the method of enumeration of upland crops was changed during the revisional survey, leading to over-estimation of the area under such crops. However, the *Season and Crop Report* for 1936 provides us suitably adjusted figures for foodgrains other than rice, and these have beeen useful in preparing the acreage estimates.

These minor caveats apart, we have to deal with the basic fact of accuracy of our interpolated figures. In construction of various series, the basic assumption is that the rate of growth (in this case exponential rate) was the same for every year interpolated in between our benchmark period, (i.e. the Survey and Settlement period) and the end period (1946–53). We have also further used the same rates to extrapolate these figures beyond the benchmark period down to 1890. How far is this assumption correct? First, for the intervening period the estimates represent the trend of acreage, but they cannot be said to reflect the annual variation of acreage.

If the official acreage statistics were only inaccurate in respect of the trend, while reflecting the annual fluctuations with some accuracy, we could have taken out the percentage fluctuations from the series and superimposed it on to our estimated acreage. But, we know for certain that the official acreage statistics had no systematic bias in so far as the trend was concerned and the annual fluctuations were abrupt and arbitrary.

We are thus left with no choice but to be satisfied with the trend estimate of acreage. Even though, we cannot estimate the exact degree of inaccuracy in our estimate, we can learn about the general directions of such inexactitude.

For instance, the amount of sown acreage would be a function of the timing and distribution of rainfall during sowing time. This factor to some extent also determines the final output. Thus, we can say, that the years in which there is a bad harvest, would also have seen a decline in the acreage and vice versa. If the assumption, that the fluctuation in acreage would be directly correlated with fluctuation in output, holds, then we can say that any estimation of output on the basis of our estimated acreage would tend to be more damped than the fluctuation in the actual output series.

Now as to the *trend* estimation; between two point estimates theoretically an infinite series of paths can be drawn, and we have chosen the exponential growth function. But could the actual trend of acreage be represented by an exponential growth function? There is no apriori reason for choosing any particular trend to describe the path of growth. In a historical series, of course, the square of the residuals provide the means for choosing the type of trend.

This being precluded, in the absence of an accurate historical series, the choice is limited to reasonable speculation. For instance, it is certain that the rate of expansion of acreage varied over time. That is, the expansion would be faster in the beginning, then it tends to slow down and finally reaches a plateau. Thus it is reasonable to suppose that the trend of acreage would follow a curve which is best approximated by the asymptotic growth curves. The equation of the curve in general is $Y = K + ab^t$ where the rate of growth of acreage is itself a function of time. There are many variants of this type of curve. Two best known are of course the Gompertz curve ($Y = K\ ab^t$) and the Logistic curve ($Y = k/1 + 10^{a+bt}$). In each of these trend curves, we have k, which represents the value of the asymptote or the upper limit of the series 'a' is a constant and 'b' is the rate of growth which keeps changing with time growing at a faster rate in the beginning and falling off towards the end. But in order to specify these three parameters we need at least three points in time. But the most we have are two points (in the Settlement period and the 1946–53 phase). Secondly, it would be possible to use these curves, if we could specify the asymptote or the upper limit. But given the variation in the rate of growth between districts and even over time, (e.g. Hazaribagh and Palamau display a for greater rate of growth after the Survey and Settlement operations than that of other districts) it would be almost useless to specify the asymptote or use the modified exponential curve.[14] Thus we are left with choosing either a simple linear trend (y = a + bt) or an exponential trend (log y = a + bt) which gives us constant rate of change. We have assumed the latter equation for our purpose.

The second problem is in extrapolation. For Chotanagpur Division as a whole, we have the acreage under rice and other food grains from 1890 onwards. How far is it correct for us to extrapolate backwards the district figures of acreage on the basis of rates of growth calculated for a later period? Specially, given that the higher rates of expansion of Hazaribagh and Palamau after the Settlement is precisely due to their stagnation earlier. We have to admit helplessness here. It is impossible to specify the rate of expansion for different districts prior to the Settlement. All we can say is that our figures for the whole division would be more accurate than that of individual districts, taking a constant rate of growth, in the extrapolated years. The reason is that if acreages in Hazaribagh and Palamau were relatively stagnant prior to the Settlement then in the other three districts it was far more vigorously expanding afterwards thus if we overestimate the rate of growth of these two districts (Hazaribagh and Palamau) in the pre-settlement period, we are also simultaneously underestimating the rate of growth of the other three districts. Then these two tendencies would counteract each other, giving us a more accurate figure at the level of the division than of the individual districts.

Condition Factor and Standard Yield

In case of rice, we can be sure of the fact that the condition factor is a reliable indication of the harvest condition at the aggregate level of the division while on the level of individual districts, it is less reliable an index.

It is expected that the mean condition factor over a long enough time should equal 100. But this is not so. The mean condition factor for the division and the districts are given below for the period 1901–48 for the three groups of crops whose estimates were

[14] For a discussion on the expansion and stagnation in acreage in Chotanagpur see P. P. Mohapatra, 'Some Aspects of Arable Expansion in Chotanagpur 1880–1950', *Economic and Political Weekly*, vol. XXVI, no. 16, 20 April 1991, pp. 1043–54.

published in the *Season and Crop Report*. We have taken the divisional condition factor as a weighted average of the district condition factor weighted by their relative acreage. Similarly for other foodgrains, the district condition factor is the weighted average of four crops whose condition factor was published in the *Season and Crop Report*, (i.e. maize, wheat, barley and gram) again weighted by their individual acreage. The divisional figure is similarly the average of estimated district figures weighted by their relative acreages of all foodgrains excepting rice. Similar method has been adopted for oil seeds (where we have figures for linseed, rape and mustard).

Table 2. Average Condition Factor: Various Crops 1901–48

	Rice	Other food grains	Oilseeds
Hazaribagh	90.2	77.6	79.7
Ranchi	93.6	80.5	85.83
Palamau	84.2	73.5	77.56
Manbhum	86.3	72.25	74.85
Singhbhum	86.0	75.02	75.35
Chotanagpur division	88.5	77.17	80.80

SOURCE: *Season and Crop Report of Bengal & Bihar* for relevant years.

It is thus evident that there was significant deviation from the theoretically normal 100 and it was on the whole less than the above figure.

Heston suggested that the series of official condition factor should be replaced by another series which measured the percentage deviation from the trend.[15]

We have retained the official condition factor series for all the groups of crops, since for many of the crops and districts we could not find a significant downward trend. It would distort our series greatly if we calculated only the percentage deviation from the trend.[16] But to take into account the below normal figure of the long run average of condition factor we have in general upgraded the normal yield by equating the average normal yield of our estimate with the long run average condition factor.

NORMAL YIELD

We have seen that the estimation of normal yield in the official series, generally had a downward trend. This was in the main

[15] *Cambridge Economic History of India*, vol. II, 1982, p. 426.

[16] Except in the case of Manbhum.

responsible for the decline in the official output figures. How do we calculate the normal yield? the simplest way is to divide the crop cutting results of 1945–8 in the *Report on Crop Survey* by the condition factor published in the respective *Season & Crop Report* and determine the normal yield. The actual yields and the respective condition factors are given in Table 3. It is evident by our method of estimation, that there is a great deal of year to year variation in the estimated normal yield. Only in Hazaribagh and Ranchi district, the direction of actual yield (for crop cutting results) and that of the condition factor coincide. While in the case of Palamau, Singhbhum and Manbhum they are completely at variance. Most of the discrepancies occur due to unreasonably low estimate of condition factor. Thus if we assume that the errors in the individual districts are generally downwards and eliminate the grossly low figures of condition factor, e.g. the figures of Manbhum and Palamau for the year 1945, and figures of Singhbhum and Manbhum for 1946, the level of discrepancy is reduced to a great extent. Then by taking the averages of the rest of the figures of each district, we arrive at a normal yield figure of each district given in column NY I. The weighted average of individual district estimates give us the Divisional average. Is the process of elimination we have chosen arbitrary? It is true that we have no basis for elimination excepting the absurdly low level of condition factor (or high level of normal yield) of some of the figures.

Table 3. Yield, Condition Factor and Estimated Normal Yield

	Actual Yield and Condition Factor (in maunds of rice per acre)				Estimated Normal Yield	
	1945	1946	1947	1948	NY I	NY II
Ranchi	7.19(96)	8.17(100)	7.98(96)	6.46(88)	7.83	7.67
Palamau	8.66(54)	7.79(96)	5.53(67)	7.02(67)	8.12	7.77
Hazaribagh	8.69(85)	9.23(89)	10.11(92)	7.2(81)	10.12	10.28
Manbhum	13.08(70)	13.67(84)	11.56(85)	11.90(85)	13.80	13.80
Singhbhum	9.48(66)	9.90(71)	9.08(78)	8.90(93)	10.82	11.13
Chotanagpur	–	–	–	–	10.42	10.48

SOURCE: *Season and Crop Report of Bihar 1945–63.*
Report on Crop Survey of Bihar 1944–8.
NY II = Actual district Yield/Average Condition Factor,
(1945–63) (1901–48).

But there is a second estimation by which we can cross check our estimation. We have the actual yield estimates through random crop cutting of rice for the period 1945–63 as published in the *Season and Crop Report of Bihar* for 1949 onwords.

Now by dividing this average yield figure with the long run average of condition factor, we arrive at another estimate of the Normal Yield (NY II). Now by comparing this figure with our estimated figure (NY I), there is only 2 per cent discrepancy between the two normal yield figures at the divisional level. For our purpose, we shall choose the estimates of normal yield given by the second method (NY II) as it is based on crop cutting results of a longer period. We have corrected some of the absurdly low figures of condition factor during 1845–8 by using the new estimate of normal yield.

Calculating Normal Yield for other Foodgrains and Oil Seeds: In calculating the normal yield for other food grains and oilseeds, we are forced to adopt the second method enumerated above, primarily because there are no random crop-cutting figures as in the case of rice for the period 1945–8.[17] The results of our estimation are given in the Table 4.

Table 4. Normal Yield of OFG and Oil Seeds
(in maunds per acre)

	OFG	Oil Seeds
Ranchi	5.27	3.29
Palamau	6.38	3.49
Hazaribagh	6.79	4.30
Manbhum	6.59	4.97
Singhbhum	5.89	3.84
Chotanagpur	6.10	3.77

SOURCE: Same as Table 3.

Here a bit of explanation is necessary. We have already cited the method of construction of condition factor for the group of crops collectively called 'other food grains'. It was done by weighting the individual crops namely wheat, maize, gram and barley by respect-

[17] The crop cutting experiments were conducted on a country wide scale by the ICAR between 1944–9 the summary results of this survey is to be found in '*Sample Surveys for Estimation of Food Crops 1944–9*, ICAR Bulletin no. 72, New Delhi, 1951. The detailed results for Bihar for three years 1945–7 can be found in *Report on Crop Survey*.

ive acreages in the settlement period. The condition factor for the whole division was the average of individual districts using the total of other food grain acreage of each district in the year 1925 as weights. It was our assumption that the condition factor would give a rough idea of the condition of harvest of all the food grains apart from rice. In actual fact, the average yield of all the food grain crops varied enormously. We studied the yield figures of each of the four crops for the years 1949–63. We find that the maize yield was consistently higher than other crops in all the years.

We calculated the average yield of maize for each individual district separately. Then taking the other three crops (wheat, gram and barley) as representative of all other food grains excepting maize, we have calculated their average yield together. Then we combined the two averages thus obtained by a weighting formula of the following kind:

$$Y_{OFG} = Y_M \text{ (Maize/Total OFG)} + Y_{WBG} \text{ (1} - \text{Maize/Total OFG)}$$

Where

Y_{OFG} = Combined average of yield of other food grains

Y_M = Average yield of maize 1949–63

Y_{WBG} = Weighted average of yield of three crops wheat, barley and gram.

In order to simplify calculations we have used the 1953 figures as constant weighting for maize and all other food grains.

The results thus obtained, we feel, are significantly better indicators of yield of Other Food Grains than a simple weighting by respective acreages of the yields of all the four crops. In the other case, the yield figure would be heavily biased towards a high yielding crop like maize and thus raise the combined average yield significantly higher than the actual yields.

The next step was to divide the individual district figures by the condition factor of Other Food Grains which gives the standard yield of each district. The weighted average of the districts (weights of 1925 acreage of other food grains) gives us the divisional yield.

For oilseeds, a similar method was used as in case of rice and other food grains. In case of oilseeds, we have the published condition factors of only three types, viz., linseed, til, rape and mus-

Table 5. Annual Average Output of Chotanagpur (in '000 metric tonnes)

	(I)		(II)		(III)		(IV)		(V)	
Years	Rice		Other food grains		Total food grains (I)		Total food grains (II)		Oil seeds	
	Qty.	Index	Qty.	Index	Qty.	Index	Qty.	Index	Qty.	Index
1890–4	772	87	276	90	1,048	88	–	–	–	–
1895–9	734	83	303	99	1,037	87	–	–	–	–
1900–4	885	100	305	100	1,190	100	1,022	100	45	100
1905–9	872	98	264	87	1,135	95	1,017	99.5	36	80
1910–4	961	109	315	103	1,275	107	1,296	127	48	107
1915–19	915	104	316	104	1,232	104	1,312	128	48	107
1920–4	1,092	123	317	104	1,409	118	1,232	120.5	50	112
1925–9	1,057	119	297	97	1,354	114	1,221	119.5	49	109
1930–4	1,075	122	288	94	1,363	115	1,322	129	44	99
1935–9	997	113	273	89	1,270	107	1,268	124	39	88
1940–4	1,041	118	248	81	1,288	108	1,297	127	38	84
1945–8	1,138	129	238	78	1,376	116	1,325	130	39	86

SOURCE: According to Table 2 and 3 of Appendix I of Mohapatra 'Chotanagpur'.

NOTE: For col. IV and V the annual average of 1901–4 is 100.

tard. For each district, then their average condition factor (weighted by their acreage in the settlement period) is taken to represent the condition of harvest of all the oilseeds. Divisional average is calculated with weights of 1925 acreages under oilseed in each district. The standard yield has been calculated by taking the weighted average yield of 1949–63 of these three oilseeds and then dividing by the long run condition factor (1901–48).

The divisional standard yield similarly is a weighted average of the district standard yield. Once the normal yield, condition factor and acreages have been suitably corrected, output can be estimated. But we must deduct a certain per cent from the acreages, the area lost to field boundaries. In Chotanagpur this area was reported to be as high as 8 per cent. The estimated output of all food grains and oilseeds are given in Tables 5 and 6. For a comparison of official figures of rice production with our estimate see figure 1.

Growth and Instability

The foodgrain production in Chotanagpur between 1890 and 1948 grew at an annual compound rate of 0.52 per cent. The major part of this growth was due to the high rate of growth of rice production (0.73 per cent), while the production of other foodgrains in fact

Table 6. Trend Rate of Growth of Output Chotanagpur Division, 1890–1948

	1890–1923	1924–48	1890–1948
Rice	1.17*	0.29†	0.73*
	(2.95)	(0.94)	(5.08)
Other food grains	0.50†	−1.11*	−0.20†
	(1.38)	(5.29)	(1.45)
Total food grains	1.00*	0.01†	0.52*
	(2.72)	(0.04)	(3.88)
Oil seeds	1.09†	−1.37*	−0.19 (a)†
	(1.44)	(4.69)	(0.92)

SOURCE: Calculated from Tables (2 and 3) of Appendix I of Mohapatra, 'Chotanagpur'.

NOTE: (*a*) the series for oilseeds commences from 1901.
(*b*) the figures in bracket are 't' statistic of the coefficient
* significant at 1% level
† not significant.

declined over this period. It is however easy to see in Figures 1–3 that the character of growth was not uniform over the whole period. Between 1890 and 1923 the rate of growth of all crops was much higher than in 1924–48; but the higher rate of growth was associated with much sharper annual fluctuations than in the period of stagnation 1924–48, which shows much greater stability. There is no doubt that the period of instability of production was more dangerous for the cultivators, and especially so for the poorer households, than the period of stagnant but stable production. This was so because the institutional structures of market and credit in Chotanagpur could not adequately alleviate the effects of fluctuations in food production.

A Test of the Production Estimates: Consumption of Foodgrain 1938–47

In conclusion we may test our production figures by comparing them to the consumption estimates that may be derived from the diet surveys carried out under the auspices of the Indian Nutrition Institute between 1938 and 1948. In Chotanagpur the surveys were mainly carried out by K. Mitra. Thirty-five surveys covered 923 rural families consisting of 4,884 persons and 701 urban and industrial families consisting of 3,544 persons. Thus over a period of 10 years, the actual dietary habits of 8,428 persons was recorded by the method of weighing of daily intake of the sample of families for an average of 10 days. The surveys were held at various times of the year and some of the areas were resurveyed to gauge the impact of massive price rise after 1943. The sample families were usually of the poor cultivators or agricultural labourers or industrial workers. This was representative of the largest section of both the rural and urban population. The details of the individual surveys are given in my thesis.[18] Here I shall only analyse the results. (1) First, a clear distinction between the dietary intake of the urban and rural population emerges from the surveys. The urban intake was higher both in terms of quantity of cereal and pulses consumed, and also in terms of calories. The weighted mean of consumption of cereals and pulses per consumption unit of urban population was 25.63 ounce or 731 grammes per day. The weighted mean of caloric intake per consumption unit was 2,740 calories per day. In

[18] Mohapatra, 'Chotanagpur', pp. 212–18.

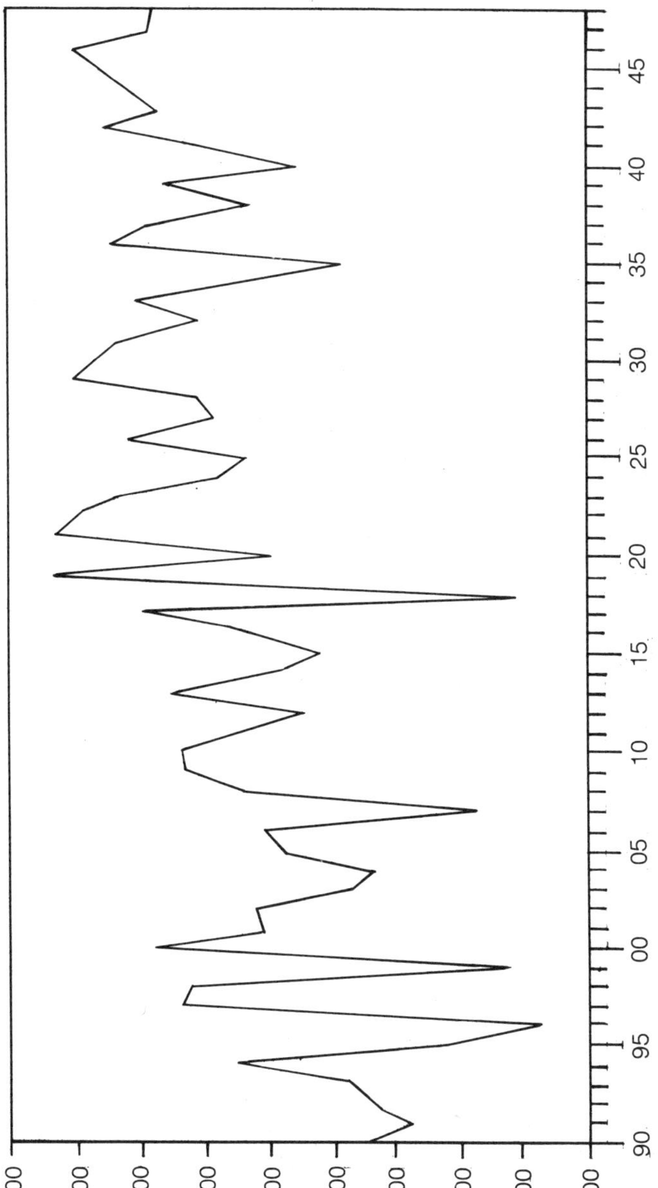

Figure 1. Estimated output of Rice: Chotanagpur 1890–1948 (in 000 metric tonnes)

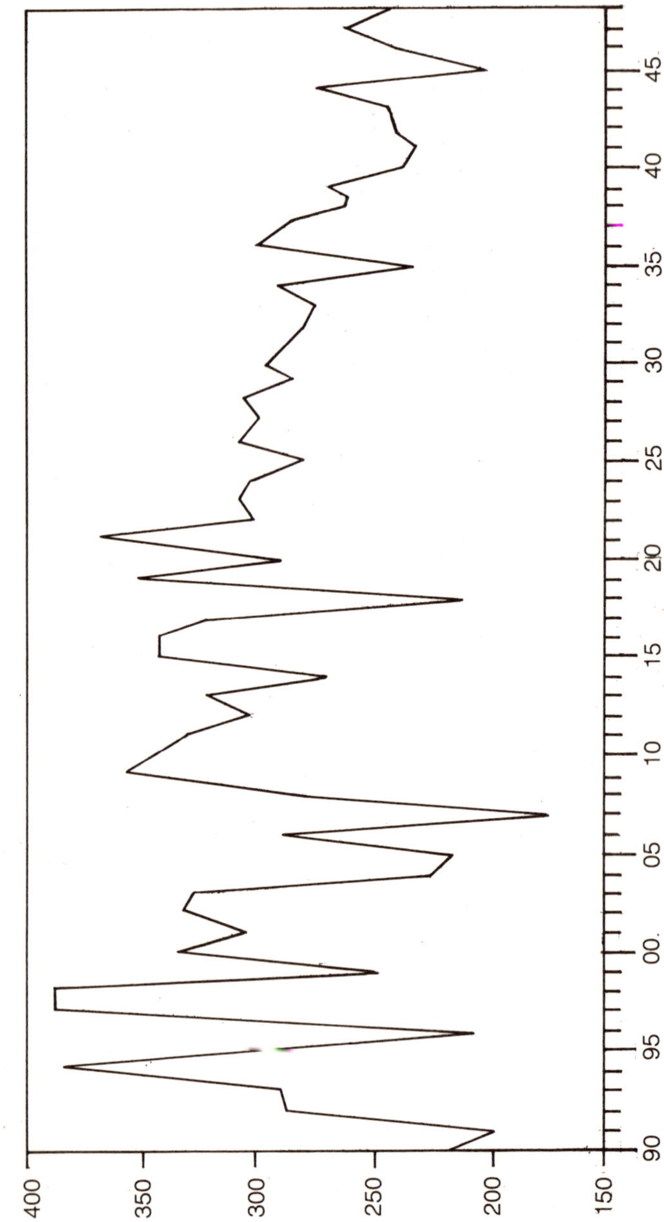

Figure 2. Estimated Output of Other Food Grains: Chotanagpur 1890–1948 (in 000 metric tonnes).

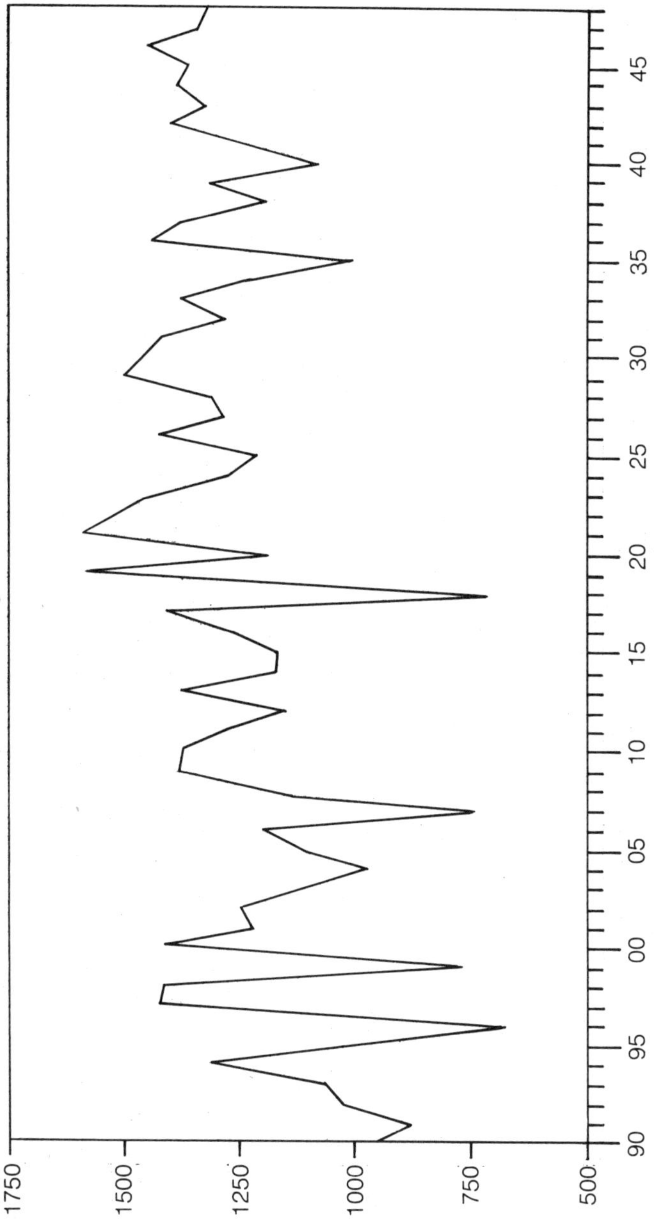

Figure 3. Estimated Output of Total Food Grains: Chotanagpur 1890–1948 (in 000 metric tonnes)

contrast amongst the rural households, the weighted mean of intake of cereals and pulses per consumption unit was 21.07 ounces or 601 grammes per day. The average intake in rural households was about 1,978 calories. Not only the level of consumption of foodgrains but also other items of food was lower in rural households.

Table 7. Average Intake of Various Food Items, Household (in grammes)

Food items	Urban	Rural
Cereals and Pulses	731.00	601.00
Leafy vegetables	33.56	23.07
Other vegetables	121.58	29.40
Fruits	10.07	0.71
Ghee and Vegetable oil	22.70	3.77
Milk and milk product	54.23	4.64
Meat,, fish and fowl	56.51	4.65
Sugar and Jaggery	10.05	6.05
Condiments	18.45	4.98
Total Calories	2740.00	1978.00

SOURCE: Mohapatra, 'Chotanagpur', Table 4.13, p. 216.

(2) Second, one can see that there was a distinct seasonal pattern in dietary intake in rural areas: being highest in the post harvest season from November to May. In the harvest and post harvest season, 13 surveys were held among rural households, and the average cereal intake per consumption unit per day was 23.83 ounces or about 680 grammes. The average caloric intake was roughly 2,350 calories per consumption unit. In the lean season stretching from June to September, in 9 surveys the average cereal consumption was 16.67 ounce or 476 grammes per consumption unit. The caloric intake was similarly lower at 1,483 calories per consumption unit per day. In contrast, in the urban areas the caloric intake difference between the two seasons was insignificant. Between November and May, in 8 surveys the average caloric intake was 2,862 calories per consumption unit. And in 4 surveys held during the lean season the calorie intake was 2,924 calories per consumption unit.

(3) There was a relationship between average income and the level of consumption. The income effect of consumption cannot be strongly established since the income data was presumably collected with less accuracy than the diet intake. The income data

was obviously much better in case of urban and industrial households. In these households, there is a clear tendency for a rise in cereal and pulse consumption up to a certain income level after which it falls. On the other hand the caloric consumption tends to increase with income, indicating that the Engel's law comes into operation with a shift from cereals and pulses to high caloric consumption of milk and milk products, meat and fish, sugar, fruits and vegetables, with a rise of income beyond a certain level.

In the rural households, the income data is given in only 13 surveys. These surveys are rendered incomparable by their being held at different times of the year and in different years. But in terms of groups in which surveys were held roughly at the same time, there was a distinct tendency for both cereal and pulse consumption as well as caloric intake to increase with income. The only case where the relation does not hold good is in Singhbhum in September 1943 (Survey Nos. 52, 53, 54, 55), which was because of the abnormal situation following a massive increase in prices and the failure of the *bhadoi* harvest resulting in a lower than normal harvest of 1942. With the exception of this case the general rate of increase in the intake of foodgrains and calories tended to increase with income in the rural households.

Estimate of Production from the Consumption Data

Since we have a fairly wide ranging sample of consumption pattern, it might be possible to compare it with the production estimates. This would act as a check on the accuracy of our production estimates. We shall take only the consumption of food grains into account. A few assumptions need to be made before we go on to compare production with consumption of food grain: (1) First, our foodgrain (cereals + pulses) consumption data are in terms of consumption units. The calculation of consumption units from total population data is dependent on accurate agewise break down of the population figures. This is a difficult task given the unreliability of age statistics. In one estimate using the 1941 age tables of India, the League of Nations estimate of coefficient of consumption was 0.75. From the All India figures of 1935–48, *Report on Survey of Diet*, the coefficient of consumption was estimated at 0.81. Mahalanobis's weighting of consumption of rice of a sample of 253 persons at Giridih showed a coefficient of consumption of 0.78. After reviewing the existing surveys, Mahalanobis came to the conclusion that the actual coefficient of consumption for the

Indian population lay between 0.75 and 0.81.[19] We shall use all these 3 coefficients namely (0.75, 0.78 and 0.81) in estimating the number of consumption units.

(2) The second point that needs to be clarified is that our consumption estimation would be only for the period 1938 to 1947, i.e. the 10 years in which the surveys were held. The average number of consumption units of these 10 years is then multiplied by the weighted mean of food grain consumption of rural population (21.07 ounces or 601 grams per day per consumption unit) and the urban population (25.61 ounces or 731 grams per day per consumption unit) to give us the average food grain consumption per year.

(3) On the production side, we have to deduct from the total production, the amount of seed grain. In this we have assumed that in the case of rice the seed grain rate is 0.693 maunds per acre and for other food grains a flat rate of 5 per cent of the annual produce.[20]

From Table 8 it can be deduced that the net food grains production of the region fell short of the total consumption by a minimum of 66,000 metric tonnes and a maximum of 1,68,000 metric tonnes. It would be simpler if we knew the average annual net import of food grains to the region. But given the trend in the earlier decades (1900–20), it does not seem improbable that the net import of food grains could have been between the range specified above.[21]

It thus seems that the estimate of production we have, is roughly accurate at least for the period 1938-48. The verification of our production estimation, of course, does not hold good for the earlier period. But nevertheless, the rough consonance with consumption figures proves that the method adopted for estimating the production series (i.e. correction of acreage, normal yield and condition factor) was correct.

[19] *National Sample Survey, General Report* 1st round, New Delhi, 1951.

[20].This is the new rate used by the agricultural monthly reports *Report on Marketing of Rice*, Agricultural marketing series, 40, New Delhi, 1940, and *Report of Marketing of Maize*, New Delhi, 1952.

[21] There is some evidence of food grain imports into Jamshedpur alone, during 1944 to 1947, the annual average being 21,330 metric tonnes. *Singhbhum District Gazetteer*, 1958, p. 348. Net imports of foodgrains into the division in 1920 announced to 102,000 tonnes. See Mohapatra, 'Chotanagpur', p. 211.

Table 8. Total Consumption and Production of Foodgrains in Chotanagpur 1938–47

Average annual consumption of food grain 1938–47				Average annual production of food grain 1938–47 (in m. tonnes)		Deficit = Net production – Consumption		
	K = 0.81	K = 0.78	K = 0.75	Total food grain prod.	Food grain available for consumption	K = 0.81	K = 0.78	K = 0.75
Rural	12,61,054	12,14,348	11,67,642					
Urban	1,14,220	1,09,989	1,05,759	13,12,397	12,07,571	1,67,703	1,16,766	65,830
Total	13,75,274	13,24,337	12,73,401					

SOURCE: Mohapatra, 'Chotanagpur', Table 4.14, p. 219.

NOTE: K = Coefficient of Consumption, total consumption unit/total population.

Annotated Bibliography

Note: This bibliography does not claim to be exhaustive; the papers reproduced in this collection have also been excluded.

Baker, C. J., 'Review of M. M. Islam *Bengal Agriculture 1920–1946*' in *Modern Asian Studies*, 14 (3), 1980. A brief but incisive critique of Islam's work. His *An Indian Rural Economy 1880–1955: The Tamilnad Countryside* (Delhi: OUP, 1984), pp. 176–7 and 508–15 offer a well-researched argument for the reality of declining yields in Tamilnad.

Dewey, C. J., 'Patwari and Chaukidar: Subordinate Officials and the Reliability of India's Agricultural Statistics' in C.J. Dewey and A. G. Hopkins (eds.), *The Imperial Impact: Studies in the Economic History of Africa and India* (London, 1978). The most important attack on the quality of the agricultural statistics themselves.

Heston, A. W., 'National Income', in The *Cambridge Economic History of India* (Cambridge, 1983), vol. II. Part 2 and Appendix 4.2 of this chapter are largely devoted to the question of the defects in agricultural statistics, and the methods of correcting them. A very well-argued essay.

Islam, M. M., *Bengal Agriculture 1920–1946: A Quantitative Study* (Cambridge and New Delhi, 1978). An attempt to reconstruct the agricultural statistics which is not wholly successful.

Mishra, S. C., 'On the Reliability of Pre-Independence Agricultural Statistics in Bombay and Punjab', in *The Indian Economic and Social History Review*, XX (2), 1983. This is an attempt to rebut Heston's criticisms of the Bombay statistics as well as Dewey's attack on the Punjab official statistics.

Panse, V. G., 'Why Crop-Cutting Surveys?', in *Indian Journal of Agricultural Economics*, XVIII (2), 1963. Argues that the revenue yields were understated and tended to underestimate variation.

Shah, C. H., 'Comparison of Yield Estimates Prepared on the Basis of Traditional and Crop-Cutting Methods', in *Indian Journal of Agricultural Economics (IJAE)*, XVII (4), 1962. This important essay compares yields generated through the revenue annawari estimates with those found by crop-cutting surveys, and finds that neither intercepts nor trends differed significantly at the Bombay State level. His 'Reply', in *IJAE*, XVIII (2), 1963, is a response to the criticism by V. G. Panse in the same journal.